RELIGION, PROTEST, AND SOCIAL UPHEAVAL

Religion, Protest, and Social Upheaval

*Matthew T. Eggemeier, Peter Joseph Fritz,
and Karen V. Guth, Editors*

FORDHAM UNIVERSITY PRESS   NEW YORK 2022

Library of Congress Cataloging-in-Publication Data available online at https://
catalog.loc.gov.

Printed in the United States of America

24 23 22   5 4 3 2 1

First edition

Contents

RELIGION, PROTEST, AND SOCIAL UPHEAVAL

Introduction

Matthew T. Eggemeier, Peter Joseph Fritz, and Karen V. Guth

In March 2020, the COVID-19 pandemic forced the imposition of worldwide lockdowns. For some, work, school, and religious participation moved online. For others, it simply ceased, as businesses and other institutions closed temporarily or even permanently. Social life came to a halt, while masked politicians and healthcare workers carried on as best they could. The economic fallout was immediate, compounding an already devastating situation marked by extensive suffering and death. Although the pandemic gave rise to various forms of solidarity, it more often than not threw societal fault lines into stark relief.

This was as true in the United States as elsewhere. The pandemic revealed glaring disparities between comparatively wealthy people who enjoy security, on the one hand, and comparatively poor people in precarious positions, on the other. Both groups experienced widespread job loss—the worst since the Great Depression of the 1930s—but the latter group suffered especially hard, given four decades of stripped social protections under neoliberalism. The "essential" status of many blue- and pink-collar jobs allowed—sometimes forced—many in these lines of work to continue. But not without significant risk of COVID-19 infection.

Then on May 25, a Minneapolis police officer killed George Floyd, an unarmed Black man. (The ex-officer has since been convicted of second- and third-degree murder and second-degree manslaughter.) Floyd's murder came on the heels of the March 13 killing of Breonna Taylor, a Black woman who was fatally shot in her own home by police in Louisville, Kentucky. Following Floyd's killing, protesters across the United States and around the world demanded an end to police brutality and systemic racism. Racial tensions hit fever pitch during the summer, stoked no doubt by the anguish and suffering caused by the COVID-19 pandemic. Before long, protests against systemic racism and police brutality grew into the largest mass uprising in U.S. history, with various religious groups participating.[1] Catholics, Protestants, Jews, Muslims, and Mormons joined in protest; white televangelists such as Joel Osteen joined, in spirit and action, along with Black church leaders such as Rev. William Barber.

The year 2020 also gave rise to counter-protests. The U.S. presidential election season coincided with the George Floyd protests, and the campaign of embattled incumbent Donald Trump inhabited a decidedly anti–Black Lives Matter (BLM), anti–George Floyd, pro-police stance. In fact, the then president ordered protesters removed (they were tear-gassed) from the vicinity of St. John's Episcopal Church so that he could pose before the church holding a Bible. Counter-protests against BLM also intersected with protests against COVID restrictions, both often populated by Trump supporters who also suffered as a result of the pandemic-induced economic downturn. These protests intersected with objections to government restrictions on occupancy in houses of worship by self-proclaimed advocates of religious freedom. In summer 2020, the fault lines strained.

We could not have anticipated these phenomena in fall 2017, when we convened the conference at the College of the Holy Cross that gave rise to this volume. But 2017 was also a tumultuous year that highlighted economic, racial, and gendered disparities and divisions. The prior fall, the United States elected Donald Trump to the presidency after a campaign featuring economic populism, dog-whistle (or perhaps foghorn) racism and xenophobia, and overt misogyny. The political left, and even political center, met his election with dismay and protest while the political right, and more notably, the far right, embraced him.

On January 21, 2017, an estimated 500,000 people participated in the Women's March on Washington, D.C. to protest Trump's presidential inauguration. The event started when one woman, Teresa Shook of Hawaii, created a Facebook event inviting her friends to march on Washington. It grew into a worldwide movement when others with similar event pages consolidated their efforts. Protestors donned so-called pink "pussy hats" (knitted hats that resemble cat ears) to reclaim the derogatory term used by Trump in an infamous 2005 remark about "grabbing women by the pussy," but also to advocate for causes including women's rights, immigration rights, abortion rights, and concern for the environment. They expressed their support for science, expressed solidarity with other movements like BLM, and defended the rights of diverse religious groups, as well as native, Black, brown, Asian, Pacific Islander, and

LGBTQ people, through nonviolent resistance and demands for more inclusive and equitable social, economic, and political structures.[2] The Women's March was, at that point (before the protests of summer 2020), the largest single-day protest in U.S. history.

Less than a week later, more protests followed. On January 27, 2017, President Trump signed Executive Order 13769, which blocked the admission of refugees into the United States and banned travel of citizens from the Muslim-majority countries of Iran, Iraq, Libya, Somalia, Sudan, Syria, and Yemen, with the stated intent to "protect the nation from foreign terrorist entry into the United States."[3] Citizens immediately protested at airports and other public places across the nation, rejecting the so-called "Muslim ban."

If these protests opposed the new Trump administration and various aspects of its agenda, others occurred in support of the new president—and of white nationalism. One such protest occurred in Charlottesville, Virginia, on August 11, 2017, when "Unite the Right" protesters paraded across the lawn of the University of Virginia, chanting "White lives matter" and "You will not replace us." On the following day, when faced with counter-protesters, the white nationalist protesters responded, among other ways, by beating DeAndre Harris and killing Heather Heyer. Before the official rally even began, Virginia State Police declared the assembly dissolved. Even though this particular protest was comparatively small and short-lived, it was particularly traumatic for people of color and their allies, and it emboldened white nationalist and other far-right groups, often Trump supporters.

By fall 2017, many of the social rifts of spring and summer 2020 were shifting just below the surface, their glints and flashes auguring current upheavals.

While situated between 2017 and 2020, this volume aims to contribute to a rapidly developing history of protest and social upheaval. Rather than offering an overarching theory of protest, it offers specific, situated reflection at the nexus of academia and activism on a variety of phenomena from scholars in religious studies, theology, ethics, and gender studies. Its analysis will be of primary interest to scholars and students in these fields, as well as religiously engaged activists.

The volume's chapters began as presentations at the Religion, Protest, and Social Upheaval conference, held at the College of the Holy Cross on November 15–17, 2017. Cosponsored by Holy Cross's Department of Religious Studies, under the leadership of Tat siong Benny Liew, and the McFarland Center for Religion, Ethics, and Culture, directed by Thomas Landy, the conference gathered an array of scholars to address this topic of pressing social significance in conjunction with the annual meetings of the American Academy of Religion being held nearby in Boston. The original description of the conference read as follows:

> The recent proliferation of social, political, and economic protest and populist expression, from Black Lives Matter to Hindu Nationalism, invites renewed exploration of religion's age-old power to fuel and shape cultural change. This conference brings together a diverse group of scholars across national and religious divides to examine the impact of religion on various social and political movements. Organized around six themes—nationalism, immigration, race, gender, ecological concern, and economics—the conference aims to illuminate the complex dynamics of religion in protest and social upheaval.[4]

The volume itself has coalesced around two concrete foci from the conference: first, distinctive forms of protest and social upheaval in the United States, and second, their intersection with two of the United States' largest religious traditions, Christianity and Islam. Even so, each of the essays has global relevance, and two specifically explore how international phenomena affect communities in the United States. Kwok Pui-lan's contribution examines the global interconnectedness of women's protests and feminist theology, and Ju Hui Judy Han analyzes queer Christian politics in Korea. The volume demonstrates the plurality of ways that the study of religion can illuminate protest and social upheaval. The contributions here include the voices of both preeminent scholars and emerging voices who study the relationship between religion and social movements. As such, this volume represents not only the best of current scholarship but also identifies important trajectories for future work.

The contributors' essays oscillate between theoretical material and more direct and practical engagements with grassroots movements, advancing theoretical conversations while fortifying protest activities. Each acknowledges the contributions of grassroots movements, prompting a rethinking of theoretical constructs. In all cases, history looms large, whether in the experiences of 2017 and 2020, or longer historical itineraries, such as the path from W. E. B. Du Bois's early twentieth century to the twenty-first, the development of women's movements from the 1960s to today, or early Christian ideas of the ascension inflecting our neoliberal present.

Given history's role in this volume's contributions, some may have judged it appropriate for the chapters, or at least this introduction, to have included reflection on events from just a few years earlier than 2017: the social upheaval wrought by the global economic collapse of 2008–2009 and the resulting protest movements in the United States, including the Tea Party; the protests of 2011, radiating out from the Arab Spring and including Occupy in the United States;

and the 2014 Ferguson uprising that followed the police killing of Michael Brown. Such reflection could have given rise to an overarching theory of protest and religion. We found, however, wisdom in the focus many of our authors took on the social moment of 2017, and in their revised chapters, of 2020.

Our contributors have responded to these moments of protest and social upheaval out of the resources of their study of religion. We recognize that not every author would explicitly identify their essay as contributing to the political project of the religious left. At the same time, the contributors all examine, from a religious perspective, interrelated forms of social and political domination that, historically, have been the focus of the American left: capitalism, environmental degradation, racism, xenophobia, and gender and sexuality.

The standard narrative about the role of religion in American politics often has focused on the significant impact of Protestant evangelicals, Catholic integralists, and other religious conservatives on politics, while characterizing the left as a predominately "secular" movement.[5] One reason for the pervasiveness of this narrative is that the religious right is a more cohesive coalition that operates by building power through traditional institutional structures and the election of religious conservatives to political office.[6] By way of contrast, the religious left operates less by building institutional structures and electing politicians, and more through critique, protest, and participation in mass social movements. Furthermore, where the religious right is largely comprised of white Christians who seek representation in the political realm (George W. Bush, Mike Pence, and so on), the religious left is a multi-racial, interfaith coalition situated within an even larger, heterogenous progressive coalition that seeks to build political power through mass movements that demand economic (Occupy Wall Street), racial (Black Lives Matter), and gender justice (the Women's March).[7]

This volume highlights the contributions that scholars of Christianity and Islam have made to a diverse set of protest and social movements on the left. Pluralism is a mark of this volume, not only in terms of the traditions our contributors analyze, but also the methodologies they employ and the strategies for social transformation they describe. The pluralism of our contributors' chapters is precisely what gives this book its distinctive coherence and import: taken together, the chapters concretely express the state of the religious left as it intersects with protest and social upheaval in the early 2020s.

Introducing the Chapters

The volume's structure offers a guide for seeing connections between essays while also highlighting their distinctive interventions. Part I groups three essays under the rubric of capitalism, analyzing Christianity and social upheaval with regard to race and class, postmodern theory, and ecology, as all of these intersect with the world's current dominant economic system. Part II gathers three essays on religion and race, with each examining the affective, poetic, or aesthetic aspect of racism and its social manifestations, and giving primary attention to Christianity. Part III includes two essays on Islam and grassroots organizing to underscore a particular form of xenophobia (Islamophobia), resistance to it, and its intersection with economic and social movements. Part IV returns to consideration of Christianity with two essays on gender and sexuality, treating religion and women's protest movements and Korean and Korean diaspora Protestant queer politics.

Part I: Upheaval under Capitalism

Mark Lewis Taylor opens the volume with Chapter 1, "Capital's 'Secret Orders': A Du Boisian Lens on the Alt-Right and White Supremacy." He argues for a critical theory that fuses race, capital, *and* U.S. empire to understand the rise of white supremacy during Donald Trump's presidency. Despite important gender-related criticisms of W. E. B. Du Bois's thought on "secret orders," Taylor argues that his account continues to challenge contemporary thinkers to develop an expansive theory of racism that addresses both capitalist exploitation and imperial domination. Taylor shows how effective resistance by Christians, religious leaders, and other people of conscience demands critique of the "U.S. corporate warrior elite" who work at the conjunction of white supremacy and capitalism.

Devin Singh argues in Chapter 2, "Protest at the Void: Theological Challenges to Capitalist Totality," that despite its globalized pretensions to totality, neoliberal capitalism is more fragile and fractured than its exponents or opponents readily admit. Maintenance of fragility is central to contemporary capitalism's operation, and Singh proposes that this behavior may have been learned from Christianity. Engaging in critical examination of the Christian doctrine of the ascension, Singh traces a genealogy of our economic present and finds a resource for Christian protest against it. If the oddity of the ascension, and all its attendant teachings and practices, funds neoliberalized capitalism's denial of vulnerability and claim to supremacy, it may also ground Christian discourse that distends capitalist structures and fosters socio-economic-political alternatives.

In Chapter 3, "As the World Burns: *Laudato Si'*, the Climate Crisis, and the Limits of Papal Power," Mary Doak explores whether the Roman Catholic Church possesses the resources and the power to address the climate crisis. She argues that Pope Francis's groundbreaking encyclical on the environment, *Laudato Si'*, features four significant developments in Catholic doctrine on the intrinsic value of nature. These developments include an expansion of the sacrament of communion to include communion with nature; the articulation of an "integral ecology" that highlights the interrelatedness of all life; a call for the reform of politics and political discourse; and conversion to a spirituality both contemplative and prophetic. While Doak acknowledges that it remains to be seen whether these developments will lead to the transformations that environmental justice demands, she sees potential in the Church's magisterial and lay power to shape public policy.

Part II: Race, Aesthetics, and Religion

In Chapter 4, "Whiteness and Civilization: Shame, Race, and the Rhetoric of Donald Trump," Donovan O. Schaefer proposes that rather than viewing Donald Trump's rise to political power as indicative of an ideological shift, it is best seen through the prism of affect. Schaefer argues that Trump's coalition was motivated by a particular configuration of white shame in the aftermath of liberal and progressive challenges to white dominance. Using affect theory, he shows that multiple sites of Trump's support—rural whites, white evangelicals, and the (white) online alt-right—combine to make an aggressive response to perceived challenges to white dignity.

Chapter 5, "Rootedness on the Slippery Earth: Migration in a Time of Social Upheaval" by Nichole M. Flores, examines the Latine protest tradition as it applies to movements for migrant justice in the United States. Acknowledging twentieth-century roots in the United Farm Workers movement and sixteenth-century roots in *la Virgen de Guadalupe*'s appearance to Juan Diego, the chapter sketches a philosophical framework for treating transitoriness and contingency within theological aesthetics. In doing so, it provides an alternative to aesthetics based on transcendentals of being to serve a social ethics of rootedness (an alternative to virtue ethics). It highlights distinctive Latine religious contributions, coming from devotions and liturgy, to democratic conversations and work toward justice for immigrants.

In Chapter 6, Jermaine M. McDonald's "Christian Responses to the 'Revolutionary Aesthetic' of Black Lives Matter" surveys the development of Black Lives Matter (BLM) as a protest movement and organizational principle. BLM's "revolutionary aesthetic" (a descriptor borrowed from Reverend Osagyefo Sekou) complicates Christian interaction with BLM. A sensibility marked by a preference for decentralization over hierarchy, for radical feminism over patriarchy, and for justice over types of reconciliation that would sustain the status quo characterizes BLM. This aesthetic may appeal to some

progressive churches, but it clashes with dominant white evangelical aesthetics (though there are prominent exceptions) and even traditional Black
church culture. McDonald ends by appealing to Christian churches to examine whether they may admit a pull toward a more revolutionary vision of Jesus
to better align them with BLM.

Part III: Migration, Labor Movements, and Islam

Chapter 7, Zayn Kassam's "Caught in the Crosshairs: Muslims and Migration" examines the contested terrain of migration politics by focusing on the
concrete experience of Muslims in the post-9/11 United States. Kassam first
traces the leading causes of global migration to the complicated entangle-
ment between neoliberal capitalism and military interventionism. She then
demonstrates how the emergence of a racialized xenophobia and Islamophobia in the United States has created a "politics of fear" that seeks to
criminalize, detain, or ban migrants from certain regions in the world. As an
alternative to this xenophobic response to migration, Kassam explores grassroots faith and civic communities in California who witness to a "politics of
compassion" through their efforts to help resettle refugees in their local communities.

Chapter 8, Melissa Snarr's "Iftars, Prayer Rooms, and #DeleteUber: Postsecularity and the Promise/Perils of Muslim Labor Organizing," shows how
organizing among Muslim American workers lays bare Protestant Christian
religious biases in purportedly secular institutions. Labor organizing surrounding nondiscrimination with regard to religious practices, such as five
daily prayers and iftars, reveals how the very structure of American workplaces
cannot accommodate Muslim practice, *not* because of the *non*religious orientation of the workplace, but because of its unstated Christian orientation.
Snarr proposes postsecularity as a category for understanding this religious
phenomenon. Postsecularity prevents the expunging of religion from public
spaces (as critics of "secularism" may fear or champions of the secular may
celebrate) and enlivens Christian resistance to these particularly Christian
forms of cooption and distortion that curtail interreligious cooperation and
authentic religious practice by Christians, Muslims, and others alike.

Part IV: Thresholds in Gender, Sexuality, and Christianity

In Chapter 9, "Slogan, Women's Protest, and Religion," Kwok Pui-lan considers three slogans from women's protests that indicate shifts in moral reasoning
influencing politics and struggles for liberation. The first slogan, "For God

and Home and the Native Land," comes from the late nineteenth century. It affirmed expansion of women's public roles in religion, economics, and politics. The racial and class-based limits of protests supported by this slogan, however, are immediately recognizable: It came from and appealed to white, married, middle-class women and upheld settler colonialism and Jim Crow segregation. The 1970s slogan, "Our bodies, ourselves," shifted beyond expansion of public roles to seek full-blown historical subjectivity for women. Women's bodies became a battleground (as the now-classic Barbara Kruger poster put it); varied women's protest movements unified in the fight. Racial, heterosexist, and geographic biases remained, and vigorous contestation in activism, the academy, and religious groups transpired through the early 2010s. The third slogan, #MeToo (first coined in 2006, without the hashtag), oriented protests from 2017 forward, shedding particular light on sexual harassment and abuse of women. Kwok examines the promise of this slogan's dissemination through social media for future, interconnected feminist activism worldwide. She ends with a special plea for progressive religious mobilization through social networks.

With the final chapter, Ju Hui Judy Han's "LGBTQ+ Politics and the Queer Thresholds of Heresy," readers encounter how struggles in some U.S. Protestant denominations have counterparts elsewhere, in this case, in Presbyterian churches in South Korea. The chapter examines the condemnation of Reverend Lim Borah for heresy (*idan*) by the largest evangelical denomination in South Korea for her contributions to queer theology and LGBTQ+ ministry. The Lim case reveals the political function of heresy. Evangelical Protestants in South Korea have employed heresy to discredit and silence dissenting minorities and demarcate the boundaries of socially acceptable behavior. Paradoxically, however, Han maintains that heresy serves not only to stifle dissent, but also to uncover it. Han contends that the exercise of institutional power reveals its limits in the Lim case by rendering visible "new queer vitalities" and by highlighting the power of dissenting movements to interrogate the legitimacy of anti-LGBTQ+ orthodoxy.

Prior versions of three chapters have been published elsewhere. The editors thank the Taylor & Francis Group for permission to print, in modified form, Donovan Schaefer, "Whiteness and Civilization: Shame, Race, and the Rhetoric of Donald Trump," *Communication and Critical/Cultural Studies* 17, no. 1 (2020): 1–18. We thank Duke University Press for permission to print, in modified form, Ju Hui Judy Han, "The Queer Thresholds of Heresy," *The Journal of Korean Studies* 25, no. 2 (October 2020): 407–28. And we recognize that parts of an earlier version of Chapter 7, Zayn Kassam's "Caught in the

Crosshairs: Muslims and Migration," appeared in Daniel Schipani, Martin Walton, Dominiek Lootens, eds., *Where Are We? Pastoral Environments and Care for Migrants: Intercultural and Interreligious Perspectives* (Düsseldorf: Society for Intercultural Pastoral Care and Counselling, 2018).

Notes

1. Andrea Shalal, "After George Floyd's Death, a Groundswell of Religious Activism," *Reuters*, June 9, 2020, https://www.reuters.com/article/us-minneapolis-police-usa-religion/after-george-floyds-death-a-groundswell-of-religious-activism-idUSKBN23G1FS.

2. See https://womensmarch.com/mission-and-principles.

3. For the full text, see https://www.whitehouse.gov/presidential-actions/executive-order-protecting-nation-foreign-terrorist-entry-united-states-2/.

4. See the conference website at https://www.holycross.edu/faith-service/mcfarland-center-religion-ethics-and-culture/events-mcfarland-center/conferences/religion-protest-and-social-upheaval.

5. *The Religious Left in Modern America: Doorkeepers of a Radical Faith*, ed. Leilah Danielson, Marian Mollin, and Doug Rossinow (New York: Palgrave Macmillan, 2018).

6. Jack Jenkins, *American Prophets: The Religious Roots of Progressive Politics and the Ongoing Fight for the Soul of the Country* (New York: Harper One, 2021).

7. Jack Jenkins, "The Religious Left isn't what the media thinks it is," *Think Progress*, April 26, 2017, https://archive.thinkprogress.org/stop-comparing-the-religious-left-to-the-religious-right-692c70490b0d/.

PART I

Upheaval Under Capitalism

1

Capital's "Secret Orders"

A Du Boisian Lens on the Alt-Right and White Supremacy

Mark Lewis Taylor

> Thus under "race" they camouflage a dictatorship of land and capital over black labor and indirectly over white labor.
> —W. E. B. DU BOIS, *Black Reconstruction in America, 1860–1880*[1]

It is one of the signs of our times that still "under race" we find camouflaged what W. E. B. Du Bois termed "a dictatorship of land and capital." In analyzing social upheaval and protest, this can be affirmed without ignoring the centrality of race, or even the primacy of the war that capital wages on Black persons directly ("Black labor")—a war also waged indirectly upon others ("white labor") and especially upon the earth's "darker peoples."[2] Looking through a Du Boisian lens, I argue in this essay that in the current period, we will not understand the strength of white supremacy in Donald Trump's rhetoric and policy, or in persisting Trumpism, without an accompanying analysis of class, capital, and empire. To make this argument, I discuss the so-called "alt-right" movements not only as manifestations of white supremacy but also, to break out from "under race," as reflective of a "dictatorship of land and capital." The forces of white supremacy and capital are operative, of course, at many sites of social upheaval, not just at those of the alt-right. Let me consider two of today's many other sites before turning to the essay's main focus on the alt-right.

Consider, first, the protest and social upheaval sites formed by Movement-4Black Lives (M4BL), a coalition of many organizations including the Black Lives Matter (BLM) movement. These movements indeed protest the callous violence of police and others against Black life; they also rightly critique the problems of "structural racism." With the 2020 George Floyd rebellion, the United States saw its largest mobilization of peoples against racial injustice.[3] Yet racial injustice is also variously *structured into* the impoverization of dispossessed working classes in the United States who are disproportionately Black, red, and brown. Some of my students assume that these protests are all about race and Black lives besieged by whiteness. Indeed, that is true, but that assumption alone tends to remain still "under race," hiding under the race concept and failing to name the always interacting "dictatorship of land and capital." This is to neglect the full complexity of what Cedric Robinson theorized as "racial capitalism"[4] and which historian Robin D. G. Kelley finds powerfully articulated in policy documents of M4BL. The core dynamic in racial capitalism is not to explain away either racist domination in terms of class exploitation or class domination in terms of white supremacy. It is to identify, resist, and transform a state system of power in which "the capitalist economy is constituted by a racial logic."[5] Note, however, that in this state system what the racial logic constitutes is a capitalist economy. So tightly intertwined are these forces within racial capitalism that we might also speak of a "racial economy" and a "capitalist logic." The theoretical challenge is to discern how white supremacism constitutes capitalist economy without losing sight of the fact that precisely that which is constituted by the racial logic is capitalism and its workings. Thus Kelley summarizes "racial capitalism" as "not the invisible hand of the market but the visible fist of state-sanctioned violence," noting that this is why M4BL frames the "ongoing processes of extraction, dispossession, and subjugation as a 'war on Black people.'"[6] To treat the alt-right and white supremacy in this essay, I will also have to respect, following Du Bois's lens, these always interplaying forces of racial logic and capitalist economy.

As a second site where today white supremacy and capital interplay, consider the COVID-19 pandemic and interpretations of the tumult and upheaval surrounding its outbreak. It is rightly noted and well-documented that Black and brown (and red/indigenous) communities bear disproportionately the toll of COVID-19 cases and deaths.[7] This is not only the result of a very real legacy of dispossession and persistent inequality that increases the spread of "comorbidity" factors in these communities. It is also due to social, political, and economic factors that keep people from these groups in positions of "essential service workers," requiring of them more person-to-person contact and fewer opportunities to retreat to isolated online salaried work. For such "essential workers," wages have to be earned in the face-to-face trenches of daily labor amid the pandemic. Again, the ways that land and capital organize social life are crucial factors shaping Black, red, and brown peoples' disproportionate suffering.[8] But to make only this point can often camouflage, again "under race," the controlling power of land and capital." Racialized groups in the United States are suffering not just "under race" but also under the control of land and capital "over black labor and indirectly over white labor" and indirectly also, over other non-Black racialized groups, this being a "political economy of racism" as Keeanga Yamahtta-Taylor analyzes it.[9]

Moreover, we also need to look toward the global dynamics that form a matrix for the COVID-19 pandemic in the United States and elsewhere. Neoliberals in the current Biden team, for example, fault the failures of the Trump regime to stem the spread of the virus to and in the United States.[10] But what the neoliberal critique often misses is that the Trump regime's neglect was not simply a callous attitude toward the virus generally or toward racial groups particularly, but also an outcome of capital's unbridled global functioning. This functioning persists whether the global roles of U.S. governments are orchestrated by Republicans or Democrats, or whether other national powers seeking global sovereignty are labeled autocratic or democratic. Specialist epidemiology journals such as *Clinical Microbiology Reviews* stress the need to examine the COVID-19 outbreak in the United States in relation to "rapid economic growth" and "global dissemination."[11] Evolutionary epidemiologists, agronomists, and disease ecologists have joined together to focus not only on communities in "outbreak zones" (say, in China, then Europe and the United States) but on ever larger "global economic actors that shape epidemiologies."[12] Sociologist Whitney Later Pirtle links racial injustice to land and capital when she focuses on "racial capitalism" as a "fundamental cause" of the pandemic, influencing multiple disease outcomes, exacerbating disease risk factors, and breaking down ecological buffers against disease.[13] Writing from MIT, Professor Kate Brown reminds us that "The Pandemic Is Not a Natural Disaster" but the result of human-induced "hurricanes," her metaphor for the destructive global circulations of capital by which humans alter their environment, and then concentrate populations, agricultural industry, and production patterns.[14] Historian and activist Mike Davis summarizes, "Economic globalization—that is to say, the accelerated free movement of finance and investment within a single world market where labor is relatively immobile and deprived of traditional bargaining power— . . . is everywhere breaking down traditional boundaries between animal diseases and humans."[15] In sum, the epidemiology and biology of death and disease in COVID-19, even when analyzed necessarily "under race," must also attend to the racial capitalist structuration of our globalization matrix. If this essay treats the alt-right under both race and capital, it is because nearly all the structural injustices of our time require this kind of dual focus.

The Alt-Right, Du Bois, and Religious Studies

This essay focuses on the "alt-right" because its newsmaking capacity during the presidency of Barack Obama in 2008 and especially with the rise of Donald Trump's presidency in 2016, awakened many observers of U.S. society and culture to persisting white supremacist currents. This was especially the case after the alt-right's "Unite the Right" rally on August 2017 in Charlottesville, Virginia. There, young white males marched, chanting "Jews will not replace us," and one young man with neo-Nazi and Trump-leaning tendencies drove his car into peacefully protesting crowds, killing one anti-racist protestor.[16] He was also affiliated with Vanguard America whose "blood and soil" nationalism lamented that "white Americans are becoming a minority in the nation they built."[17] The alt-right phenomenon, which was one of the points of upheaval that generated the conference from which this book's chapters arise, has widely been treated "under race," but the alt-right also provides a site to observe white racism's mutual entailment in cultures of U.S. wealth.

The origin of the term "alt-right" is usually attributed to "white identity" spokesman Richard Spencer, who himself places his coinage of it in 2008 as occurring soon after discussions of alternative right movements with "paleo-conservative" Paul Gottfried.[18] The "alt-right" is described by almost all scholars as a loose concatenation of persons and ideas. Matthew Lyons of *Political Research Associates* summarizes its key features as "a *contempt* for both liberal multiculturalism and mainstream conservatism, a *belief* that some people are inherently superior to others" and "*a self-presentation* as being new, hip and irreverent." Lyons also notes that the central emphasis is on "white nationalism" and advocacy of a white "ethnostate." This is frequently combined with antisemitism, xenophobia, and misogyny.[19] The commitment to forms of "white nationalism" is a constant if one reads across studies of the "alt-right." This white nationalism reflects what the Southern Poverty Law Center (SPLC) terms a growing "deep fear of demographic change" in white America.[20] The loss of America's majoritarian whiteness was triggered especially by Obama's rise to commander-in-chief in 2008 and expressed still more desperately through the 2016 rise of Trump's campaign and anti-Obama discourse. Sociologist Ashley Jardina links these fears of demographic change to broad concerns by whites to preserve the linkage of majoritarian whiteness to U.S. national citizenship. This is part of today's "politics of white identity," she documents, which is "not wholly or even primarily rooted in economic disenfranchisement; it is far broader and pervasive."[21] Just one manifestation of it was a robocall during the Trump campaign by a white nationalist in Massachusetts. The message was emphatic: "The white race is being replaced by other peoples in America and in all white countries. Donald Trump stands strong as a nationalist."[22]

U.S. liberal concerns intensified with the Tiki-torch carrying alt-right marchers in Charlottesville. Biden foregrounded concerns with the threat of white supremacy in the 2019 videos by which he announced his candidacy for president, a fight he intoned for "the soul of the nation."[23] This is, again, to parse the problem of rising white supremacism largely "under race." Rarely does this liberal rhetoric include careful reference to the conjoining of capital's structures with our racially divided American terrain. A Du Boisian lens assists precisely in gaining understanding of this conjuncture. Why, though, do these issues of race and class, viewed through a Du Boisian lens on the alt-right, become important for religious and theological studies, or perhaps also those of humanist and secular colleagues of spirit and conscience for whom the values of equality and justice are often of paramount concern?

The significance for religious and theological studies is twofold. First, turning to these issues prevents religious and theological reflection from a long tradition of intellectual failure to treat the realities of class stratification in the United States, what Susan Brooks Thistlethwaite and Peter Hodgson dubbed a "problem of problemlessness." American religion scholars and theologians often turn "a blind eye to the problem of classism."[24] To think and work only "under race" while silent about corporate capital risks a theology that cannot break free from a liberal multiculturalist paradigm. Such a paradigm mainly spawns multiculturalism as a "management of difference" within and for today's exploitative capitalist milieu. Rarely within that paradigm are those rendered or affirmed as "different" also actually empowered to resist their marginalization and repression. We need what I have discussed elsewhere as a "political theology of liberation,"[25] a reflection that promotes practices that work toward Black and Brown peoples' resistance and flourishing against white supremacy *and also* against the commodification of their bodies worked by the transnational capital that is rooted in centuries of colonialism and still active today.[26] Strategically, this means not only challenging alt-right and Trumpian white supremacist "insensitivity" and their "crude" and racist tweets, as liberals and Democrats daily do in social media. It means also organizing movements against the institutional carriers of these discourses. These carriers include the institutions for policing, imprisoning, and surveillance and also those of corporate capitalism that service U.S. imperial drives for global sovereignty. Liberals and Democrats are often servile sycophants to these larger powers at work in the media and the academy even when they criticize Trump and their Republican rivals. It is no surprise that the U.S. Democratic Party establishment, and other progressives, often remain disastrously silent about war and capitalism even when lamenting white supremacy. Religious thinking and theology in the United States needs to do better.[27]

Second, it is important for theological and religious studies to take up these concerns because of the diverse ways that white racism develops strategies of "secrecy." Often, white racism's beliefs are animated and made appealing by secrecy. Especially in the United States, white racism has been and remains not only blatant, crude, and often visibly displayed, but also so disseminated throughout ordinary practices and institutions that it becomes hidden to or unnoticed by many (especially those who are not its primary sufferers). The connections of alt-right and other racist groups to the organization of capitalist wealth is a further development of this hiddenness. This development makes it appear "economic," not "racist." Paradoxically, the hiddenness or secrecy is often quite open for those who care to look. Scholars have identified white supremacy in police forces, for example, as a phenomenon "hidden in plain sight."[28] Moreover, in a society presenting itself as democratic there is often unease about persistent white supremacism, thus an *intentional* hiding of white supremacist proclivities, however boldly demonstrative they can be. The hiding of wealthy persons' contributions to white supremacist groups, or groups that hide themselves online and in the "deep web" exemplify the penchant for secrecy in white supremacy.

I will explore racial capitalism's penchant for secrecy in a later section of the chapter. Here, I am merely emphasizing that religion and theology should engage this secrecy, caught up as these fields often are in study of what is claimed or experienced by adherents to be hidden and secret — to be what a number of scholars term "esoterica." As comparative religions scholar Hugh Urban notes, "approaches to secrecy in the history of religions" have had an important place in religious and theological reflection across many traditions.[29] It is not only the more mystical or sacramental traditions that show penchants for the hidden. Protestant thinkers, too, such as Luther and Calvin, work with a God "revealed" yes, but also as "hidden" — "*Deus absconditus.*"[30] Even closer to the interests of this chapter, when Protestant evangelical Christians in the United States have taken governmental power, as during the presidency of George W. Bush (2001–09), secrecy and religion interacted in unique ways. Bush was a member of the well-known Yale secret society "Skull and Bones," and his administration continually orchestrated a relationship between "secrecy and dissimulation" on the one hand, and his "avowed commitment to a religious faith that values honesty and truth" on the other. The mysteries of faith that Bush claimed to revere went hand in hand with a clearly articulated belief by his neoconservative allies who deployed the political philosophy of "neocon" theoretical guru, Leo Strauss, who taught that state leaders need the powers of secrecy and religion.[31]

White supremacy and the alt-right to which we turn here thrive at the conjuncture of secrecy, religion, and state power. Racial capitalism breathes in the rarified air of that conjuncture. Not surprisingly, then, Du Bois used the term "secret orders" in his historical analysis and theoretical framework in *Black Reconstruction in America, 1860–1880*. Du Bois's 1935 book is a close study of the U.S. Civil War, but predominantly of the post–Civil War era of "Reconstruction." The "secret orders" were the 1865/1866-birthed Ku Klux Klan and other groups such as Knights of the White Camellia, White League, Southern Cross, and The Innocents.[32] His book never separates these white supremacist formations from the milieu of capital's formation.

Why Du Bois's Study of the Reconstruction Era?

In Du Bois's study, "capital" referred to both the Southern planter elite (in its different forms before and after the war) and also to Northern industry, which, by the end of Reconstruction, rose to power as a world commercial force, strengthened by its eventual alliance with the resurgent post–Civil War South. Before the war, the North had ridden the power of the South's unfree forced labor's production of the astonishingly global cotton trade: "Slavery stood at the center of the most dynamic and far-reaching production complex in human history."[33]

Indeed, several periods in U.S. history might enable study of this interplay of white supremacy and capitalist formation. But the Reconstruction era is especially illuminating because it throws into stark relief the historical functioning of U.S. white supremacy and capital as antagonistic dynamics and structures that endure. The starkness of these forces in post-war "Reconstruction" is due, first, to the sheer magnitude of ruin left in the Civil War's wake. With the ruin so extensive, with previous complex institutions of the South so disrupted, the newly "reconstructed" rising powers are on display in stark relief. Second, the period also features the drama of key legislation that promised emancipation for the previously enslaved four million Blacks in the United States. In quick summary, this legislation included the 13th Amendment announcing a claim to abolish slavery and indentured servitude (1865), the 14th Amendment claiming to guarantee rights to citizenship and due process to Blacks and all others (1866), and the 15th Amendment proclaiming to guarantee the right to vote without restrictions of "race, color or previous condition of servitude."[34] Third, Reconstruction was the period for consolidating patterns of U.S. industrialization that created the domestic coalition necessary for U.S. imperial adventuring abroad. By the end of Du Bois's life, he termed this U.S. mode of governing abroad a "colonial imperialism," one that had turned Blacks and working poor of all backgrounds into "a colour caste of serfs."[35] These three reasons are sufficient for warranting our return today to Reconstruction. Du Bois himself stressed repeatedly in *Black Reconstruction* such points of significance. The Reconstruction era constituted "an economic revolution on a mighty scale and with world-wide reverberation."[36]

Enduring respect for Du Bois's text and its timeliness does not mean there is no need for criticism or revision. Most notably, Black feminists and others have been critical of Du Bois's insufficient attention to slave women's resistance in what he called the "General Strike," the mass uprising by slaves with multiple strategies of resistance that broke out at the start of the Civil War and throughout.[37] Thus, a fuller treatment of Du Bois requires a theorization of sexuality and gender as undertaken in Black and other feminist treatments of white supremacy and capitalism. This essay will point to the significance of that treatment by referencing the masculinist character of much of the "alt-right" and its corporate sponsors. A number of current studies highlight the gendered and sexual dynamics at play in the alt-right "manosphere." It is crucial to emphasize with Black and other women-of-color theorists that a sex/gender politics is also co-constitutive of the state violence worked by "racial capitalism."[38] As historian Sarah Haley reminds readers in her analysis of Black women's experience of punishment in U.S. carceral systems, racial capitalism needs to be analyzed as "*gendered* racial capitalism."[39] At best, Du Bois offers only fleeting provocations toward this latter notion, but they are significant provocations.[40]

The following sections of this chapter lift out the five key elements in Du Bois's analysis that are instructive for us. These I propose as a template for reflecting on race and capitalism in today's race-in-capitalism complex. My comments become more contemporary only as I move into the second of Du Bois's five elements.

A Tale of Two Oligarchies

In the aftermath of the Civil War, the political scene featured not simply a victor and vanquished, a triumphant North and a defeated South. One sees a divided capitalism. Du Bois tells throughout his book what I call a "tale of two oligarchies." Throughout *Black Reconstruction*, these are referred to as "two forces of Northern and Southern capitalists."[41] Although "with the Civil War the planters died as a class,"[42] afterward they maintained most of their land while having lost their slaves and wealth. Before the war, the Southern planter entrepreneurs had become "the richest class of white people in the U.S., and perhaps the world."[43] From the fiery furnace of slave-based cotton Southern aristocracy, embers of the Old South still glowed in the ashes of the Civil War. Both white supremacy and capitalism would fan those embers to flame, into a new fierce system of exploitation in the United States and abroad.

Crucial here is the other oligarchy triumphant after the war: the Northern capitalists. They were delighted not so much by emancipation of slaves as by the reduction of Southern capital as a competitive force. During Reconstruction, as Du Bois observes, Northern industry lobbied against reduction of the tariffs on the South and for taxation on imports. This had fattened Northern industry during the Civil War.[44] The tariff and taxation policies had supported a class monopoly by Northern industrialists at the expense of both Northern agriculture and rising and struggling Southern agriculture.[45] Throughout the Civil War and deep into Reconstruction, there occurred a struggle between these two oligarchies. Again, Du Bois's own words are important:

> It was a battle between oligarchy whose wealth and power had been based on land and slaves on the one hand; and on the other, oligarchy built on machines and hired labor. The newly organized industry of the North was not only triumphant in the North but began pressing in upon the South. . . .[46]

Interaction between the two oligarchies is an important dynamic throughout the book. Permit me now to move quickly to the second element of the Du Boisian framework before turning to the current period.

The "Abolitionist" Oligarchy

A persistent thread in Du Bois's *Black Reconstruction* concerns the phenomenon of "abolition-democracy" during Reconstruction. On the one hand, this phenomenon features for Du Bois a set of positive, genuinely abolitionist, and democratic forces working to empower former slaves and end all vestiges of slavery. This set of positive forces could include the mighty oratory of Thaddeus Stevens and Charles Sumner in the U.S. Senate. Du Bois designates them and others as Northern "crusaders with a great cause and meticulously honest."[47] Especially worth considering are the many efforts of Blacks themselves to institutionalize emancipation by building schools and securing elected office, among other means. Crucial here was the Freedmen's Bureau, which for a time enjoyed the backing of U.S. military forces in the South.[48]

On the other hand, there were more negative forces in the abolition-democracy movement. These rendered only tepid support of abolition and democratic reconstruction for Blacks and poor whites in the South. Among these negative forces were the Northern industrialists. As financiers who enjoyed the monopoly I mentioned previously, these "had in self-defense to join with abolition-democracy in forcing universal suffrage in the South, or submit to the reassertion of the old land-slave feudalism with increased political power."[49] Across his book's more than 700 pages, Du Bois highlights the significant role of this brutal disingenuousness of Northern industry, an "effective combination . . . both curious and contradictory."[50] The Republican Party in the 1860s and 1870s (from the start of the Civil War to the collapsing of Reconstruction) built its platform to serve Negro freedoms and also the desires of Northern industry. Du Bois comments, "Thus a movement which began primarily and sincerely to abolish slavery and insure the Negroes' rights, came coupled with a struggle of capitalism to retain control of the government as against Northern labor and [against] Southern and Western agriculture."[51] This Northern oligarchy is what I term an abolitionist oligarchy—"abolitionist," of course, only as a self-interested pose—that could be dismantled by advocates of abolition themselves when such advocacy no longer served the interests of Northern economic and political power.

So it is that Du Bois's exposure of this Northern "abolitionist" oligarchy prompts us to consider a phenomenon certainly not limited to Du Bois's time. Indeed this is, I suggest, especially pertinent to current U.S. national politics. I refer to the phenomenon of "humanitarian, generous, democratic," even "emancipatory," advocacy by forces of capital. The more blatant examples include the U.S. military business interests' assault on Iraq in 2003,[52] with claims even that its intervention would be greeted by Iraqis as a liberation.[53] World Bank and International Monetary Fund leaders often lead with language of "inclusive development" and even "liberation."[54] Many philanthropic liberalisms speak of "helping the poor," and "developing" poorer communities while never questioning the corporate structures that perpetuate the interests of a small class of wealthy nations that sustain global hierarchy.[55]

At this point, the most important lesson for us is just the distinction—indeed often a division—in today's capitalist class. On the one hand, there is a blatant, chauvinistic, daringly racist sector of ruling class wealth that is then also often imbibed at all levels of society. On the other hand, there is a more sophisticated group that poses as anti-racist, full of inclusive-sounding rhetoric, and at times even espouses ideals of racial liberation. With this division in mind, we might distinguish, as I have in an earlier work, between two corporate cultures of power: "corporate libertarian profiteers" and "corporate liberal cosmopolitans."[56] The libertarian profiteers are usually unrestrained in announcing their unbridled pursuit of profit. They see few if any problems with class hierarchy, racist attitudes, or the global division of labor and power.[57] Cosmopolitan liberals are more reticent about allying with such extreme chauvinistic rhetoric. They cloak their profit-making in advocacy of economic "development" and liberal philanthropy as uplift, promotion of democracy, and empowerment (recall Bill Clinton's "empowerment zones"[58]).

Turn now to racism considered in relation to this division in current capitalism. Today's alt-right leans toward the more blatant racism of corporate profiteers. Alt-right leader Richard Spencer's promotion of white identity and forms of a "white ethnostate" would seem far removed from either the corporate profiteers or the corporate cosmopolitans. But as the alt-right came to widespread notice, its links to the blatant corporate profiteers and their chauvinisms (racial and misogynous) were evident, especially via its connections to Breitbart News. Steve Bannon served as Breitbart News's executive chairman from 2012 to 2018, except for seven months of that time when he was Trump's White House Chief Strategist. On the eve of Bannon's short tenure in the White House, he announced in 2016 that Breitbart News is "the platform of the alt-right." Later, though, Bannon backed away from that claim, instead advocating an *economic* nationalism" and stating, "Bigotry or white supremacy in any form is blasphemy against the American creed."[59] After the alt-right showed its even uglier politics of racism to lethal effect in Charlottesville, Bannon derided the alt-right as a "collection of clowns" and "losers."[60] Which is it? Bannon was politically savvy enough to play it both ways. He could state that his news site's aims were "economic nationalism" while making pitches to racist whites in the alt-right with his claims to be their platform. He also continued to run stories that were xenophobic, claiming to document extensive "Black crime," and championed the flying of the Confederate flag. Whatever Bannon's backtracking and ambiguous rhetoric, there was little doubt about his willingness to risk being seen as a racist and an ally to the alt-right. Bannon's advocacy of the alt-right while also backtracking from it may make him a promoter of what has been called the "alt-lite." Political scientist George Hawley describes the "alt-lite" as those "people whose views on immigration and race relations partially overlap with those on the alt-right yet do not cross the line into open white nationalism . . . The alt-lite believes in the superiority of Western culture and values (including some values, such as tolerance, which many on the alt-right reject), but it does not necessarily believe nonwhites are incapable of thriving in Western countries."[61] Because of Breitbart News's alt-right/alt-lite boundary position—and because its policies and publications usually refuse to repudiate white supremacism and in fact promote the most blatant of white supremacist symbols (the Confederate flag)[62]—I will term this side of the division in capitalism the "corporate racists."

These can be contrasted with what I will term the "corporate anti-racists," those whose rhetoric often lifts up frequent criticisms of white supremacy and even of exploitative economic conditions. The problem is that these same critics are often unmindful or duplicitous about how the very structure of capital is and has been white supremacist. Hillary Clinton may be the key example here, especially with her campaign speech against Trump and his supporters, indicting Trump's hiring of Bannon, especially for Breitbart News's article "Hoist It High and Proud: The Confederate Flag Proclaims a Glorious Heritage."[63] Clinton makes no mention of how U.S. corporate and imperial formation are often part of the very white supremacy she decries.

What one sees in this class division, then, are two different kinds of racism. In Joel Kovel's language, the corporate libertarian profiteers, those who give support to groups with blatant racist positions, display a "dominative racism."[64] This is an explicit acting out of bigoted viewpoints and policies that overtly target Blacks and people of color and immigrants from the global South. Kovel sees this tendency as historically belonging to the Old South in the United States. Contemporary defenses of the Confederate flag highlight this historical lineage of dominative racism. This lineage lives whenever threats to white supremacy are met with white rage, enforced policies of separatism and supremacy, and the threat or realization of white violence (by mobs or state forces such as the police).

The other kind of racism Kovel terms "aversive racism." It is just as powerful but does not act out directly. Its basic tendencies are to respond to threats by Black and Brown peoples with aversion, avoidance, denial (color-blindness claims, for example)—often with coldness and silence. According to Kovel, this was and is the racism of the North, although this racism no more than the first flows only in accord with geographical region.[65] It is manifest in Senator Clinton's at times maternalizing condescension to Black Lives Matter activists, in her and her family's support for mass incarceration, especially worsened by Bill Clinton's crafting of new limits on prisoners' rights to appeal their convictions. This latter development was paramount for keeping thousands of people behind bars for longer periods.[66] Proponents of these policies may often condemn the blatant chauvinisms of dominative racism. They do little, however, to dismantle the structures of corporate power and discriminatory patterns that routinize outcomes of social policy in ways detrimental to people of color.[67] The aversive racists, again primarily among corporate liberal cosmopolitans, throw a patina over white supremacy, such that the worst of it can easily be resurgent under the next dominative racists who may assume power. As French philosopher Alain Badiou intoned about governance by oligarchs vying with one another: "In the chambers of state the adversary's bed must always be made."[68] So the aversive racists often make the beds for the dominative racists, as often the liberal cosmopolitans do for the libertarian profiteers—and yes, as Clintonian neoliberalism has done for Trumpian authoritarianism.[69]

Both dominative and aversive racisms reinforce one another to entrench what Kovel terms white supremacy's "metaracism."[70] This is a more elusive kind of racism that permeates the media, our technological society, and often the impersonal cultural patterns of everyday life. Metaracism is the matrix and milieu wherein dominative and aversive racism coalesce. Crucially, both racisms are diffused throughout capitalist and late-capitalist society. Today's "alt-right" needs to be analyzed in this matrix of metaracism. Without this perspective, the alt-right is only a sector of crazy "white boys," and we fail to grasp the full force of what is before us. In Hawley's terms there is an "overlap" of the alt-right with the alt-lite.[71] The two mutually enable one another. In other words, elements of dominative racism in the alt-right become more palatable as aversive racism through alt-lite toleration (as in Bannon's deceptive and ambiguous Breitbart News articles). The alt-right's "overlapping" with the alt-lite creates an enabling dialectic; together they form an ideology that enables white racism to permeate capitalist society in ways that reinforce both "aversive racism" and "dominative racism" in a metaracist, capitalist system.

When the Oligarchies Coalesce

This brings us to one of the most significant elements of Du Bois's analysis of the end of Reconstruction. What dealt Reconstruction its death blow, ending hopes for the effective post–Civil War institutionalizing of emancipation, were the dynamics that brought the two oligarchies, Northern and Southern, into coalition. White supremacy (as social practices working against Blacks and indirectly other groups of color) *and* capitalism (as social practices working against labor, both Black and white, and in both the North and South) were insurgent together. As two of Du Bois's chapter titles put it, the end of Reconstruction became under the power of this coalition, a "Counter-Revolution of Property" as well as a move "Back to Slavery."

At first, immediately after the Civil War, this coalescence of Northern and Southern oligarchies was masked. Northern oligarchs' pressure on Southern oligarchs took the form of its advocacy against the South of "abolition-democracy." At the same time, what Du Bois identifies as the Northern oligarchy's "advance guard" went to work in the South as "small Northern capitalist and office-holders who sought to make quick money in raising cotton and taking advantage of the low-priced labor and high cotton prices due to war famine."[72]

By 1876, however, the North sensed that the Southern oligarchy was at a competitive disadvantage. At this point Northern industrialists let go of their "abolitionist" postures and withdrew their support for the U.S. troops who were enforcing policies consistent with the emancipatory amendments. Du Bois saw these troops in the South as a legitimate temporary "military dictatorship"[73] needed to defend the constitution for the Black vote, Black land, and representation—in short, for the emancipation promised to them. When the troops were withdrawn, writes Du Bois, the United States "ceased to sustain the right to vote of half the laboring power of the South and left capital represented by the old planter class [of the South], the new Northern capitalist, *and* the capitalist that began to rise out of the poor whites." The result was "a control of labor greater than in any modern industrial state in civilized lands."[74]

Thus, Du Bois shows a coalition of both the Northern and Southern oligarchs—in the South, a "new oligarchy" fused with the North and built upon "the tottering depleted foundations of the [South's] old oligarchy."[75] In the late nineteenth century and extending into the Jim Crow period, the South's new rulers became "more ignorant, intolerant and ruthless because of their inferiority complex."[76] The North welcomed these new rulers, having itself "never been thoroughly converted to the idea of Negro equality," save when the Northern liberal cosmopolitans struck their abolitionist-democracy pose to weaken the South's hold on land and wealth. So weakened, the Southern oligarchy, by 1880 grafted into Northern industry, offered a "capitalistic dictatorship of the United States, which became the most powerful in the world and which backed the new industrial imperialism and degraded colored labor the world over."[77] The notion here of worldwide degradation of "*colored* labor" prompts us now to consider the role Du Bois attributed to "race" in these developments.

The "Race Philosophy" in the Capitalist Matrix

Du Bois treated the construct of race in two closely related ways. This two-fold treatment is clear especially in his "Back to Slavery" chapter, where he presents race as both an "element" and as an entire, more comprehensive "philosophy." As *element* it was a tool, functioning with the strategic aim of exploiting Negro labor, doing this with the assistance of white workers who were enlisted to aid white capitalists' exploitation by dividing them from their Black coworkers. But to achieve this, a more expansive, all-permeating *race philosophy* was needed, one disseminated everywhere from folklore to science and designed to create an ethos of assumed "Black ineptitude" in the Reconstruction period. Blacks were said to not work efficiently, to be uneducated and unable to teach, and to be incapable overall of acting responsibly. Nor could they hold office to govern well or with distinction. In fact, Blacks were increasingly held responsible for the entire failure of Reconstruction, so much so that in the 1930s when Du Bois was writing *Black Reconstruction*, this alleged "ineptitude" of Blacks was the common reason circulated in North and South, and by many historians themselves, for Reconstruction's demise.[78] Thus, a more comprehensive function of the race philosophy was "to make labor unity or labor class-consciousness impossible." It was an attack on the entire possibility of a united powerful labor movement in the South of white and Black workers. With that attack there emerged a new promulgation of white worldviews about Blacks as lacking capacities for living well or leading others.[79] The result was the dissemination of a white supremacist metaracism permeating views of society and work, such that the nation was propelled into later historical periods of continuing cultural and institutional racism: into the Jim Crow era of the late nineteenth and twentieth centuries, into the government repression of Black freedom movements in the mid-twentieth-century era of civil rights and Black Power, and into today's era of "the New Jim Crow" with its racialized mass incarceration and police violence.[80] In today's context, these are not just criminal justice problems or racial injustice issues. They remain also an economic problem. Some fifty million U.S. citizens are in poverty or "near poverty."[81] The resultant insecurity creates perfect conditions for the surveillance and war industries of today's U.S. neoliberalism.[82]

This metaracist "race philosophy" is especially important to recall and theorize today. Instead, however, mainstream U.S. media tend to keep their focus on discrete racist acts largely perpetrated by individuals with bigoted intentions. Even "the liberal Left" plays along with foregrounding rhetoric about racially bigoted individuals, with many versions of headlines like "Here are the 13 Examples of Trump Being Racist." Sure, these and other of Trump's remarks *are* racist as are those by alt-rightists, by Charlottesville's marchers and chanters, and by individual authors writing at Breitbart News. But the power of these examples of "dominative racism" to hold good, to put down roots and to endure, comes from their interaction within a metaracist and capitalist system within which aversive racism circulates in cultural settings where often even "anti-racist liberals" move with alleged respectability, sophistication, and "civility."

It should come as no surprise then that today some of the most effusive spending that supports alt-right platforms comes from those in the highest echelons of corporate power. This corporate milieu is not as far removed from the alt-right worlds as some might think. Perhaps a key and exemplary link here is evident in Robert Mercer and the way he has funded key voices of white supremacist rhetoric.[83]

Mercer, a wealthy hedge-fund tycoon, co-CEO of Renaissance Technologies, was "a brilliant computer scientist," according to investigative journalist and author Jane Mayer. He "helped transform the financial industry through the innovative use of trading algorithms."[84] He invested $5 million in Cambridge Analytica, a firm that "mines online data to reach and influence potential voters."[85] One of Mercer's own associates at Renaissance was fired, writes Mayer, for concluding that Mercer was a white supremacist. A lawsuit filed by this associate alleges Mercer opining that before the Civil Rights Acts infantilized them, Black people were doing fine and that "the only remaining racist people in the U.S. were black."[86]

Mercer denies any allegiance to white supremacism, but white supremacist proclivities are intimated by his giving more than $10 million to *Breitbart News*. Bannon, with co-founder Andrew Breitbart, received early support for starting the news site with millions of dollars from Mercer. He is said to have "out-Koched the Koch brothers" (Charles and David) in campaign funding influence. With his politically interventionist daughter Rebekah Mercer by his side, Mercer may have single-handedly rescued Trump's candidacy when his campaign was floundering in summer 2016.[87] Robert's funding support for Trump was reportedly waning in 2018 due to a falling out with Bannon.[88] But in 2020, he renewed his support to Trump's campaign with a $355 million donation, thus joining others among Trump's corporate supporters. These others included magnate Sheldon Adelson and his wife (giving $1.2 million), New York Stock Exchange Chairman Jeffrey Sprecher and his wife, Georgia Republican Senator Kelly Loeffler ($580,600), casino and resort CEOs and the chief executive of private-equity firm Blackstone Group ($3 million).[89] Both Robert and Rebekah Mercer strongly supported Jeff Sessions as U.S. Attorney General, with Rebekah serving on Trump's transition team. The owner of the conservative Newsmax Media, which saw a surge in Trump viewers in 2020, once described Rebekah as "the First Lady of the alt-right," largely because of her and her father's financing of Breitbart News's site, keeping it on the rise to ever greater notoriety. Mayer notes that "according to ComScore, a company that measures online traffic, the *Breitbart News* site attracted 19.2 million unique visitors in October."[90]

One final point about Mercer. His Renaissance Technologies, writes Mayer, "according to Andrew Lo, a finance professor at M.I.T.'s Sloan School of Management, is . . . 'the commercial version of the Manhattan Project.' Intensely secretive and filled with people with Ph.D.s, it has been sensationally profitable. Its Medallion Fund, which is open only to the firm's three hundred or so employees, has averaged returns of almost eighty percent a year, before fees. Bloomberg News has called the Medallion Fund 'perhaps the world's greatest moneymaking machine.'"[91]

Whether the Mercers as individuals are racist or not, their advocacy of withdrawing all state limits on white supremacist venues and their organized resistance to state regulations on capital in the name of Ayn Rand libertarianism, function to spur systematic white racism embedded in social practices. This is especially evident in their funding of Breitbart News to send support to the alt-right, even though this is often done through a kind of "alt-lite" media discourse. Again we see Breitbart News as a site whose enabling of the alt-right/alt-lite dialectic thereby services a metaracist ideology and strengthens the rule of white supremacy and capital.[92]

So we have an extraordinarily wealthy and politically influential family from financial capitalism's wealthiest stratum, which facilitated Trump's campaign and political coverage by bringing into being and sustaining one of the most accessed online news sites, Breitbart News, which functioned as an alt-right/alt-lite platform. Corporate wealth continues to mainstream the alt-right, strengthening metaracist dynamics and structures. At the time of this writing in 2021, the corporate funding of white supremacy seems to be metastasizing; the wealth of corporately connected donors continues to find its way into white supremacist groups, into the alt-right and others, as groups like "Amazon, PayPal and Spotify often inadvertently fund white supremacists," as do also, perhaps, some established charities with corporate connections."[93] In the wake of the January 6, 2021 storming of the U.S. Capitol by many members of white supremacist groups, representatives of major corporations (Facebook, Google, and so on) withdrew enabling funds and social media platforms. Still, in the aftermath of the white riot, it became evident how important is the funding provided by wealthy donors such as the Mercers to white supremacist groups.[94]

It is not anachronistic to observe that current capitalism's nurture of this white supremacist ethos plays the role that Du Bois discerned in his analysis of coalescing capitalist oligarchies' use of "race philosophy." Of course, "philosophy" is too distinguished a term for what is, in fact, a loosely constructed white supremacist ideology for capitalist oligarchies that profit still from a racially divided American populace of workers and the unemployed.

The penchant for secrecy among corporate funders of white supremacists permeates the esotericism that often links the Christian Right to U.S. corporate culture and the U.S. government. I return to this theme in the next section. Here, it is important to mention the near secret religion among the "KEK" and "Pepe" memes proliferating among devotees of the young white alt-right groups, which fascinate and titillate the young online racists.[95] There is also the secrecy of Mercer family projects, especially its secretive Medallion Fund.

The Mercers have also provided hundreds of thousands of dollars to another secretive group, the Council for National Policy (CNP), which nurtures connections between powerful conservatives in corporate culture and key figures on the Christian Right.[96] U.S. presidential candidates such as George W. Bush in 1999 have presented major speeches before this council, and yet as multiple venues have reported, these speeches remain unavailable to the public, even when given by one running for the nation's highest electoral post.[97] While serving as Vice President in 2007, Dick Cheney made a quick trip to give a "confidential" speech to a CNP meeting in Salt Lake City, Utah.[98] Mayer writes that "the group swears participants to secrecy. But a leaked 2014 roster revealed that it included many people who promoted anti-Clinton conspiracy stories, including Joseph Farah, the editor of WorldNetDaily [WND]."[99] The Mercers joined the CNP at the Council's invitation. Working in the group also has been L. Brent Bozell III, of the Media Research Center (MRC). According to Mayer, from 2011 to 2014, "the Mercers gave nearly eleven million dollars to the MRC," an advocacy group whose "sole mission," according to its website, "is to expose and neutralize the propaganda arm of the Left: the national news media." Mayer concludes, "The Mercers have been among the MRC's biggest donors, and their money has allowed the group to revamp its news site, and it now claims to reach more than two hundred million Americans a week."[100] Others in the CNP include Christian Right leaders from James Dobson's group, Focus on the Family. Tony Perkins, a Christian "Pro-Life" and "Pro-Family" advocate from the Family Research Council, is now President of the CNP. The CNP also played the role, writes Mayer, of bringing the Mercers into proximity with two others at the Trump White House: Kellyanne Conway, who was on CNP's executive committee, and Bannon.[101] The penchant for secrecy, whether in the CNP, in the Mercers' Renaissance Technologies and Medallion Fund, or in the online gaming of alt-righters, takes me to the final element from the Du Bois framework.

Capital's Secret Orders

In this context, I can now introduce the notion of capital's secret orders. These orders are, we might say, "the stormtroopers" of the race philosophy and white supremacist ideology, but in service *also* to capital. They are often invisible to many—until they're not. Du Bois writes that the secret orders' purpose was "to fasten the dictatorship of property over labor upon the South." This began immediately at the Civil War's end in 1865.[102] Poor whites enlisted into the secret orders and thus did "the dirty work of revolution" for the coalescing oligarchies destroying Reconstruction. "This was the birth and being of the Ku Klux Klan."[103] After capital's division of Black and white labor by the race philosophy, it was the secret orders that "beat the black laborer into subjection."[104] The secret orders were bands of "regulators"[105] for capital, emphasized Du Bois, "which systematized the effort to subordinate the Negro."[106] It was the secret orders that eventually implanted a nearly routine vigilantism against Blacks. They also often came down hard on whites who sided with Blacks.[107]

It is important when we recall this vigilantism in Reconstruction that we not think of the KKK, as it is often discussed today, as forceful but relatively occasional and contained.[108] In Reconstruction, it blossomed from and extended beyond what we see today. In Du Bois's language, the KKK, which started in Tennessee, became "a larger and more inclusive secret order."[109] Crucial to its enlarging and growing inclusivity was the race element and the "new unity" that the race philosophy afforded it. In his 2017 biography of Ulysses S. Grant, Ron Chernow shows under the Grant Presidency (1868–76) that as thousands of Blacks were murdered and maimed, the Klan went from "social club" to "quasi-military organization," or from a "free-floating network of thuggish white groups" to movements enlisting former soldiers (Confederates),[110] to then a "comprehensive movement that spanned the entire white community" in key states. It soon also constituted, writes Chernow, a "grand system of criminal associations pervading most of the Southern States."[111] Chernow reports that Grant managed to indict 3,384 Klan agents and convicted over a thousand. And even when the North's industrial powers moved against Grant's Attorney General Amos Akerman to have him removed, the Grant administration still pressed aggressively its war against the Klan.[112] Eventually, Grant, under pressure from the North's oligarchic forces, also grew weary of supporting the military troops in the South.[113]

The important point here is that when we hear Du Bois's word "vigilantism," or even "routine vigilantism," we need to note that he referenced a *system-wide* secret order that needed exposing, not only an informal and *ad hoc* development. As system-wide it was often orchestrated by the highest levels of official governance. To fight the Klan in his day, Grant's officials and military personnel even had to remove governors of states, as they did Louisiana's Governor James M. Wells, a vigorous opponent of Reconstruction.[114] This meant that from the lower levels to the highest levels, the problem was not just scattered vigilante groups but also those catalyzing and growing within a metaracist system of white supremacy and capital that involved agents at the highest levels. One may retort, "some 'secret'!" Indeed, we are again back to the notion of secrecy as "open secret" as "hidden in plain sight."[115]

Throughout *Black Reconstruction* Du Bois subjected this systemic complex of white supremacy to an analysis that revealed its political and sinister social-psychological character. In this character dynamics of fear and secrecy work in tandem. He argued that white vigilantism and resultant mob rule needed to be viewed within a system of "fear" that both capital and white supremacy created and sustained. Strikingly for Du Bois, the "inner nucleus" of this fear was the "fear of unemployment." He developed this point in an especially rich passage reflecting on fear's relation to mob rule and racist violence. White mob rule is motivated by fear, he suggested. Du Bois pushes further: but fear "of what?" He responds: "Of many things, but usually of losing their jobs, being declassed, degraded, or actually disgraced; of losing their hopes, their savings, their plans for their children; of the actual pangs of hunger; of dirt, of crime. And of all this, most ubiquitous in modern industrial society is that fear of unemployment."[116]

Is the alt-right such a "secret order?" The secrecy and online clubs of trollers and quasi-religious meme-sharing make them seem so. But they only approximate the forces Du Bois traces when they are seen in relation to a race philosophy that pulses more silently in alt-lite modalities, in aversive racism permeating structures of both white supremacy and capitalism. Indeed, many of the alt-right's online trolls and devotees prefer online anonymity and thus also seem capable of being shamed, as when after the events in Charlottesville, several white participants were outted by online movement to expose their racist actions in the streets.[117] After Charlottesville, as Angela Nagle documents, the alt-right was also exposed as whites who had been expressing "Millennial Woes" (the name of one alt-right website). These "woes" were driven by "forces behind the movement" such as "the rapid demographic transformation of the Western world" and a failure to deliver on "the promise of material progress." Nagle even suggests that the best way to fight the alt-right, those young "lost boys" now growing old without a sense of having any future, might be to bring back "a spirit of class solidarity."[118] This is certainly consonant with Du Bois's analysis of what is necessary for fighting "the race philosophy." The secret orders are powered by the fear of material woes that both white supremacism and Western capitalism create.

Because the problem with the secret orders is this extensive and deep—whether we think of the Klan or the varied and changing formations of the alt-right and white supremacy today—redressing it means we need to look beyond the outted and shameable white boys online and beyond the "loose concatenation" of white identarian forces called the alt-right. We need to look elsewhere than to even Spencer's on-campus shock speeches, however much they are crucial parts of capitalism's continually disseminated "race philosophy" dividing the populace, atomizing and individualizing them in ways that serve market interests. The 2021 civil suit that was won against Spencer and other white supremacists was a valuable step.[119] But there is also a need to be vigilant about how the alt-right can metastasize through the so-called "alt-lite" within the aversive racism that is society-wide and that carries dominative racism into structures of capital that shape white supremacy and its routinized violence. We need to look to those powers catalyzing or catalyzed by white supremacism today that can become "a grand system of criminal association" as it was faced, in one example, by Grant's administration.[120]

Thus, if one wants to expose capital's secret orders, in Du Bois's sense of the term, we need to keep to the fore the patterns at work in corporately supported racist groupings, "elite class thugs" in high places and elsewhere. These include not only the likes of Mercer of the Medallion Fund and Renaissance Technologies but also perhaps especially the collective elite groups like the secretive CNP that intentionally coordinates mingling and co-planning of Christian rightists with U.S. corporate leaders and with political warrior elite figures. Not only do they pray together, but they also plot and prey on others to defend racial capitalism.[121] These secret societies formed among governing elites should not be set outside the realm of those secret orders that function as veritable stormtroopers of capital and white supremacy. Their meetings are held in secret as is the money circulating to and through them for their policies—"dark money," a term used by Jane Mayer to describe the way hidden, untraceable funds often power the ideologies of the rich through "social welfare organizations."[122]

Beyond this task of exposing these secret societies in U.S. corporate ranks, which I have only begun here, I suggest that we look in two other directions as well.

First, we do well to continue monitoring the armed white militias, which did not receive quite as much attention in the early days of the Trump presidency as did the alt-right online white boys of that period. In the waning weeks of the 2020 presidential election, however, Trump began signaling ever more overtly his support of white supremacist groups. He remained largely silent, for example, when the Michigan militia hatched plots to kidnap the governor of Michigan.[123] Militias were also present at the Charlottesville marches and counter-protests, but they kept a low profile compared to alt-right marchers, even if they gave off a greater menacing specter due to their display of firearms at the August 2017 march where the media tended to foreground the alt-right.[124] These militias were the most heavily armed groups at the march event, often better armed than the police on hand. We should not be surprised. The SPLC has been tracking such militia groups for years. When reporting on the 2014 standoff of the Federal government with the white militia groups in the Nevada desert and on the later 2016 Oregon takeover of a Federal building, the SPLC "identified 276 militia groups—up from 202 in 2014, a 37% increase."[125] Most of these white militia groups deny connections to the alt-right and white supremacy, and also to Neo-Nazis, but they still hold views of the United States as having lost its way and being primarily under attack by Islam.[126] The alt-right online "lost boys" share much of this rhetoric. After Charlottesville, the militia groups increasingly inserted themselves into 2020 electoral politics, showing familiar white nationalist proclivities.[127]

Second, we need to focus on the standing and legally sanctioned, but barely accountable, forces and officers in U.S. police departments. The killing of Black and Brown youth, usually in urban cities, and of Native Americans by police on reservations and elsewhere, is even more exemplary of the type of secret orders about which Du Bois writes. These killings, of Blacks in urban spaces and American Indians in rural spaces, are often intricately connected to contemporary capital's drive to "gentrify" or "develop" poor communities, or to extract natural resources from their lands. Such "development" and "extraction" requires destabilization, control, and often dispossession of communities in those areas. All this makes the recent violent actions of police understandable, as they perform the dirty work of capital, reinforcing a systemic subjugation of the poor, who are disproportionately Black, Brown,[128] and also "Red."[129] Just as the alt-right have their secret memes and mythologies online to enhance white identity, the police have their largely secret lodges and sometimes logos and insignia, which function to bond them in a white identity while carrying out their "public service." Nevertheless one does not need to go looking for secret societies *within* the police, when in fact an already pervasive "code of silence" or "blue wall of silence" among standing U.S. police departments makes of their normal operations a kind of secret order in the U.S. body politic.[130]

One might especially consider today the Fraternal Order of Police (FOP). As Paul Butler, a prosecutor and law professor at Harvard and Georgetown Universities notes, the FOP is "the nation's largest police association, boasting more than 300,000 members" and "within its 2,000 local chapters its national leadership is made up of seven white officials." While claiming that 30 percent of its members are officers of color, its white leaders continue to provide racist defenses for police shootings or descend to calling the Black Lives Matter movement—as did the head of the FOP in Philadelphia at a "Back the Blue" rally—a "pack of rabid animals."[131] Thus, as Butler writes, it should be of concern that a capital-bought[132] government in Washington and increasingly in state governments is now facilitating the transfer of new shipments of surplus military equipment to police programs, this under the 1033 program that "would give local police departments surplus military equipment including bayonets, tanks, and grenade launchers."[133] Militarized police have also been supplemented in 2020 by SWAT teams from U.S. Immigration and Customs Enforcement (I.C.E.), used against Black Lives Matter's peaceful protestors in, for one example, Portland, Oregon.[134]

The absence of associations organized within or by police personnel explicitly to support Black Lives Matter or to generate public critique of racialized police killings, renders the entire U.S. police force a largely silent and secret order for the killing and repression of the Black, Brown, and poor—again, as Michael German writes, this order is "hidden in plain sight."[135] Historically, it is a matter of record that U.S. police and other officials (judges, ministers, lawyers, and businessmen) were participants in the Klan and other secret orders.[136] That the police would itself become a secret order servicing both capital and white supremacy is no surprise. And if one further recalls that the bulk of police history can be traced to slave patrolling and Indian removal and containment, then we can see the police as a kind of secret order securitizing capital's interests in slavery, land, and markets.[137]

In short, heavily armed white militias throughout the country, *and* militarily reinforced police on U.S. city streets, are forces that must be engaged—exposed and resisted—if we are to resist "capital's secret orders." In a sense, after the white mob assault on the United States Capitol of January 6, 2021, major aspects of "the secret" are now exposed. Previously kept on the fringe of the mainstream media, news reports on white supremacism are now more prominent. White supremacist groups are shown now to enlist many types of people from white communities. Members of those communities feature a mélange of predominantly white everyday folk, mixed with members of militia groups, law enforcement, correctional officers, and military veterans. At this writing it looks like the assault mob was, at least in part, enabled by preliminary orders from the Trump administration, formal or informal, to delay approvals for deploying the Washington D.C. National Guard on January 6 to the Capitol building.[138] Moreover, any such deployments of the D.C. Guard would have had to be approved, if not by Trump himself, then by favored personnel that he himself had placed atop the Department of Defense just after he had lost the election and was facing the end of his presidency.[139] In these ways, paramilitary and military personnel, supported by corporate power at work in the highest levels of national governance, often strengthen the whole complex of racial capitalism.

Much of this will remain shrouded to U.S. citizen observers. Secrecy among official and semi-official orders and groups has been essential to statecraft throughout the history of governing powers. It is, writes Du Bois, "a method as old as humanity."[140] Secrecy, he further noted, heightens terror, as when white sheets not only "hid" the official status of agents riding in the night. Secrecy had additional functions. Whether in the alt-right or especially in the white militias and the police, it encourages participants to risk doing what they might fear to do in the light of day. Pertinent to understanding the power of secrecy in white supremacy today is Du Bois's reminder in *Black Reconstruction* that secrecy often "attracts people who otherwise could not be reached." What he terms "the outrage of maiming and murder," an outrage people are usually "afraid and ashamed to do openly," is accomplished when done "secretly, masked or at night." Fear, in Du Bois's view, among people who are deeply anxious about their pending losses or replacement, drives them to shameful acts that when done under a "veil of darkness" often also take on an aura of attractive mystery, even "glamor."[141]

In sum, the threat of white supremacy cannot be fought by obsessing over the "alt-right" and bringing it alone into the light of day. The forces that fasten *the dispossessions of capital* upon working people and form the related *daily repressions of white supremacy* are at work in places already heavily armed, and often cloaked in ideologies of respect and reverence (the police and military, at work in the United States and abroad). Any religion, any people of faith who are committed to resisting white supremacy, cannot stop with exposing and resisting the alt-right today. They must also direct their interests into the center of the race-in-capitalism complex that Du Bois foregrounded. It is a complex that has been stubbornly persistent in U.S. history. Ultimately, that complex lies in that region so many U.S. citizens dare not admit: the space where our militant wars on racialized peoples at home and abroad are related to the powers of big capital. This entire complex is an ominous power, one whose secrecy is often left unchallenged by many in religious communities. We ignore that complex today at the peril of any real hopes for justice, social equality, and peace.

Notes

1. W. E. B. Du Bois, *Black Reconstruction in America, 1860–1880*, first published 1935 (New York: The Free Press, 1992), 535.

2. W. E. B. Du Bois, "The Souls of Black Folk," in *W. E. B. Du Bois: Writings*, Library of America (New York: Literary Classics of the United States, 1986), 372.

3. Matthew Countrymen, "2020 Uprisings, Unprecedented in Scope, Join a Long River of Struggle in America," *The Conversation*, June 20, 2020, https://the conversation.com/2020-uprisings-unprecedented-in-scope-join-a-long-river-of-struggle -in-america-139853.

4. Cedric J. Robinson, *Black Marxism: The Making of the Black Radical Tradition*, 3rd edition (Chapel Hill: University of North Carolina Press, 2021), 9–28.

5. Robin D. G. Kelley, "Foreword: Why Black Marxism? Why Now?," in Robinson, xiii.

6. Kelley is citing M4BL's document "A Vision for Black Lives: Demands for Black Power, Freedom & Justice," https://m4bl.org/policy-platforms/.

7. Tony Kirby, "Evidence Mounts of the Disproportionate Effect of COVID-19 on Ethnic Minorities," *The Lancet* 8, Respiratory Medicine (May 8, 2020): 547–48.

8. Zinzi D. Bailey, Nancy Krieger, Madina Agénor, Jasmine Graves, Natalia Linos, and Mary T. Bassett, "Structural Racism and Health Inequities in the USA: Evidence and Interventions," *The Lancet* 389 (April 8, 2017): 1453–63.

9. Keeanga-Yamahtta Taylor, *From #Blacklivesmatter to Black Liberation* (Chicago: Haymarket Books, 2016), 205–9.

10. One of the more even-handed analyses of the failures of the Trump regime, occurring in the *New York Times* was performed and written by those who have also been critical of the Obama regime. See Eric Lipton, David E. Sanger, Maggie Haberman, Michael D. Shear, Mark Mazzetti, and Julian E. Barnes, "He Could Have Seen What Was Coming: Behind Trump's Failure on the Virus," *New York Times*, April 11, 2020. For the Obama critic among these writers, see David E. Sanger, *Confront and Conceal: Obama's Secret Wars and Surprising Use of American Power* (New York: Crown, 2012).

11. Vincent C. C. Cheng, Susanna K. P. Lau, et al., "Severe Acute Respiratory Syndrome Coronavirus as an Agent of Emerging and Reemerging Infection," *Clinical Microbiology Reviews* 20 (October 2007): 660, 683.

12. Rob Wallace, Alex Liebman, Luis Fernando Chaves, and Rodrick Wallace, "Covid-19 and Circuits of Capital: New York to China and Back," *Monthly Review* 72, no. 1 (May 2020): 1–15, 6.

13. Whitney N. Laster Pirtle, "Racial Capitalism: A Fundamental Cause of Novel Coronavirus (COVID-19): Pandemic Inequities in the United States," *Health Education & Behavior* 47, no. 4 (April 2020): 504–8.

14. Kate Brown, "The Pandemic Is Not a Natural Disaster," *The New Yorker*, April 13, 2020, https://www.newyorker.com/culture/annals-of-inquiry/the-pandemic -is-not-a-natural-disaster.

15. Mike Davis, "Mike Davis on Pandemics, Super-Capitalism and the Struggles of Tomorrow," interview with Sharif Abdel Kouddous (fellow The Nation Institute, member of media collective Mosireen), in *Mada Masr*, March 30, 2020, https:// www.madamasr.com/en/2020/03/30/feature/politics/mike-davis-on-pandemics-super -capitalism-and-the-struggles-of-tomorrow/.

16. Jonah Engel Bromwich and Alan Blinder, "What We Know About James Alex Fields, Driver Charged in Charlottesville Killing, *New York Times*, August 13, 2017, https://www.nytimes.com/2017/08/13/us/james-alex-fields-charlottesville-driver-.html.

17. Bromwich and Blinder, see video insert with this article at the 0:51 second mark.

18. George Hawley, *Making Sense of the Alt-Right* (New York: Columbia University Press, 2017), 51–52.

19. Matthew N. Lyons, "CTRL-ALT-DELETE: The Origins and Ideology of the Alternative Right," *Political Research Associates: Challenging the Right, Advancing Social Justice*, January 20, 2017. Angela Nagle in a December issue of the *Atlantic* writes that "the Alt-Right is a fractious, fluid coalition comprising bloggers and vloggers, gamers, social-media personalities, and charismatic ringleaders like Spencer, who share an antiestablishment, anti-Left politics and an enthusiasm for the political career of Donald Trump." Angela Nagle, "The Lost Boys," *Atlantic*, December 2017, https://www.theatlantic.com/magazine/archive/2017/12 /brotherhood-of-losers/544158/.

I especially wish to express my appreciation for extensive research done by research assistant and doctoral candidate Maggie Elwell, who collected for me enormously helpful materials on the alt-right, only a few of which have been cited in this chapter but all of which were crucial to ideas formulated here.

20. Southern Poverty Law Center, *The Year in Hate and Extremism. 2019 Report* (Montgomery, Ala.: Southern Poverty Law Center, 2019), 9.

21. Ashley Jardina, *White Identity Politics* (New York: Cambridge University Press, 2019), 9.

22. David Neiwert, *Alt-America: The Rise of the Radical Right in the Age of Trump* (New York: Verso Books, 2018), 2.

23. Molly Nagle, "Biden Cites Charlottesville and Saving 'Soul' of U.S. in 2020 Presidential Bid," ABC News, April 25, 2019, https://abcnews.go.com/Politics /joe-biden-announces-2020-run-president/story?id=62579665.

24. Susan Brooks Thistlethwaite and Peter Crafts Hodgson, "The Church, Classism and Ecclesial Community," in *Reconstructing Christian Theology*, ed. Rebecca S. Chopp and Mark Lewis Taylor (Minneapolis: Fortress Press, 1994), 303–25, 305.

25. Mark Lewis Taylor, "Political Theology: Reflecting on the Arts of a Liberating Politics," in *Theological Perspectives for Life, Liberty and the Pursuit of Happiness: Public Intellectuals for the Twenty-First Century*, ed. Ada María Isasi-Díaz, Mary McClintock Fulkerson, and Rosemary P. Carbine (New York: Palgrave Macmillan, 2013), 83–98. See especially pages 83–85.

26. Howard Winant, *The World Is a Ghetto: Race and Democracy Since World War II* (New York: Basic Books, 2002), and Denise Ferreira da Silva, *The Global Idea of Race* (Minneapolis: University of Minnesota Press, 2007).

27. For my previous attempts to focus religious reflection as resistance to imperial and capitalist formation, see Mark Lewis Taylor, *Religion, Politics and the Christian Right: Post-9/11 Powers and American Empire* (Minneapolis: Fortress Press, 2005).

28. Michael German, "Hidden in Plain Sight: Racism, White Supremacy and Far-Right Militarism in Law Enforcement," *Brennan Center for Justice*, August 27, 2020, https://www.brennancenter.org/our-work/research-reports/hidden-plain-sight -racism-white-supremacy-and-far-right-militancy-law.

29. Hugh B. Urban, "The Torment of Secrecy: Ethical and Epistemological

Problems in the Study of Esoteric Traditions," *The History of Religions* 37, no. 3 (February 1998): 209–48, 212.

30. B. A. Gerrish, "'To the Unknown God': Luther and Calvin on the Hiddenness of God," *Journal of Religion* 53, no. 3 (July 1973): 263–92.

31. For this quoted material, see Hugh B. Urban, "Secrets of the Kingdom: Spiritual Discourse and Material Interests in the Bush Administration," *Discourse* 27, no. 1 (Winter 2005): 141–65, 149, and 150.

32. For one example in Du Bois's treatment of Louisiana and Mississippi, see *Black Reconstruction*, 474.

33. Sven Beckert, *Empire of Cotton: A Global History* (New York: Alfred K. Knopf, 2014), 244.

34. Note that I write that these amendments "claimed" or "proclaimed," not that they actually effected what they claimed. On the thirteenth amendment's claimed "abolition" of slavery and on the perpetuation of slavery or conditions "worse than slavery," see Dennis Child's *Slaves of the State: Black Incarceration from the Chain Gang to the Penitentiary* (Minneapolis: University of Minnesota Press, 2015).

35. W. E. B. Du Bois, in Bill V. Mullen and Cathryn Watson, eds., *W. E. B. Du Bois on Asia: Crossing the World Color-Line* (Jackson: University Press of Mississippi, 2005), 188. Lisa Lowe, citing Du Bois and Cedric Robinson's work on "racial capitalism" expands on this Du Boisian world focus. See Lowe, *The Intimacy of Four Continents* (Durham: Duke University Press, 1914), 141–44, 149–50, 165–74.

36. See Du Bois's repeated claims on pages 358, 390, 401, 405, 408, but especially the long summary from pages 346–47:

> Reconstruction was an economic revolution on a mighty scale and with world-wide reverberation. Reconstruction was not simply a fight between the white and black races in the South or between master and ex-slave. It was much subtler; it involved more than this. There have been repeated and continued attempts to paint this era as an interlude of petty politics or nightmare of race hate instead of viewing it slowly and broadly as a tremendous series of efforts to earn a living in new and untried ways, to achieve economic security and to restore fatal losses of capital and investment. It was a vast labor movement of ignorant, earnest and bewildered black men whose faces had been ground in the mud by their three awful centuries of degradation and who now staggered forward blindly in blood and tears amid petty division, hate and hurt, and sur-rounded by every disaster of war and industrial upheaval. Reconstruction was a vast labor movement of ignorant, muddled and bewildered white men who had been disinherited of land and labor and fought a long battle with sheer subsistence, hanging on the edge of poverty eating clay and chasing slaves and now lurching up to manhood. Reconstruction was the turn of white North-ern migration southward to new and sudden economic opportunity which followed the disaster and dislocation of war, and an attempt to organize capital

and labor on a new pattern and build a new economy. Finally, Reconstruction was a desperate effort of a dislodged, maimed, impoverished and ruined oligarchy and monopoly to restore an anachronism in economic organization by force, fraud and slander in defiance of law and order, and in the face of a great labor movement of white and black, and in better strife with a new capitalism and a new political framework.

37. See Farah Jasmine Griffin's "Black Feminists and Du Bois: Respectability, Protection and Beyond," *The Annals of the American Academy of Political and Social Science* 568 (March 2000): 28–40; and Alys Eve Weinbaum, "Gendering the General Strike: W. E. B. Du Bois's Black Reconstruction and Black Feminism's 'Propaganda of History,'" *South Atlantic Quarterly* (Summer 2013): 437–63.

Eric Foner's book on Reconstruction perhaps remains definitive for many historians, and Foner acknowledges in his new introduction to the 2014 edition of his 1988 book how important to him was Du Bois's work. (See Foner, *Reconstruction: America's Unfinished Revolution 1863–1877*, Updated edition [Harper Perennial Modern Classics, 2014].) For other historians' "corrections" of Du Bois, see David Levering Lewis, Introduction, in Du Bois, *Black Reconstruction*, xv–xvii. It should be stressed that since the Reconstruction period of over a century ago, significant transformations have occurred. Capital's later development and phases since can be told in many ways but surely would have to include late-nineteenth-century and twentieth-century wars of rising capital against U.S. labor movements, the end of one "period of globalization" in the Great Depression of the 1930s, the revisions of Keynesianism (economic and military), and the financialization of speculative capital and current neoliberal capitalism in Asia, Africa, Latin America, and the Caribbean. Then, too, *white supremacy* itself can be tracked through the consolidating of Jim and Jane Crow after Reconstruction, into eras of resistance in civil rights and Black Power movements of the 1950s to 1970s, toward the post-1980s years of today's mass incarceration, and resurgent police violence amid current "color-blind racism" or what sociologist Eduardo Bonilla-Silva terms "the new racism." See Eduardo Bonilla-Silva, *Racism without Racists: Color-Blind Racism and the Persistence of Racial Inequality in America* (Rowman and Littlefield, 2018), 17–52.

38. Robinson, *Black Marxism*, 2, 3, and 9–28.

39. Sarah Haley, *No Mercy Here: Gender, Punishment, and the Making of Jim Crow Modernity* (Chapel Hill: University of North Carolina Press, 2016), 4–6.

40. For an example of such provocation, see Alys Weinbaum: "For even though Du Bois only fleetingly casts female slaves as workers who elected to take their labor power out of circulation, in placing *Black Reconstruction* and black feminism into dialogue we can begin to recognize that slave women's protest against the exploitation of their sexual and reproductive labor—against rape and the work of breeding—was as central to the struggle against slavery in the nineteenth century as it might yet be to the struggle against contemporary biocapitalism." Alys Eve Weinbaum, "Gendering the General Strike: W. E. B. Du Bois's *Black Reconstruction*

and Black Feminism's 'Propaganda of History,'" *South Atlantic Quarterly* (2013): 112 (3): 440.

41. Du Bois, *Black Reconstruction*, 482–83.

42. Du Bois, *Black Reconstruction*, 54.

43. Edward Baptist, *The Half Has Never Been Told: Slavery and the Rise of American Capitalism* (New York: Basic Books, 2014), 143.

44. Du Bois, *Black Reconstruction*, 210.

45. Du Bois, *Black Reconstruction*, 269–70, and 625.

46. Du Bois, *Black Reconstruction*, 349.

47. Du Bois, *Black Reconstruction*, 349.

48. Du Bois, *Black Reconstruction*, 220–30.

49. Du Bois, *Black Reconstruction*, 240.

50. Du Bois, *Black Reconstruction*, 240.

51. Du Bois, *Black Reconstruction*, 214. Bracketed term added for clarity of Du Bois's argument.

52. See the argument and sources in Naomi Klein, *Shock Doctrine: The Rise of Disaster Capitalism* (New York: Metropolitan Books, 2007), 325–59.

53. Vice President Dick Cheney, Meet the Press, NBC News, Moderator Tim Russert. Transcript for September 14, 2003, https://www.nbcnews.com/id /wbna3080244.

54. See James D. Wolfensohn of the World Bank, "The Challenge of Inclusion," To the Boards of Governors of the World Bank, September 23, 1997, https://openknowledge.worldbank.org/bitstream/handle/10986/26154/multiopage .pdf?sequence=1&isAllowed=y; and on the International Monetary Fund, see Ivan Petrella, *The Future of Liberation Theology: An Argument and Manifesto* (Orbis Books, 2006), 8–9.

55. Still one of the best, most nuanced summaries of this global hierarchy is by economist William Tabb, *The Amoral Elephant: Globalization and the Struggle for Social Justice in the Twenty-first Century* (New York: Monthly Review Press, 2001).

56. Taylor, *Religion, Politics and the Christian Right*, 78–80.

57. James Mittelman, *The Globalization Syndrome: Transformation and Resistance* (Princeton: Princeton University Press, 2000), 31–108.

58. Sarah F. Liebschutz, "Empowerment Zones and Enterprise Communities: Reinventing Federalism for Distressed Communities," *Publius* 25, no. 3 (Summer 1995): 117–32.

59. Eric Levitz, "Steve Bannon's Nationalism Is Not about the Economy, Stupid," *The Intelligencer*, September 11, 2017, https://nymag.com/intelligencer/2017/09/steve -bannons-nationalism-isnt-about-the-economy-stupid.html.

60. Graham Lanktree, "Steve Bannon Calls Alt-Right 'Losers' and Says Government Rivals are Wetting Themselves," *Newsweek*, August 17, 2017, https:// www.newsweek.com/steve-bannon-calls-alt-right-losers-and-his-government-rivals -are-wetting-651767.

61. George Hawley, *Making Sense of the Alt-Right*, 143–44.

62. Gerald Warner, "Hoist It High and Proud: The Confederate Flag Proclaims a Glorious Heritage," *Breitbart*, July 1, 2015, https://www.breitbart.com/politics/2015 /07/01/hoist-it-high-and-proud-the-confederate-flag-proclaims-a-glorious-heritage/. Warner's original title, shown here in this note, was later changed to "The Confederate Flag Proclaims a Historical Heritage."

63. Transcript: Hillary Clinton's Full Remarks in Reno Nevada, August 25, 2016, *Politico*, August 25, 2016, https://www.politico.com/story/2016/08/transcript-hillary -clinton-alt-right-reno-227419.

64. Joel Kovel, *White Racism: A Psychohistory* (New York: Columbia University Press, 1984), ix–x, 54–5, 211–30. Kovel's is one of the few books that treats white supremacist "psychohistory" in relation to political, economic, and racial histories. Freud *and* Marx, *and* Fanon receive their due.

65. Kovel, *White Racism*, 54–55.

66. Michelle Alexander, "Why Hillary Clinton Doesn't Deserve the Black Vote," *The Nation*, February 29, 2016, https://www.thenation.com/article/archive/hillary -clinton-does-not-deserve-black-peoples-votes/.

67. For a summary of these policies, see sociologists Bonilla-Silva, *Racism without Racists*, cited previously, and also Joe Feagin, *Racist America: Roots, Current Realities and Future Reparations* (New York: Routledge, 2014).

68. Alain Badiou, *Polemics*, trans. with an Introduction by Steve Corcoran (New York: Verso, 2006), 80. With Cécile Winter contributing Chapter 8 in Part II of this work.

69. Mark Lewis Taylor, "The Time Is Now: To Defeat Both Trump and Clintonian Neoliberalism," *Counterpunch*, July 2016, https://www.counterpunch.org /2016/07/19/the-time-is-now-to-defeat-both-trump-and-clintonian-neoliberalism/.

70. Kovel, *White Racism*, 209–10.

71. Again Hawley, *Making Sense of the Alt-Right*, 144.

72. Du Bois, *Black Reconstruction*, 349.

73. Du Bois, *Black Reconstruction*, 610, 616.

74. Du Bois, *Black Reconstruction*, 630.

75. Du Bois, *Black Reconstruction*, 633.

76. Du Bois, *Black Reconstruction*, 633.

77. Du Bois, *Black Reconstruction*, 630.

78. Du Bois attacks this assumption directly in Chapter XVII, "The Propaganda of History," in *Black Reconstruction*, 711–38.

79. To be sure, even at the time of this "promulgation," but especially later, Black and white workers *did* unite for resistance. See Robin D. G. Kelley, *Hammer and Hoe: Alabama Communists During the Great Depression* (Chapel Hill: University of North Carolina Press, 1990). On the possibilities of working-class whites and Blacks sharing leadership in resistance to capitalism, see Oliver Cromwell Cox, *Caste, Class and Race: A Study in Social Dynamics* (New York: Monthly Review Press, 1959), 572–83.

80. Michelle Alexander, *The New Jim Crow: Mass Incarceration in the Age of Color-Blindness*, Tenth anniversary edition with a new Preface by the author (New York: New Press, 2010), 25–75.

81. Charles Hokayem and Misty L. Heggeness, "Living in Near Poverty in the U.S., 1966–2012," Current Population Reports (U.S. Census Bureau, 2014), 3–5, https://www.census.gov/prod/2014pubs/p60-248.pdf. "Near poverty" for a family of four is defined as those earning annual incomes less than $29,104 but more than the poverty level threshold of $23,283.

82. For two different ideological perspectives, consider the earlier 2004 essay by Mark P. Mills, "The Security-Industrial Complex," *Forbes*, November 29, 2004, https://www.forbes.com/forbes/2004/1129/044.html?sh=641717694dd9; and then the 2016 essay by Thibalt Henneton, "The Security-Digital Complex," *Le Monde diplomatique*, April 2016, https://mondediplo.com/2016/04/10siliconarmy.

83. Other figures in addition to Mercer could be foregrounded. See, for example, Sarah Anderson, "The Noxious Combination of Racism, the alt-right and the Upper Class," *AlterNet*, August 17, 2017, https://www.alternet.org/2017/08/noxious-combination -racism-alt-right-and-upper-class/. Another source from the world of U.S. big business is William Regnery, who, in 2005, founded the National Policy Institute that is now headed by alt-right figure Richard Spencer. See the *Southern Poverty Law Center*, "William H. Regnery, II," https://www.splcenter.org/fighting-hate/extremist-files /individual/william-h-regnery-ii.

84. Jane Mayer, "The Reclusive Hedge-Fund Tycoon Behind the Trump Presidency," *The New Yorker*, March 27, 201, https://www.newyorker.com/magazine /2017/03/27/the-reclusive-hedge-fund-tycoon-behind-the-trump-presidency. Mayer is also author of *Dark Money: The Hidden History of the Billionaires Behind the Rise of the Radical Right* (New York: Doubleday, 2016). This book is essential also for tracing corporate funders' support for white supremacist organizations. Mayer focuses on the Koch brothers, Charles and David, especially.

85. Mayer, "The Reclusive Hedge-Fund Tycoon."

86. Judd Legum and Danielle McLean, "These Wealthy Institutions Are Quietly Funding White Nationalism," *Think Progress*, October 19, 2017, https://archive .thinkprogress.org/these-wealthy-institutions-are-quietly-financing-white-nationalism -5313db89b185/.

87. Steven Perlberg, "CMO Today: Mercer Family Set to Become Washington Power Brokers," *Wall Street Journal*, January 9, 2017, https://www.wsj.com/articles /cmo-today-mercer-family-set-to-become-washington-power-brokers-1483964872.

88. Rosalind S. Helderman, "Mercer Issues Rare Public Rebuke of Former Ally Bannon," *Washington Post*, January 4, 2018, https://www.washingtonpost.com/news /post-politics/wp/2018/01/04/mercer-issues-rare-public-rebuke-of-former-ally-bannon/.

89. Michelle Ye Hee Lee and Anu Narayanswamy, "GOP Megadonor Robert Mercer Made His First Six-Figure Donation to Trump's Reelection, New Filing Shows," *Washington Post*, April 16, 2020, https://www.washingtonpost.com/politics

/gop-megadonor-robert-mercer-made-his-first-six-figure-donation-to-trumps
-reelection-new-filing-shows/2020/04/16/b4dac5cc-7f90-11ea-9040-68981f488eed
_story.html.

90. Mayer, "The Reclusive Hedge-Fund Tycoon." In April 2018, the Mercers' Cambridge Analytica was revealed as having "improperly acquired the private Facebook data of millions of users" in its function as a "voter-profiling firm co-founded by [Robert Mercer] and used by the Trump campaign." Nicholas Confessore and David Gelles, "Facebook Fallout Deals Blow to Mercers' Political Clout," *New York Times*, April 10, 2018, https://www.nytimes.com/2018/04/10/us /politics/mercer-family-cambridge-analytica.html.

91. Mayer, "The Reclusive Hedge-Fund Tycoon."

92. For another analysis of Breitbart, see Stephen Piggott, "Is Breitbart.com Becoming the Media Arm of the 'Alt-Right'?" at the Southern Poverty Law Center, Hatewatch, April 28, 2016, https://www.splcenter.org/hatewatch/2016/04/28 /breitbartcom-becoming-media-arm-alt-right. Piggott writes, "Breitbart has always given a platform to parts of the radical right, most notably elements of the organized anti-Muslim and anti-immigrant movements."

93. Alex Kotch, "Funding Hate: How Online Merchants and Payment Processors Aid White Nationalists," *PR Watch*, Center for Media and Democracy, April 28, 2020, https://www.prwatch.org/comment/45641. Also see Caitlin Dewey, "Amazon, PayPal and Spotify Inadvertently Fund White Supremacists. Here's How," *Washington Post*, March 2015, https://www.washingtonpost.com/news/the-intersect /wp/2015/03/17/amazon-paypal-and-spotify-inadvertently-fund-white-supremacists -heres-how/; Lizzy Dearden, "British Far-Right Extremists being funded by international networks, report reveals," *The Independent*, May 31, 2019, https://www .independent.co.uk/news/uk/home-news/far-right-uk-identitarian-movement -alt-right-defend-europe-isd-research-nazis-national-action-a8013331.html; "The Millionaire and Billionaires Funding White Supremacy," *The Northwest Accountability Project*, June 9, 2020, https://www.independent.co.uk/news/uk/home -news/far-right-extremism-terrorism-tommy-robinson-funding-international-a8937116 .html; Christopher Matthias, "The White Supremacist and Extremist Donors to Trump's 2020 Campaign," *Huffington Post*, October 24, 2020, https://www.huffpost .com/entry/white-supremacist-donors-trump-campaign-2020_n_5f9336c7c5b6494b a13be8d8; and Alex Kotch, "Nation's Biggest Charity Is Funding Influential White Nationalist Group," *Sludge*, November 22, 2019, https://readsludge.com/2019/11/22 /nations-biggest-charity-is-funding-influential-white-nationalist-group/. On the high marks received by *Sludge* for factual reporting, see "Media Bias/ Fact Check," August 17, 2020, https://mediabiasfactcheck.com/sludge/.

94. Matthew Cunningham-Cook, "Rebekah Mercer Raised Specter of 'Armed Conflict' in 2019 Book," *The Intercept*, January 27, 2021, https://theintercept.com /2021/01/27/rebekah-mercer-book-capitol-riot/.

95. Hawley, *Making Sense of the Alt-Right*, 2–3, 68, 70. See also Michelle Goldberg, "The Khakis and Tiki Torches: The Middle Class, Clean-Cut Racism

of Richard Spencer's Acolytes," *Slate*, August 14, 2017, https://slate.com/news-and
-politics/2017/08/the-middle-class-clean-cut-racism-of-richard-spencers-acolytes.html.
For an examination of the interplay of secrecy and religion in something like an
alt-right esotericism, see David Neiwert, "What the Kek?: Explaining the Alt-Right
'Deity' Behind their 'Meme Magic,'" Southern Poverty Law Center, Hatewatch,
May 8, 2017, https://www.splcenter.org/hatewatch/2017/05/08/what-kek-explaining-alt
-right-deity-behind-their-meme-magic.

96. On the Council for National Policy (CNP), see Sarah Posner, "Secret
Society," AlterNet, March 1, 2005, https://www.alternet.org/2005/03/secret_society/.
For a recent investigative report on the CNP, see Robert O'Harrow, Jr., "God, Trump
and the Closed Door World of a Major Conservative Group," *The Washington Post*,
October 25, 2021, https://www.washingtonpost.com/magazine/2021/10/25/god-trump
-closed-door-world-council-national-policy/?itid=ap_roberto%27harrowjr. For a
book-length treatment, see Columbia University research scholar Anne Nelson,
Shadow Network: Media, Money and the Secret Hub of the Radical Right (New York:
Bloomsbury, 2019).

97. On the "confidentiality" maintained around Bush's speech, see Mark J.
Ambinder," Inside the Council for National Policy," ABC News, January 6, 2006,
https://abcnews.go.com/Politics/story?id=121170&page=1.

98. Nathan C. Gonzalez, "VP Cheney Makes Quick Trip to Utah to Address
Secretive Conservative Policy Group," *The Salt Lake Tribune*, September 28, 2007,
https://archive.sltrib.com/article.php?id=7028160&itype=NGPSID.

99. The SPLC writes of WND that it serves up "a daily dose of conspiracy
theories, apocalyptic alerts, and anti-gay rhetoric. WND was ranked by Alexa in 2012
as the 1,832nd most popular website in the world and the 423rd in the U.S. That
ranks just above Nickelodeon and a few spots below Victoria's Secret," https://www
.splcenter.org/fighting-hate/extremist-files/group/worldnetdaily.

100. Mayer, "The Reclusive Hedge-Fund Tycoon." On the CNP as site of
interaction between the Christian Right and corporate culture, see Taylor, *Religion,
Politics and the Christian Right*, 60–61.

101. Mayer, "The Reclusive Hedge-Fund Tycoon." For a photo of Rebekah
Mercer, posing with Kellyanne Conway and Steve Bannon at the 2017 inauguration
of Donald Trump, see the second photo in Confessore and Gilles, "Facebook
Fallout Deals Blow to Mercers' Political Clout," https://www.nytimes.com/2018/04
/10/us/politics/mercer-family-cambridge-analytica.html.

102. Du Bois, *Black Reconstruction*, 679.

103. Du Bois, *Black Reconstruction*, 623.

104. Du Bois, *Black Reconstruction*, 670.

105. Du Bois, *Black Reconstruction*, 676.

106. Du Bois, *Black Reconstruction*, 677.

107. Du Bois, *Black Reconstruction*, 494. A Democratic State Central Committee
in Louisiana wrote this about whites siding with Blacks: "And we would earnestly
declare to our fellow-citizens our opinion that even the most implacable and ill-

disposed of the Negro population, those who show the worst spirit toward the white people, are not half as much deserving our aversion and non-intercourse with them as *the debased Whites* who encourage and aid them, and who become through their votes the office-holding oppressors of the people . . ." See Du Bois, *Black Reconstruction*, 474 (italics added).

108. Although today's KKK has an estimated 3,000 members in over 40 chapters across 22 states (up a bit since 2016), those numbers are unstable, with members joining and withdrawing. Membership levels have still not reached the extensive nature as in post–Civil War Reconstruction. See "In Spite of Internal Turmoil Klan Groups Persist," *The Anti-Defamation League*, June 2017 Report, New York, https://www.adl.org/sites/default/files/documents/CR_5173_Klan%20Report_vFFF2.pdf.

109. Du Bois, *Black Reconstruction*, 679–80.

110. Ron Chernow, *Grant* (New York: Penguin, 2017), 588.

111. Chernow, *Grant*, 708.

112. Chernow, *Grant*, 711.

113. Chernow, *Grant*, 710–11.

114. Chernow, *Grant*, 589.

115. German, "Hidden in Plain Sight: Racism, White Supremacy and Far-Right Militarism in Law Enforcement," https://www.brennancenter.org/our-work/research-reports/hidden-plain-sight-racism-white-supremacy-and-far-right-militancy-law.

116. Du Bois, *Black Reconstruction*, 678.

117. Emma Grey Ellis, "Whatever Your Side, Doxing Is a Perilous Form of Justice," *Wired*, August 17, 2017, https://www.wired.com/story/doxing-charlottesville/.

118. Angela Nagle, "The Lost Boys," *The Atlantic*, December 15, 2017, https://www.theatlantic.com/magazine/archive/2017/12/brotherhood-of-losers/544158/.

119. James Doubek and Vanessa Romo, "Jury Finds Rally Organizers Liable for the Violence that Broke Out in Charlottesville," National Public Radio, November 23, 2021, https://www.npr.org/2021/11/23/1058024314/charlottesville-unite-the-right-trial-verdict.

120. Chernow, *Grant*, 708 and 1005n92.

121. Again, see Taylor, *Religion, Politics and the Christian Right*, 60–62, and Posner, "Secret Society." On secrecy and Christian religion during the George W. Bush presidency, see Hugh Urban, "Religion and Secrecy in the Bush Administration: The Gentleman, the Prince and the Simulacrum," *Esoterica*, journal, Michigan State University, and his book, Hugh Urban, *Secrets of the Kingdom: Religion and Concealment in the Bush Administration* (Lanham, Md.: Rowman and Littlefield, 2007). For an engagement with sociologist Edward Shils's study of governmental secrecy, see also Hugh B. Urban, "The Torment of Secrecy: Ethical and Epistemological Problems in the Study of Esoteric Traditions," *Journal of the History of Religions* 37, no. 3 (February 1998): 209–48.

122. Jane Mayer, *Dark Money: The Hidden History of the Billionaires Behind the Rise of the Radical Right* (New York: Doubleday, 2016), 229, 248.

123. Nathan Layne, Gabriella Borter, "Militia Members, others charged in plot to kidnap Michigan Governor; she says Trump complicit," *Reuters*, October 7, 2020, https://www.reuters.com/article/us-michigan-whitmer/militia-members-others-charged-in-plot-to-kidnap-michigan-governor-she-says-trump-complicit-idUSKBN26T2ZF.

124. Sam Jackson, "Don't Assume the Militias at the Charlottesville Rally Were White Supremacists," *Washington Post*, September 8, 2017, https://www.washingtonpost.com/news/monkey-cage/wp/2017/09/08/remember-those-militias-at-the-charlottesville-unite-the-right-rally-heres-what-they-believe/.

125. Southern Poverty Law Center, "Anti-Government Militia Groups Grew by More than One-Third in the Last Year," January 4, 2016, https://www.splcenter.org/news/2016/01/04/antigovernment-militia-groups-grew-more-one-third-last-year.

126. Jackson, "Don't Assume the Militias" (see Jackson's penultimate paragraph on "Islamophobia"). On the long history, antedating the formation of the United States, of Islamophobia, see Robert Allison, *The Crescent Obscured: The United States and the Muslim World, 1776–1815*, new edition (Chicago: University of Chicago Press, 2000).

127. Hampton Stall, Roudabeh Kishi, and Clionadh Raleigh, *Standing By: Right-Wing Militia Groups and the U.S. Election.* The Armed Conflict Location and Even Data Project (ACLED), October 2020, https://www.jstor.org/stable/pdf/resrep26641.7.pdf.

128. Mumia Abu-Jamal, *When Have Black Lives Ever Mattered* (San Francisco: City Lights Press, 2017).

129. Stephanie Woodward, "The Police Killings No One Is Talking About," *In These Times*, A Special Investigation, October 17, 2016, https://www.democracynow.org/2016/10/19/the_police_killings_no_one_is.

130. *Chicago Tribune*, "Editorial: Judgment Day for Police Code of Silence," August 17, 2016, https://www.chicagotribune.com/opinion/editorials/ct-chicago-police-laquan-mcdonald-emanuel-edit-20160817-story.html.

131. Paul Butler, "The Fraternal Order of Police Must Go," *The Nation*, October 11, 2017, https://www.thenation.com/article/archive/the-fraternal-order-of-police-must-go/. On the Philadelphia FOP statement on video, see Sebastian Murdock, "Philly Police Union President Calls Black Lives Matter Activists a 'Pack of Rabid Animals,'" *Huffington Post*, September 2, 2017, https://www.huffpost.com/entry/philly-police-union-president-calls-black-lives-matter-activists-a-pack-of-rabid-animals_n_59aacc02e4b0dfaafcf0bc55. The FOP President also defended a police officer who sported a Nazi tattoo.

132. Michael Beckell and Jared Bennett, "12 Ways that *Citizens United* Has Changed Politics," *Center for Public Integrity*, January 21, 2015, https://publicintegrity.org/politics/12-ways-citizens-united-has-changed-politics/.

133. Beckell and Bennett, "12 Ways."

134. Mark Hosenball, "U.S. Homeland Security Confirms Three Units Sent

Paramilitary Officers to Portland," *Reuters*, July 21, 2020, https://www.reuters.com
/article/us-global-race-protests-agents/u-s-homeland-security-confirms-three-units
-sent-paramilitary-officers-to-portland-idUSKCN24M2RL.

135. See German, "Hidden in Plain Sight."

136. Wyn Craig Wade, *The Fiery Cross: The Ku Klux Klan in America* (New York:
Oxford University Press, 1987).

137. Robin D. G. Kelley, "'Slangin' Rocks . . . Palestinian Style,' Dispatches from
the Occupied Zones of North America," in *Police Brutality: An Anthology*, ed. Jill
Norton (New York: Norton, 2000), 21–54, especially 25–32.

138. Paul Sonne, "Pentagon Restricted Commander of D.C. Guard Ahead of
Capitol Riot," *Washington Post*, January 26, 2021, https://www.washingtonpost.com
/national-security/dc-guard-capitol-riots-william-walker-pentagon/2021/01/26
/98879f44-5f69-11eb-ac8f-4ae05557196e_story.html.

139. Aaron Mehta, "As Term Winds Down, Trump Shifts Pentagon Line of
Succession," *The Defense News*, December 11, 2020, https://www.defensenews.com
/pentagon/2020/12/11/as-term-expires-trump-shifts-pentagon-line-of-succession/.

140. Du Bois, *Black Reconstruction*, 677.

141. Du Bois, *Black Reconstruction*, 677–78.

2

Protest at the Void

Theological Challenges to Capitalist Totality

Devin Singh

What is the point of protest in an age of capitalist supremacy? Where and on what ground can one stand in a period where the system appears all-encompassing, as it works to co-opt and to commodify gestures of resistance?[1] What role has religion played in contributing to this present order, and what resources if any does it retain to push back and seek transformation? This chapter explores these questions by interrogating the problem of an "outside" to global capitalism under neoliberalism. It initiates a search for footholds that we might grasp and stand upon to pull ourselves out of the cave of capitalist totalization.

I proceed by first reviewing this dynamic of totalization, examining the claim of capitalism's purported role as the governing framework and horizon of our age. I then follow inquiries that challenge such a presentation. Indeed, I suggest, the image of capital as total and monolithic is actually constructed in response to its vulnerability and fragility. The system requires constant shoring up, defense, and enforcement. Such modes are often immanent and subtle, dealing with micro-practices of self-formation and discipline, affect, and life orientation. But capitalist enforcement also operates systemically, at a macro level, following tried and true institutions of sovereignty and coercion such as law, war, and policing.

Drawing on theological genealogy and archaeology, I consider some of the theological sources mobilized in capitalism, asking how they convey systemic vulnerability. Teasing out the threads and finding useful correspondences and analogues between theology and economy, I consider how these may be mobilized around the cracks and fissures in the system. Are there loose sutures to the present order, and can we pull them apart?

I consider the doctrine of the ascension as a possible resource for such suture-pulling. The ascension marks one site of central vulnerability and fragility in Christian tradition: The risen and exalted lord upon which the movement is founded is nowhere to be found. Claims to divine supremacy, power, and exaltation are met with the reality of resounding silence and enduring absence. Worshipping at an empty throne, Christianity longs for the return of the king. Coping with the trauma of such abandonment, Christian thought and practice initiated a series of strategies to manage its vulnerability. Such vulnerability is glimpsed at pivotal moments in relation to capitalism, such as the much-discussed anxiety of Calvinist believers before their inscrutable sovereign God, an anxiety that generated a certain mode of entrepreneurial productivity.

While gestural and exploratory, this chapter considers the patterns of vulnerability and the concomitant policing of fragility that this theological imaginary may have conveyed to capitalism. I argue that meaningful Christian theological confrontation with capitalist fragility comes not from attempts to demonstrate religious supremacy or to grasp at masks of theological imperviousness, but through embrace and acknowledgment of Christianity's own fragility and vulnerability. In so doing, Christianity might reckon with the effects of its own history of denying fragility and speak in humble protest against capitalism's own denials and the injustices caused in its wake.

The Lost Outside

One current question relating to protests over economic injustice is whether we have lost all grounds for counternarratives and viable alternative visions for the future. Pundits across the political spectrum either celebrate or lament the supposed lack of alternatives to global capitalism as well as the absence of any obvious fulcrum points from which to leverage change. Francis Fukuyama infamously hailed the end of history after the fall of communism around the globe, identifying capitalism as the totalizing, closed system we now inhabit.[2] History was over because we now lack agonistic polarities, the differences that would drive history forward dialectically and agitate for change. Given the supposedly economic foundation to historical alteration, the absence of real difference and polarization to propel shifts in the dominant mode of production means a kind of stasis. Fukuyama's was merely a late scholarly intervention into the earlier proclamation that "there is no alternative" to capitalism, bandied about by the Thatcher administration and catapulted into prominence under Reagan.[3] If we cannot offer alternatives and if capitalism is not snowballing toward its inevitable crisis engendered by its internal contradictions, what escape is possible?

This mythology of closure has prompted, among other things, a return to discourses of hope and other forward-looking affective postures and forms of subjectivity. If there is no future we can construct, and if we are stuck in an atemporal, capitalist homeostasis, is there anything for which to hope?[4] The responses fall on a spectrum from dogged retrievals of theological transcendence as the only fulcrum for change, to attempts to think hope and radical transformation within immanence. Indeed, global capital as totalizing seems to align neatly with an immanent frame, which further solidifies the image of the economic system squelching out other horizons of the good. In other words, arguably, the age of capitalism coincides with the ostensibly secular age of immanence, such that the two reinforce each other. This portrayal, of course, requires investigation.

Related critiques of the deformed hopes perpetuated by neoliberalism— such as Lauren Berlant's notion of "cruel optimism"—consider the ways that the system perversely generates forward-looking postures of anticipation that serve to extend the life of the system itself while foreclosing meaningful escape.[5] With bitter irony, neoliberalism actually produces mockeries and empty husks of hope, mingled with a desire fiercely disciplined by advertising. The result is constant "leaning in" toward the future, a dystopian horizon of endless accumulation, market returns, increased profit margins, fictional leisure time, mythical work/life balance, or a more productive self.[6] These visions of the future and the selves they interpolate, however, are intrinsic to the market's endless quest for new realms to colonize and new sectors of life to marketize.[7]

Capitalism thus appears as a governing framework for relationships today, one that aligns with neoliberalism as the primary philosophy of life and of state. Neoliberalism exalts markets and the price mechanism, seeking to extend the calculus of rational utility into as many sectors of society as possible. Indeed, neoliberal defenders wed rational utility to optimism in language that both disciplines emotive hope while inculcating supposedly calculative future anticipation, masquerading as coolly rational while forging new affective postures under capitalism.[8] As the Marxist literary critic Jean-Joseph Goux claims, capitalism also appears quintessentially "postmodern" in its endlessly fluid capacity to transform, redefine, co-opt, and respond to efforts at intervention and change.[9] Exalting in play and at least feigned difference and diversity, it promulgates its unceasing logic of the same, amassing in commodified abundance its endless chain of signifiers that always lead back to the engines of alienation, exploitation, and profit accumulation.

Given a totalization that not only appears social and political but also epistemological, what foundations, spaces, or exits can we find to gain the necessary critical distance from the regime to offer alternatives? A first step requires a closer look at capitalism's feigned totality and supremacy. For lingering spaces, fissures, and cracks remain.

The Capitalist Façade

Anthropologist Karen Ho provides a close analysis of the financial industry as a key driver of global capitalism, both institutionally and ideologically.[10] As she notes, it is customary for such firms to extol their global reach and present a vision of unified channels and flows of capital among international financial centers.[11] This ideology is useful for presenting a cohesive transnational effort to secure the best returns for clients, delving into untapped and emerging markets with unique investment opportunities. It also offers a view that the aims for capital returns know no borders or cultural differences, presenting a united front. In other words, it is in the interests of global capital to present itself as total and totalizing, and thus boost investor confidence.

Ho challenges and critiques leftist lamentations over the economic system's totalizing power. She questions whether such views simply take up and accept capital's self-presentation, uncritically acquiescing to its framework and perspective. Does decrying global capital as the only option simply mirror the ideological self-portrayal of this system itself? As an anthropologist, Ho is interested in offering close-up inspections, informed by ethnography and concrete studies, that reveal the many cracks and fissures in this self-professed total system. Rather than an impenetrable monolith, global capitalism and neoliberal ideology reveal themselves to be traversed with varied layers and contradictions.

Approaching matters from a different vantage point, political theorist William Connolly likewise seeks to demonstrate what he sees as the fragility and vulnerability of the neoliberal order and global capitalism.[12] He notes the attempts by the neoliberal machine to be all-pervasive. Neoliberalism as an alteration of classical liberalism moves beyond laissez-faire views of the market's spontaneous and independent existence. While many neoliberal pundits continually reiterate this view, what is manifest on the ground are concerted, coordinated, and multipronged attempts to ensure that the state and non-governmental organizations create and sustain the market of private interests. Such efforts inculcate neoliberal techniques and calculus within broad swaths of civil society, including churches and schools.

Neoliberalism appears decentered and yet totalizing, seeking to draw in as many attitudes, practices, and institutions from society as possible to support its agenda. It represents a concerted effort to advance beyond the classical liberal model, which shared similar faith in markets, and yet eschewed state intervention and espoused libertarian principles of personal freedom. Neo-liberalism expands amoebically beyond this purview, recognizing the faith of its founding fathers as unsustainable. Markets do not self-regulate or emerge spontaneously. They require construction, maintenance, and defense.[13]

The COVID-19 global pandemic has brought the irony of the neoliberal façade of market self-regulation into vivid relief. Wedded to a doctrine of market fundamentalism, which holds to a simplistic and rigid set of tenets about market self-correction and non-interventionism, the Trump administration was slow to use state resources and mandates to mobilize a response. They left the production of personal protective equipment (PPE) to private industry despite precedent for invoking the Defense Production Act as a federal mandate to spur production of needed equipment during times of national crisis. Tied to the now disrupted global supply chains, themselves incentivized by neoliberal and broadly capitalist priorities for cheap labor, private production of life-saving equipment including ventilators has not responded to clear need and demand. Relying on intrinsic market signals and forces appears insufficient, belying the doctrinaire assumptions of a perfect market system that requires no support.[14]

The neoliberal drive toward totalization is predicated upon an awareness of vulnerability and fragility. The move toward drawing all aspects of life into its orbit is neoliberalism's recognition that its view of the market requires as many props and stabilizers as it can muster. Rather than an inevitable rationality that overcomes all opposition and instability, as the system presents itself, its fragile and tenuous nature requires disciplinary structures and enforcement. It requires the state and the various institutions of the ideological state apparatus. Vulnerability is inherent in the system. The anxious proclamations by pundits of capitalist supremacy, while invoking the power of the state to enforce such supremacy, betray an awareness of such systemic vulnerability and of the mythic nature of capitalist totality that elides its many fissures. Market fundamentalism, like its religious and theological counterparts, betrays a dogged rigidity that is as much an anxious response to threats—both internal and external—as it is a naïve and brash confidence in its own truth.

Ho's and Connolly's interventions help us to see that, on the ground and in actuality, capitalism is not a monolithic, smoothly functioning single entity. Cracks and fissures in this myth signal difference, diversity, and contradiction. They reveal the constant attempts through such mythology to shore up these openings, seen as vulnerabilities, and instead articulate a unified horizon of the single purpose and destiny toward which the system moves. To be sure, academic disputes and debates among economists reveal such multiplicities, and most economists are aware of the constructed nature of market dynamics and the competing possible arrangements of market systems. Yet this diversity is papered over when various economic insights are translated into public discourse and policy by politicized defenders of a particular market theory.

Institutionalized Precarity

The structures of precarity and vulnerability within capitalism raise the possibility that capitalism also creates and reproduces vulnerable communities. Indeed, precarity has so come to characterize life under modern political economy that social theorists have identified—or at least labeled—a new social class: the precariat.[15] Echoing Karl Marx's proletariat, the class label of precariat signals not only wage labor but also the unpredictability of access to work itself, and hence to the monetary wages that circulate as the lifeblood of the present system. The precariat displays a radical vulnerability that comes when even the meager buffer of access to basic wages cannot be counted upon. As casual, contingent, and disposable labor, the precariat is not merely vulnerable to shocks in the system—rather, the system itself is the shock, for it creates and sustains the vulnerabilities of the precariat. Precarious existence is the norm, when considered from the perspective of the lived experience of the global majority. Not only is this experience neither marginal nor peripheral, such precarity is increasingly characterizing all wage labor and the life of the middle class.[16]

The production of the precariat class appears directly tied up with the vulnerability and fragility of capitalism and its attempts at denying this reality. Capitalism's own precarity causes it to create pathways to deflect its own vulnerability, and the production of pools of low-wage labor and slave labor have been two primary means by which capitalism grasps hold on its unstable legs, with a variety of intended and unintended consequences and collateral damage. Capitalism's need for low-wage labor means that, as the fragile system persists, it will continue to produce vulnerable communities that depend upon it, laboring for exploitative wages in order to survive.

At its inception, capitalism took root by creating precarity through the violence of primitive accumulation. If capital is necessary in order to produce further capital, whence the initial capital that fueled the rise of industry in early-modern markets? To answer this question, the classical political economists provided a convenient founding myth, which to Marx plays "about the same part as original sin in theology."[17] According to this "just-so story," humanity can be divided into those naturally given to industry and commerce and those given to indolence and a lack of ingenuity. The former created opportunity and incentive for the latter. If the latter had no vision for innovation, they could at least be coerced to work, offering their labor power as their only commodity.

Against such mythology, actual primitive accumulation involved possession of church and public land and goods by states and new corporate actors, the enclosure and privatization of such land, excluding peasants from it and changing their access to the means of production—now mediated through wage labor. Marx writes:

> The capital-relation presupposes a complete separation between the workers and the ownership of the conditions for the realization of their labour. As soon as capitalist production stands on its own feet, it not only maintains this separation, but reproduces it on a constantly extending scale. The process, therefore, which creates the capital-relation can be nothing other than the process which divorces the worker from the ownership of the conditions of his own labour . . .[18]

Thus, the founding acts by the agents of capital were those of the manufacture of precarity, as serfs were tossed off feudal and ecclesial land, and could only return now as "free" laborers seeking a wage to survive amidst relations increasingly mediated by money.

This is not to pretend that preceding serfdom was idyllic. Certainly, this feudal mode of production exhibited its own forms of precariousness and the creation of vulnerable communities. Yet capitalism radicalized these dynamics and created new permutations of precarity. As Marx summarizes: "The spoliation of the Church's property, the fraudulent alienation of the state domains, the theft of the common lands, the usurpation of feudal and clan property and its transformation into modern private property under circumstances of ruthless terrorism, all these things were just so many idyllic methods of primitive accumulation."[19] "And the history of this," Marx concludes, "is written in the annals of [hu]mankind in letters of blood and fire."[20]

While state and corporate actors enclosed lands and excluded serfs, who were then required to return to the land as wage laborers, capitalism gained traction through another mode of creating precarity: slavery. In the phase of primitive accumulation, the capitalist class funded much industry and new entrepreneurial expansion through unpaid, forced labor and the extraction of resources from the New World.[21] While these power brokers still recognized former European serfs as part of the social fabric (if precariously so), including them in economic circuits via the wage relationship, such capitalists underscored the exclusion and radical vulnerability of native and African peoples through imposed slavery, with no recompense or wage recognition. Colonized peoples and chattel slaves subsisted as barely within the system, as

existing on its borders and outer skin in a way that came to define its limits
and its growth edge, underlying its expanding foundations. Slaves as the limit
case of precarity prove to be capitalism's grounding possibility. This is why, as
C. L. R. James notes, we must understand the slave as the counterpoint and
complement to—and in a certain sense the condition of possibility for—the
new European proletariat.[22] We must think the land enclosure and the plantation together in the history of capitalism and the construction of precarity.[23]

The link between primitive accumulation and enclosure—both as the
closing of the commons and enforcement of the *encomienda* and plantation
systems—also suggests links between these concrete, historical, material acts
of enclosure and the ideological projection of a closed system for capitalism
itself. This suggests that the use of force on the ground to create boundaries
and a sense of immobile territorial fixity (even while creating mobile and
precarious labor) subtends the forceful projection of capitalism as a fixed and
total system, something closed off and indeed enclosed. Capitalism's image
as an inevitable and enclosed totalization of space thus refracts the enclosure
as a micro practice of managing and policing space.

Policing takes place at all levels of the system, both to secure enclosure and
to ensure that the image of totality and stability paper over the many cracks
and fissures of the system. Ideological and conceptual policing continually re-
asserts the market's totality and inevitably, and presents its logic as normal and
commonsensical. Policing also occurs at the level of subjectivity and affect,
as economic pundits portray ideal market actors as calm and rational, coolly
suppressing anxieties about market instability and calculating future returns
in the face of chaos. And of course, the system polices subjects directly and
materially, as police forces intervene in anti-capitalist protests or brutalize
subjects in poorer neighborhoods that capitalism has rendered vulnerable and
marginal. The nationwide reckoning currently underway, through the leadership of Black Lives Matter and allied organizations, highlights how police violence and the racialized protection of private property—capital appropriated
through the long history of slavery and wage exploitation—travel inextricably
together.[24]

The condition of precarity signals a state or situation of fragility, vulnerability, and dependence. "Precarious" comes from the Latin *precari*, to pray.
Precarius originally meant "obtaining by prayer or pleading" (OED). The
term's archaic links to prayer and petition invoke a state of radical vulnerability and need, such that only a god would hear and deign to help. Precarity
invokes circumstances so fragile and desperate that all one has left is a prayer
or supplication. The link to prayer is useful here because it raises the question
of how theological and religious backgrounds might be related to modern

constructions of precarity. While it does not necessitate this link, it invites us to consider what theological traces might linger in the production of vulnerable communities, the transference of systemic vulnerability, and the need to conceal it. This possibility adds additional layers for consideration of the theological context for the early modern ideas associated with capitalism's rise and its deployment in the West.

Capitalism and Theological Fragility

From a theological genealogical perspective one might consider how early apologists for capitalism appropriated and transformed prevailing theological paradigms of their day that proved useful in developing market ideas. Christian theology and forms of natural theology derived from Christianity were much discussed among the early economists.[25] Indeed, the first or so-called "classical" economists, such as Adam Smith, were primarily moral philosophers interested in new theories of society and life together.

Early modernity witnessed a series of significant transitions and developments with regard to questions of God's relationship toward, management of, and intervention into creation. We can discern a new focus on the apparently rational structure of the created universe, its governance by predictable and regularized laws. Whether in deistic construals of an absent divine watchmaker, or Reformed theistic models of an inscrutable sovereign God who no longer intervenes miraculously, the world was portrayed as clearly patterned, regimented, evacuated of mystery, and hence ultimately observable, measurable, and predictable. It was this vision that aided the rise of the modern natural sciences.[26]

Such paradigms also influenced the rise of economics as a discipline. Founding thinkers of political economy transferred ideas of the regularized and predictable patterns of nature—themselves derived from providence— into a sphere newly described as the market. Most centrally, these economists set forth a theory of *equilibrium*, depicting the market and its various and at times agonistic exchanges as somehow balancing out when seen from a high level—or God's eye view.[27] Various market transactions, however selfish and self-interested, would contribute to the net gain and common good of society. Adam Smith's famous notion of the "invisible hand" assumed and revised the idea of God's hand of providence, repressing explicit senses of an active creator orchestrating events and instead shifting agency toward the immanent market. The paradigm of providence, therefore, came to inform and continues to influence fundamental assumptions about market self-calibration and efficiency.[28]

While these classical theorists were designing a providentially informed model of market efficiency, they were also marshaling Christian doctrines of salvation. Although, to be sure, diversity persists in this area of theology, arguably many of the dominant strands of soteriology declare that God has established a type of peace with humanity and among humankind based on a saving transaction that took place in the death and resurrection of Christ. We see hints of this focus on soteriology at work in the new claims made by philosophers of the market who argued that commercial transactions bring peace and forge the bond of civil society. During this age of transition from Christendom to the emergence of nation states, thinkers proffered the economy as a possible third way—distinct from religion and politics—that might ground peaceful coexistence after centuries of religious warfare.[29] We find the remarkable insistence that commercial transaction leads toward a lessening of aggressive impulses and a channeling of desires toward productive self-interest. Traditional soteriologies of divine *commercium*, a transaction that liberated sinful humanity and prepared it for right relations with God and neighbor, subtly merged with new language of exchange and economy to yield the conclusion that economic exchange brings peace.[30] Thus, providence and salvation contributed to the conceptual matrix around the rise of capitalism, allowing market theorists to argue for the tendency for markets to calibrate and achieve equilibrium, as well as the market capacity to enable peace and social stability.

Max Weber's famous observations about the Protestant ethic address the psychology and anxiety of believers grappling with the implications of both providence and salvation. The question of predestination—which Weber claimed motivated Calvinist commercial efforts to demonstrate one's elect status—hinges on belief in a sovereign God who plans and orchestrates history in particular ways (i.e., providence) and who makes central in such planning or decree a determination of who will be saved (i.e., soteriology). While most reflection has focused on the role of providence in this story of Calvinist anxiety over election (God's sovereign, inscrutable, and eternal decree), soteriology and concern about one's destiny as elected (i.e., salvation or damnation) are just as crucial as sites of investigation. In this way, both providence and soteriology form twin nodes around which we might examine the nexus of theological ferment and market thinking.

Certainly, themes of providential equilibrium and redemptive commerce remain present today, as pundits hail stable democracy and capitalism as handmaidens, and support market globalization as a route toward global political peace. One soteriological example is the bold and oft-repeated mantra of capitalist mogul Steve Forbes: "Only Capitalism will save us."[31] Another infamous example of this pacifying sentiment is Thomas Friedman's claim that no two countries with a McDonald's have ever gone to war with one another.[32] Societies united by the common bond of capitalist markets should be societies that cooperate rather than fight, echoing "the peace that passes all understanding" enabled by Christ (Phil 4:7), who served as a payment for human iniquity, reconciling humans to God and to one another.

We see fragility and vulnerability coursing through these systems. Even as classical economists and early modern political theorists marshaled the market ideal as offering stability to a fragile and vulnerable time of conflict, the ideal market subject required self-discipline and policing of the passions. We can see the myth of the market as a tenuous overlay on unstable social relations, and its origins relied on ideas of the hand of God for stability. For what role does providence play if not to provide a sense of solace and order in the face of suffering and the chaos of life?

Similarly, what role does equilibrium play in market logic, if not to calm the anxieties raised by the continual shifts and changes—in short, the unpredictability and disorder—of commercial exchange? Without the stabilizing ideologies of the divine sovereign and providential governor, along with the rationally governed market actor, the fear appears to be that market relations may devolve into chaos. The doctrine of equilibrium—as part of the statement of faith in neoclassical economics— preserves the myth of internal stability. Despite the increasingly obvious norm in recent years that *crisis* is the true *stasis* of capitalism, neoliberal economic pundits maintain a dogged faith in equilibrium, proclaiming the inevitable return of economic peace and stability.[33]

The Calvinist anxieties that Weber and others have famously documented as one potential driver of early capitalism betray a sense of a precarious and vulnerable existence. Fear about one's elect status and one's sense of radical dependence on the eternal decrees of an inscrutable God foment entrepreneurial activity as the secular vocation that might confirm one's salvation. Here the doctrine of providence activated by concerns over salvation interpolates capitalist affective postures of anticipation, "leaning in" toward the future, and amassing capital to bring order and assurance to a precarious state of dependence on God. The incessant drive for accumulation, reinvestment, and further capital expansion that fuels the system connects to this quest to negotiate eternal precarity.[34] And certainly, this anxious need for constant growth and finding ways to weather the uncertainty of the economic system lead to endless innovations in labor exploitation.

The Calvinist dependence upon God, the inscrutable sovereign, in the face of a precarious eternal destiny, manifested in an entrepreneurial energy that displaced the anxieties of precarity onto the laborers it employed or enslaved. Such doctrine followed unique trajectories in the American context, in particular, in brands of evangelicalism and dispensationalism that emphasized Christ's imminent, literal return, and the radical transformations this would bring. Such Millenarianism and millennial eschatology are noteworthy because they inscribe precarity in history and within historical time. Everything may soon change on a dime and be altered in an instant when the elect are "caught up in the clouds" as the "first trumpet" sounds from heaven (1 Thess 4:17).

Such beliefs and attitudes support an intentional and strategic precarity: On one hand, the conditions of labor do not matter that much because Christ will transform all; on the other, one has limited time to accumulate wealth and thus labor processes must be increasingly efficient and extractive. Thus, the neglect and disregard of the environment, which ecological activists critique in these dispensational and millennial theologies, may parallel their indifference to the conditions of labor. If all will soon burn when the Lord Jesus comes on the clouds, slaves should calmly obey their masters and laborers should be satisfied with minimal wages.

While one may construe this posture of awaiting Christ's imminent return as a kind of hope, it reflects anxiety that stems from the uncertainty of salvation. Although such dispensationalists typically express a proud assurance of salvation that departs from the humility of early Calvinist believers, soteriological anxiety emerges here on the historical plane in endless end-times speculation and emphasis on the suddenness of rapture, tribulation, and divine judgment.[35] Struggling for assurance and stability amidst such theological-existential vulnerability, these American theologies that support capitalist political economy perpetuate precarity and form vulnerable communities as they mask the fragility of their own belief systems and institutions.

Fragility, Void, and Protest

In signaling repressed anxieties about the vulnerabilities of capitalism, I have gestured to two moments of anxiety, among many others, manifest in Christian thought as it connects with economic practices around work and capital accumulation. Both the early Calvinist and later evangelical and dispensational anxieties intersect in surprising and unintended ways with labor and with vulnerable communities. Both engender structural instabilities and efforts to manage such fragility that in turn lend tactics and techniques to the management of economic relations. And both signal a much more undergirding, central, and perennial anxiety within Christianity that is marked by the ascension of Christ.

Theologians have given little attention to the ascension as a point of doctrine, and it functions as an afterthought to the resurrection, which is certainly not short on engagement.[36] Thinkers have also focused on *Parousia*, or the return of Christ, which relates to our aforementioned dispensationalists—as well as any number of millenarian movements across history. But Christian thinkers have devoted less reflection to the rather significant movement in the Christological drama of Christ's removal and absence from history. My suspicion and wager are that the ascension and absence of Christianity's founding figure produce a systemic fragility, vulnerability, and concomitant anxiety in the concepts, practices, and institutions of Christian tradition. To put it in terms of this chapter: What are the theologies, politics, and economics that Christ's absence produces, an absence that renders *vulnerable* the entire Christian project and shows the *fragility* of its claims? How much do this vulnerability and the coping strategies it engenders help us understand Christianity's own relationship to the economic realm?

What do I mean that the ascension marks Christianity's vulnerability? Ascension is the place-holder and mask for the problem that the church faces: Its risen and exalted lord is nowhere to be found. The king's body is absent.[37] The throne is empty.[38] Believers and those steeped in theology and church tradition will be quick to protest that the risen Lord remains in, for instance, the church and community of believers, or in the Eucharist. But these simply are not the risen Christ. These are at best signs and markers of his absence, contested ones, for even the church cannot agree on its ecclesiology or sacramentology. These conceptual claims and attendant practices are but the tip of the iceberg in a series of coping strategies for the loss of Christ.[39]

Ascension is a marker of absence, loss, void, and attendant trauma and melancholia. Yet the scant theological engagements with ascension that I have seen suggest a triumphalism typical of denial. Covering up or failing to engage the trauma of loss, resurrection doctrine moves directly to forced celebration of the apparent exaltation of Christ.[40] Following the trajectory of resurrection, with its celebration of victory over death, this upward movement of Christ out of the grave is seen to carry forward seamlessly with his upward movement into the clouds and away from earth, history, and materiality. But difference remains. The joy, celebration, and bewilderment seen in the disciples' reunion with their risen lord stand in contrast to the shocked posture of longing toward heaven as their risen lord then departs.[41]

What sort of politics does this absence and its repression generate? Church tradition, ecclesial structure, and cooperation with empire building are efforts to fill the void and to stabilize a vulnerable structure. They are attempts to lend legitimacy to the claims of an institution that proclaims the presence and power of an absentee ruler. Charged with manifesting the presence of the absent Christ in the world, the church enacts the rule of the risen Lord, stumbling clumsily between enforcing the kingdom on earth and awaiting its true manifestation upon Christ's return. The proliferation of ecclesial bureaucracy, with its diversity of roles and offices, declarations and doctrines, attempts to bring form, substance, and support to the church's fragile project.

Can we chart a route through Christianity's own vulnerability here? Might we find points of resonance and connection with other systemic vulnerabilities in our present?[42] What links emerge to the vulnerability of capitalism and neoliberal order? Given capitalism's debt to many Christian theological concepts, practices, and institutions, might economic doctrine have also inherited these theological vulnerabilities? Could Christian attempts to cover up the fragility of their claims to divine presence generate echoes in capitalist moves to dissimulate the market's fragile disequilibrium?[43]

Let us consider three examples of major responses to abandonment by Christ: the church as the lingering body of Christ, declarations of Eucharistic real presence, and focus on the miraculous and on the sacramentality of the natural order as marks of divine presence. These three are deeply interrelated and mutually reinforcing: The Eucharist as the real presence of Christ—itself a miracle—grounds the church as manifesting Christ's body on earth in word and deed.[44] These doctrines present differently across Christian history and have always been contested. All three seek a solution to the absent Christ; all three offer covering and structure to the embarrassing void and absence—and hence vulnerability—at the heart of the church's proclamation.

Despite 1500 years of debate and diverse presentations, the Reformers radically transformed these postulates in ways with which the current, modern, Western order continues to reckon. They declared the age of miracles long closed, concluded with the apostolic age. Some of their (admittedly diverse) thought systems helped to desacralize and desacramentalize the world, presenting nature as a rational functioning system, ordained by the wise creator and requiring no miraculous intervention. Such a line of thinking also facilitated deism, which underscored divine absence and lack of intervention. The Reformers also rejected Catholic notions of Eucharistic real presence, offering variations on memorialization that rendered the bread and body signs but not material manifestations of the absent and ascended Christ. This ascended body remained safely hidden in heaven, and was not to be perpetually divided and distributed in communion in any real sense. Finally, of course, the Reformers initiated radically new ecclesiologies while shifting political realities reconfigured the body of Christ.[45] Church borders no longer aligned with the territorial borders of Christendom and, following the breakup of the

Holy Roman Empire, the church as a social body underwent transformations in relation to the new, emerging social body of the nation state.[46]

I recount these changes here as neither a story of decline nor loss. Rather, these doctrinal and ecclesial shifts represented new ways of reckoning with divine absence and the embarrassment of ascension. The preceding history is also one of such reckoning as well as denial. The point here is that these shifts and reconfigurations of absence, with their attendant attempts to mask or elide Christian theological precarity, coincided with the formalization of conceptual, economic, and political systems that structured modern life. These key moments of juncture invite consideration of potential transference and resonance, even while keeping in mind that the counter-Reformation and forms of Catholic and Protestant re-enchantment must also be considered in genealogies of modernity.

As recounted earlier, market thinkers during this era marshaled capitalism ideologically as a mediator among emerging nations and as a governing mode of commerce and relationality between modern subjects. Ideas of the body of Christ and of the real presence that establishes peace within that body despite its absent lord provided the seedbed for new and increasingly popularized ideas about how symbols of money, capital, and value might enact a tenuous peace among the nations. The redemption and ransom for which Eucharist was a chief sign provided conceptual fodder for themes of literal redemption and ransom exchange in the market. Echoes of God's providential management of the world, a world now denuded of miracles that functioned according to rational laws, in turn supported faith in the equilibrium of the market. A diverse set of theologians, philosophers, and economists conveyed structures, practices, and concepts dedicated to shoring up the void left by the absent Christ to a worldview intent on masking its own precarity through a salvific myth of market expansion.

These resonances present possible sites where theology and economy coincide. Interrogating them and offering the startling alternative of a theology unashamed of and non-defensive about the absence at its heart might provide the seedbed of possibility to begin immanent and internal deconstructions and redirections within the economic system. Such theology acknowledges and embraces its vulnerability and the precarity of its claims, given its absent lord. Rather than search for an outside, the place of transcendent difference where an exalted sovereign lord easily stands over against the system in judgment, we might pursue the hidden fissures of internal and genealogical vulnerability. Repatterning Christian theologies after the manner of vulnerability and fragility may offer perspective on the implicit theologies of the current system, revealing their violence in enforcing its mask of inevitability, and moving toward recoding the system's DNA. Such subtle and incremental changes may then provide space for light and for new life and growth to flourish in the cracks of this terror-producing façade. [47]

Notes

1. On this dynamic see, for example, Thomas Frank and Matt Weiland, *Commodify Your Dissent: Salvos from "The Baffler"* (New York: Norton, 1997).

2. Francis Fukuyama, *The End of History and the Last Man* (New York: Free Press, 1992).

3. See, for example, Eric J. Evans, *Thatcher and Thatcherism*, 4th ed. (London: Routledge, 2019).

4. David Harvey, *Spaces of Hope* (Berkeley: University of California Press, 2000); Vincent Crapanzano, "Reflections on Hope as a Category of Social and Psychological Analysis," *Cultural Anthropology* 18, no. 1 (2003): 3–32; Hirokazu Miyazaki, *The Method of Hope: Anthropology, Philosophy, and Fijian Knowledge* (Stanford, Calif.: Stanford University Press, 2004); Jonathan Lear, *Radical Hope: Ethics in the Face of Cultural Devastation* (Cambridge: Harvard University Press, 2006); Hirokazu Miyazaki, "Economy of Dreams: Hope in Global Capitalism and its Critiques," *Cultural Anthropology* 21, no. 2 (2006): 147–72.

5. Lauren Berlant, *Cruel Optimism* (Durham: Duke University Press, 2011). Historical precedents are explored in Jordana (Jordy) Rosenberg, *Critical Enthusiasm: Capital Accumulation and the Transformation of Religious Passion* (New York: Oxford University Press, 2011); Jordana (Jordy) Rosenberg, "'Accumulate! Accumulate! That Is Moses and the Prophets!': Secularism, Historicism, and the Critique of Enthusiasm," *The Eighteenth Century* 51, no. 4 (2010): 471–90.

6. Kathi Weeks, *The Problem with Work: Feminism, Marxism, Antiwork Politics, and Postwork Imaginaries* (Durham: Duke University Press, 2011); Linn Marie Tonstad, "Debt Time Is Straight Time," *Political Theology* 17, no. 5 (2016): 434–48.

7. Randy Martin, *Financialization of Daily Life* (Philadelphia: Temple University Press, 2002).

8. Devin Singh, "Irrational Exuberance: Hope, Expectation, and Cool Market Logic," *Political Theology* 17, no. 2 (2016): 120–36.

9. Jean Joseph Goux, "General Economics and Postmodern Capitalism," *Yale French Studies* 78 (1990): 206–24.

10. Karen Z. Ho, *Liquidated: An Ethnography of Wall Street* (Durham: Duke University Press, 2009).

11. Karen Z. Ho, "Situating Global Capitalisms: A View From Wall Street Investment Banks," *Cultural Anthropology* 20, no. 1 (2005): 68–96.

12. William E. Connolly, *The Fragility of Things: Self-Organizing Processes, Neoliberal Fantasies, and Democratic Activism* (Durham: Duke University Press, 2013).

13. Recent evaluations of neoliberalism extend the picture of it as an ideology

committed to enlisting state power for enforcement. See, for example, Wendy Brown, *Undoing the Demos: Neoliberalism's Stealth Revolution* (New York: Zone Books, 2015); Adam Kotsko, *Neoliberalism's Demons: On the Political Theology of Late Capital* (Stanford, Calif.: Stanford University Press, 2018).

14. Devin Singh, "COVID-19 is Exposing Market Fundamentalism's Many Moral and Practical Flaws," *Washington Post*, April 4, 2020.

15. Guy Standing, *The Precariat: The New Dangerous Class*, revised ed. (London: Bloomsbury Academic, 2016).

16. Noam Chomsky, "Plutonomy and the Precariat: On the History of the U.S. Economy in Decline," *The Huffington Post*, May 8, 2012.

17. Karl Marx, *Capital: A Critique of Political Economy*, trans. Ben Fowkes, vol. 1 (London: Penguin Books, 1976), 873.

18. Marx, *Capital*, vol. 1, 874.

19. Marx, *Capital*, vol. 1, 895.

20. Marx, *Capital*, vol. 1, 875.

21. Of the countless studies, one classic statement is Eduardo Galeano, *Open Veins of Latin America: Five Centuries of the Pillage of a Continent* (New York: Monthly Review Press, 1997). See also, for example, Edward E. Baptist, *The Half Has Never Been Told: Slavery and the Making of American Capitalism* (New York: Basic Books, 2014).

22. C. L. R. James, *The Black Jacobins: Toussaint l'Ouverture and the San Domingo Revolution*, 2nd ed. (New York: Vintage Books, 1963).

23. For one lucid attempt to think these forms of labor together, see Nancy Fraser, "Expropriation and Exploitation in Racialized Capitalism: A Reply to Michael Dawson," *Critical Historical Studies* 3, no. 1 (Spring 2016): 163–78.

24. On capitalism, law, criminality, and policing see, for example, E. P. Thompson, *The Making of the English Working Class* (New York: Vintage, 1963); Michael Tigar, *Law and the Rise of Capitalism* (New York: Monthly Review Press, 2000); Jackie Wang, *Carceral Capitalism* (Pasadena, Calif.: Semiotexte, 2018).

25. See, for example, Paul Oslington, ed. *Adam Smith as Theologian* (New York: Routledge, 2011); David Singh Grewal, "The Political Theology of *Laissez-Faire*: From *Philia* to Self-Love in Commercial Society," *Political Theology* 17, no. 5 (2016): 417–33; Lisa Hill, "The Hidden Theology of Adam Smith," *European Journal of History of Economic Thought* 8, no. 1 (2001): 1–29.

26. Ian Hacking, *Scientific Revolutions* (Oxford: Oxford University Press, 1981); Michel Foucault, *Archaeology of Knowledge* (London: Routledge, 2002); Amos Funkenstein, *Theology and the Scientific Imagination from the Middle Ages to the Seventeenth Century* (Princeton, N.J.: Princeton University Press, 1986). This standard narrative of disenchantment is not without its problems, and forms of re-enchantment and arguably of "misenchantment" are discernible, as claimed in Eugene McCarraher, *The Enchantments of Mammon: How Capitalism Became the Religion of Modernity* (Cambridge: Harvard University Press, 2019).

27. Bill Maurer, "Repressed Futures: Financial Derivatives' Theological

Unconscious," *Economy and Society* 31, no. 1 (2002): 15–36; Jacob Viner, *The Role of Providence in the Social Order: An Essay in Intellectual History*, Jayne Lectures for 1966, American Philosophical Society (Princeton, N.J.: Princeton University Press, 1972). See now Benjamin Friedman, *Religion and the Rise of Capitalism* (Cambridge: Harvard University Press, 2021).

28. See, for example, Hill, "Hidden Theology of Adam Smith."

29. These dynamics are richly documented in Albert Hirschman, *The Passions and the Interests: Political Arguments for Capitalism Before its Triumph* (Princeton, N.J.: Princeton University Press, 1977); see also Albert Hirschman, "Rival Interpretations of Market Society: Civilizing, Destructive, or Feeble?," *Journal of Economic Literature* 20 (1982): 1463–84.

30. Early Christian ideas of ransom are further explored in Devin Singh, *Divine Currency: The Theological Power of Money in the West* (Stanford, Calif.: Stanford University Press, 2018).

31. See Steve Forbes and Elizabeth Ames, *How Capitalism Will Save Us: Why Free People and Free Markets are the Best Answer in Today's Economy* (New York: Crown Business, 2009).

32. Thomas Friedman, *The Lexus and the Olive Tree* (New York: Anchor Books, 2000).

33. On capitalism as crisis and shock see Naomi Klein, *The Shock Doctrine: The Rise of Disaster Capitalism* (New York: Metropolitan Books, 2007).

34. One can open any issue of *Forbes* today and find CEOs still proclaiming the mantra: "If you're not growing as a company, you're dying." This ideology of endless and unquestioned growth is now being rethought and challenged from within capitalism as well. See, for example, Paul Jarvis, *Company of One: Why Staying Small Is the Next Big Thing for Business* (Boston: Houghton Mifflin Harcourt, 2019). For a provocative and insightful argument for the ultimate irrationality of the capitalist drive for accumulation, see Elettra Stimilli, *The Debt of the Living: Ascesis and Capitalism* (Albany, N.Y.: SUNY Press, 2017).

35. From the influential end-times film *A Thief in the Night* (1972) to the even more popular *Left Behind* (1995–2007) series by Time LaHaye and Jerry Jenkins, American evangelicalism and dispensationalism remain profoundly marked by such apocalyptic anxieties.

36. Of the scant studies on ascension, see, for example, Douglas Farrow, *Ascension and Ecclesia: On the Significance of the Doctrine of the Ascension for Ecclesiology and Christian Cosmology* (Grand Rapids, Mich.: Eerdmans, 1999); Douglas Farrow, *Ascension Theology* (London: T&T Clark, 2011). One recent engagement with ascension in Asian American perspective is Neal D. Presa, *Ascension Theology and Habakkuk: A Reformed Ecclesiology in Filipino American Perspective* (New York: Palgrave Macmillan, 2018).

37. Eric L. Santner, *The Royal Remains: The People's Two Bodies and the Endgames of Sovereignty* (Chicago: University of Chicago Press, 2011).

38. Giorgio Agamben, *The Kingdom and the Glory: For a Theological Genealogy*

of Economy and Government, trans. Lorenzo Chiesa and Matteo Mandarini (Stanford, Calif.: Stanford University Press, 2011).

39. As I have suggested previously, there "emerges the possibility of construing the ascension of Christ not as exaltation or triumphant expansion of authority but rather as abandonment. The legacy of political theology can be seen in part as a series of coping strategies for the trauma of such loss." See Devin Singh, "Anarchy, Void, Signature: Agamben's Trinity Among Orthodoxy's Remains," *Political Theology* 17, no. 1 (2016): 41.

40. Against this tendency, Linn Marie Tonstad reads the resurrection through ascension precisely as sustaining loss and absence, and develops an important initial sketch of a non-reproductive and even abortive ecclesiology, where the church attests to the absent Christ rather than attempts to be his body. See Linn Marie Tonstad, *God and Difference: The Trinity, Sexuality, and the Transformation of Finitude* (New York: Routledge, 2016), 254–77. On trauma, loss, and failure in Christian theology more broadly, see Karen Bray, *Grave Attending: A Political Theology for the Unredeemed* (New York: Fordham University Press, 2020); Shelly Rambo, *Spirit and Trauma: A Theology of Remaining* (Louisville, Ky.: Westminster John Knox Press, 2010); and Marika Rose, *A Theology of Failure: Žižek against Christian Innocence* (New York: Fordham University Press, 2019).

41. Coupled with the ascension are problems of the missing body of the savior, seen in engagements with the Gospel of Mark and its original ending. The narrative ends not with encounter with the risen lord but with a missing body and the fear of the disciples. One recent engagement with this trope and the trauma it marks is Michael J. Thate, *The Godman and the Sea: The Empty Tomb, the Trauma of the Jews, and the Gospel of Mark* (Philadelphia: University of Pennsylvania Press, 2019).

42. Connolly has also discerned "resonances" between the two vulnerable systems. See William E. Connolly, *Capitalism and Christianity, American Style* (Durham: Duke University Press, 2008).

43. One might also compare the political transfer of this absence, where political theorists filled the negative space of the absentee sovereign God of the old order of monarchy with immanent alternatives. See Claude Lefort, "The Permanence of the Theologico-Political?," in *Political Theologies: Public Religions in a Post-Secular World*, ed. Hent de Vries and Lawrence Eugene Sullivan (New York: Fordham University Press, 2006).

44. One classic examination of the political implications of the shifting definitions of Eucharist and the church as body of Christ is Ernst Kantorowicz, *The King's Two Bodies: A Study in Medieval Political Theology* (Princeton, N.J.: Princeton University Press, 1957). For further reflections on the politics engendered by recognition of the fragile and porous church as body, see Devin Singh, "Until We Are One? Biopolitics and the United Body," in *"In Christ" in Paul: Explorations in Paul's Theology of Union and Participation*, ed. Kevin J. Vanhoozer, Constantine R. Campbell, and Michael J. Thate, WUNT/II (Tuebingen: Mohr Siebeck, 2014).

45. See Christopher Elwood, *The Body Broken: The Calvinist Doctrine of the*

Eucharist and the Symbolization of Power in Sixteenth-Century France (New York: Oxford University Press, 1999).

46. Several studies have engaged the impact of the Reformation on political and economic ideas in modernity, including Brad S. Gregory, *The Unintended Reformation: How a Religious Revolution Secularized Society* (Cambridge: Belknap Press of Harvard University Press, 2012). This is not to say that the Reformation was wholly responsible for such massive epistemic and socio-political shifts. Much has also been made, for instance, of the influence of nominalism arising centuries earlier within Catholic thought as an important precursor to the watershed changes that the Reformation set into motion. See, among many studies, Michael Gillespie, *The Theological Origins of Modernity* (Chicago: University of Chicago Press, 2008).

47. Small portions of this chapter reproduce with permission material published in Devin Singh, *Economy and Modern Christian Thought* (Leiden: Brill, 2022).

3

As the World Burns

Laudato Si', the Climate Crisis, and the Limits of Papal Power

Mary Doak

Our climate crisis is, in fact, a climate emergency. Levels of CO_2 and other greenhouse gases in the atmosphere are more than one-third higher than the highest pre-industrial average from the last 800,000 years; moreover, these levels are increasing as humans continue to burn fossil fuels. The average global temperature has risen 2 degrees Fahrenheit, with significant effects on the planet. The glaciers are shrinking, sea levels are rising, agriculture is disrupted, coral is dying, and droughts, floods, and hurricanes are becoming more severe.

Even more worrisome, there is serious danger of a "feedback" loop in which the effects of global warming themselves lead to further warming. The melting of sea ice and glaciers, for example, may well send temperatures even higher as the planet absorbs solar heat previously deflected by ice sheets. Given how much polar ice has already been lost, along with the fact that CO_2 stays in the atmosphere and continues to warm the earth for decades after it is released, we may be nearing a climate change "tipping point" that triggers an unstoppable chain of environmental reactions.[1] Climate scientists advise the immediate reduction of atmospheric greenhouse gases if humanity wishes to avoid the life-threatening and civilization-altering transformation of this planet's climate.[2]

The good news is that renewable and clean energy sources, especially of wind and sun, are plentiful, and the technology to harvest this energy is improving. The 2014 report of the Intergovernmental Panel on Climate Change announced that switching to non-fossil-fuel energy sources was not only possible but could be done without damaging the economy.[3] Although averting climate change will require interrupting economic habits of heedless consumption and the pursuit of maximal profits without regard to consequences, the real economic threat is not the cost of switching to sustainable energy sources. The greater danger to the economy is the enormous expense of extreme weather events, increased disease, agricultural loss, and international conflicts due to climate change.

What is most seriously lacking is not the technology, which is increasingly available, but rather the political will to enact the substantial changes needed to reduce and ultimately to eliminate greenhouse gas emissions. While personal choices can make some difference, the requisite transformation of global energy infrastructures depends on concerted local, national, and international action. Unfortunately, in the United States today, our politics is in disarray, marked by polarization and mutual suspicion, a lack of agreement on basic facts, and a strong tendency to look to market forces rather than political action to solve our common problems. Added to this is an active climate denial industry dedicating to sowing confusion about the scientific consensus, worries about losing economic advantage, and the plans of influential fossil fuel companies, which have considerable interest in ensuring that their fossil fuel reserves do not become stranded assets without economic value.

To a large extent, then, the climate crisis is a values crisis, demanding that humanity decide whether it cares enough about the future of life on earth to expend the effort and face the risks involved in making the necessary economic changes. This climate crisis is also a political challenge, as Pope Francis has pointed out, because effective political action requires relatively healthy political institutions and habits, structures for international cooperation, and perhaps above all, the capacity for sustained political attention. After all, passionate reactivity to whatever topic is temporarily dominating the 24/7 stream of news and scandals is too ephemeral to allow for the development of adequate solutions to serious and complex problems such as climate change. The climate crisis tests the viability of democratic politics at all levels in the twenty-first century.

Can religious communities make a difference? Faith has shown itself at various times in history to be a powerful motivator, and we certainly need all of the motivation we can get to overcome the considerable obstacles to reducing greenhouse gas emissions. Yet our religious communities are also politically polarized. Christians in the United States, for example, are often more deeply divided over whether they are politically liberal or conservative than over denominational membership or doctrinal interpretations and, unfortunately, concern about climate change has become a partisan issue. One recent and rather thorough study demonstrates that young people in the United States tend to choose their political party first, and then adopt the religious beliefs deemed appropriate to that political identity.[4] While this conclusion about the priority of political over religious commitment contradicts much of what people claim about their religio-political positions, the study sheds significant light on alignments of faith and politics in the contemporary United States.

Dedicating an entire papal encyclical to the topic of Christian responsibility for nature, Pope Francis wagers that religion can be a positive motivating factor and that, as pope, he has enough authority to bridge partisan divides, establish common ground, and inspire people to act together for the good of the planet and all on it at this critical juncture. Furthermore, Francis not only sees the importance of clarifying Catholic doctrine on the intrinsic value of nature but also recognizes that doctrinal reform alone is insufficient. He analyzes the deformations of much contemporary political culture, calling for the development of a politics responsive to human problems and committed to directing the economy to serve the common good. Even more fundamentally, Francis challenges his readers to a different way of being, to a life grounded in a spirituality of interconnectedness from which we can construct healthier politics and economics. The "integral ecology" that Francis defends as the solution to the environmental, personal, political, and social crises humanity faces depends not merely on right doctrine or even on right action but also, Francis argues, on living in deep awareness of our radical relationality.

Pope Francis's vision as developed in his 2015 encyclical *Laudato Si': On the Care of Our Common Home* is an urgent appeal not only to Christians but to all people to change the way we relate to nature, including the way we relate to one another (for we, too, are a part of nature).

The most pressing question, however, is whether this encyclical will be a difference that truly makes a difference. Ultimately, of course, only time will tell. But enough time has passed to assess some of *Laudato Si'*'s impact as well as the obvious obstacles—especially in the United States—to the full reception of this document's contribution to the necessary religious, political, and economic transformations. I argue that Pope Francis makes four significant developments to Catholic doctrine on the intrinsic value of nature in *Laudato Si'*: an expansion of the mission of the church to include communion with nature; the articulation of an integral ecology that highlights the interrelatedness of all life; a call for the reform of politics and political discourse; and identification of the need for a contemplative and prophetic spirituality. I then evaluate the limited capacity of papal teaching to mobilize people, especially Catholics, to act on climate change in a manner consistent with essential Christian beliefs. I conclude by considering U.S. Catholic responses thus far, especially the inadequacy of the United States Conference of Catholic Bishops (USCCB)'s teaching on the environment, and the importance of lay Catholic commitment in developing appropriate and effective Catholic engagement with the current climate crisis.

The Contribution of *Laudato Si'*

Lynn White famously accused Christianity (already in 1967!) of teaching an anthropocentrism that fostered environmental devastation.[5] Christian human-centeredness, White argued, is rooted in the Biblical creation stories' support for human dominance over a natural world described as created for humanity's benefit.[6] Many Christian thinkers—including Pope Francis in *Laudato Si'*—have rejected White's contention, noting that the reference to dominion in Genesis 1 is better interpreted as stewardship, as care for the earth on God's behalf, rather than as a lordship that allows humanity to do whatever it wants with nature.[7] In fact, there is much in the Bible to encourage care for creation, especially the Hebrew Bible laws constraining abuse of land and animals. Pope Frances mentions a few of these laws in *Laudato Si'*, including the extension of Sabbath rest to one's ox and donkey.[8] We might also note the biblical visions of a perfect future harmony among humans and nature, as in the oft-cited Isaiah passage foretelling a time when "the wolf shall live with the lamb, the leopard shall lie down with the kid . . . and a little child shall lead them" (Is 11:6).[9]

Nevertheless, White has a valid point. Regardless of how the Bible *should* be interpreted, Christians have often understood the Bible as giving humans the right to do whatever we please to the earth. In my own undergraduate days, a Catholic theology professor announced rather matter-of-factly that God had given humans an unlimited "dominion" over nature, as though such was the clear and obvious meaning of Genesis 1.

Perhaps more influential than the interpretation of a single biblical passage, however, is the Christian focus on a divine-human drama of salvation that sidelines the rest of creation while emphasizing God's concern for humanity to the point of becoming human to save humanity from its sin. Indeed, even into the late twentieth century, official Catholic documents continued to assert that the human being is the "only creature on earth that God willed for itself," suggesting that the rest of creation has no intrinsic value but exists only for humanity's sake, and is thus available for economic exploitation.[10]

Of course, this disregard for nature has not gone unchallenged within the Christian tradition, especially in recent decades. The Ecumenical Patriarch Bartholomew has been an indefatigable champion of Christian responsibility to the environment, and many Christian denominations now have official statements on care for the earth as a moral obligation.[11] In the Catholic

Church (my focus here), Pope St. John Paul II condemned environmental degradation, as did his successor Pope Benedict XVI.[12] Regional councils of Catholic bishops, including the USCCB, have taken up the issue, forming environmental justice committees and issuing documents reminding Christians that "if we harm the atmosphere, we dishonor our Creator and the gift of creation."[13]

Unfortunately, this teaching did not have the impact one might have hoped. A 2015 study published by the Yale Project for Climate Change Communication before the release of *Laudato Si'* found that, although fifty-seven percent of Catholics agreed that human activity is largely responsible for climate change, only twenty-two percent of Catholics considered this a serious moral issue and astonishingly few (only five percent!) judged this to be a major religious concern.[14] While Catholic theologians and environmental activists have welcomed official magisterial support for environmental concerns, the broader Catholic community, especially in the United States, did not seem to have been significantly affected by these various church statements.

Could *Laudato Si'* be the game changer that energizes Christian, especially Catholic, environmental activism? This is, after all, the only encyclical dedicated entirely to the environment as a moral and religious concern, and the fact that the pope issued an encyclical on this topic underscores that he considers this an important matter to Christian faith. Minor statements by popes can easily go unnoticed amid the overwhelming output of papal addresses, writings, and sermons, and parishioners may reasonably suspect that any specific papal comment has been taken out of context or given undue weight to serve the political agenda of the one brandishing the quotation. The documents of regional episcopal conferences are also numerous, so that few non-professionals keep up with them; in any case, the authority of such documents has been called into question, especially by Joseph Cardinal Ratzinger (later Pope Benedict XVI, the immediate predecessor of Pope Francis).[15] The publication of a papal encyclical, however, is indisputably a major Catholic event, and encyclicals are sufficiently authoritative to garner attention in the secular media as well as in the Catholic community. Of course, Catholics generally are not required to agree with the content of encyclicals since these papal documents rarely include infallible teaching. Nevertheless, by devoting an entire encyclical to the environment, Pope Francis has ensured that reasonably attentive Catholics who may have been unaware of past magisterial teaching about the environment are likely to know at least that Pope Francis considers care for creation to be a Christian moral imperative. Such Catholics might even recognize that the pope accepts the scientific consensus on climate change (which is, unfortunately, a big deal in the United States).

Because papal encyclicals do not read themselves, the extent of their impact ultimately depends on Catholics' willingness to engage—and embody—the text's teachings. Local ecclesial leadership can also make a difference, calling for study of the document and its teachings, or focusing diocesan resources on other matters (a topic I will discuss shortly). Still, as we have seen, a papal encyclical devoted entirely to the environment has a claim to the attention of Catholics, gets widely reported in the press, and contributes to spreading the idea (still foreign to too many) that care for the environment is an integral element of Christianity.

That the pope issued an encyclical on the environment is in itself significant; what he actually says is even more challenging to those (especially Christians) who dismiss the moral imperative of caring for the natural world. To be sure, much of what Pope Francis articulates in *Laudato Si'* is present in earlier papal and episcopal documents. In accordance with the long-standing Catholic tradition of affirming faith *and* reason, he engages science seriously and respectfully, and the Catholic social principles of the common good, solidarity, and option for the poor are evident here as in past magisterial teachings (cited throughout *Laudato Si'*). Francis joins the previous popes, St. John Paul II and Benedict XVI, in reminding readers that the earth's resources are intended for all, and that Christian solidarity with future generations and the poor, who are most vulnerable to climate catastrophes, makes stewardship of the environment a moral imperative.[16]

There is, however, one Catholic principle frequently emphasized in earlier magisterial documents on the environment that is *not* prominent in *Laudato Si'*: the principle of prudence. In one notable example, the USCCB cited prudence as central to its call for action on climate change in the 2001 statement *Global Climate Change: A Plea for Dialogue, Prudence, and the Common Good.*[17] The reason *Laudato Si'* neglects prudence is not, I submit, that Francis is indifferent to this virtue, but rather because climate change and environmental degradation are, in his view, no longer merely risks to be weighed against other possible negative outcomes of our action or inaction. He sees climate change and other forms of abuse of the earth as evident realities demanding immediate action. Where others have talked about likely dangers, Francis observes rather forthrightly, "We need only take a frank look at the facts to see that our common home is falling into serious disrepair," adding that "we can see signs that things are now reaching a breaking point, due to the rapid pace of change and degradation."[18] Yet there are more substantive theological shifts in *Laudato Si'* that add up to a genuine—and significant—development of Catholic doctrine on the intrinsic value of nature, which is the first of four major contributions I will focus on from this encyclical.

Communion with Nature

Eschewing a human-centered evaluation of creation, Pope Francis emphasizes that the church's call to be a sacrament of communion includes communion with nature. The faithful should embody and foster a relationship
of mutual belonging in which humanity and the rest of creation enrich each
other.[19] Pope John Paul II had earlier noted the interrelationship between
humans and nature, asserting that mistreatment of the environment is rooted
in a "profound moral crisis" in which both human life and the natural world
are devalued.[20] However, John Paul II's remarks on the environment remain
human-centered, with concern for the environment deemed essential because it contributes to the good of humanity. An anthropocentric approach
also dominates the USCCB defense of environmentalism as fundamental to
the common good of humanity and to solidarity with the poor and future
generations. Care for the planet is necessary, these bishops argue, because we
have moral obligations to other human beings who do or will depend on the
resources of the earth.[21] Pope Francis, on the other hand, underscores that
humanity is called to a communion not only with God and other humans, but
also to a communion with nature that refuses to reduce creation to a resource
for economic exploitation. Citing the stories of creation and fall in the beginning of Genesis, the pope reminds us that sin is a rejection of this network of
relations, introducing disharmony on all three levels: with God, within the
human community, and in humanity's relations with nature. As the increase
in dehumanizing work conditions suggests, abuse of the environment leads to
abuse of humans, as Francis contends, just as abuse of humans leads to abuse
of animals and the environment.[22]

From this perspective, it is completely wrongheaded to set concern for
humanity and concern for the environment against each other as so many are
tempted to do, whether by prioritizing human well-being over that of non-
human nature or by prioritizing the well-being of nature over that of humans.
Rejecting this common binary, Francis challenges Christians to recognize
and embody a more adequate and a more biblical approach in which humanity and the rest of the natural world are understood to be so interrelated that
they can flourish only together.

Francis's emphasis on communion with nature takes on an even greater
significance given that, since the Second Vatican Council, the church's purpose in history—its mission—has been defined in terms of communion. Both
Lumen Gentium and *Gaudium et Spes*, major documents (or "constitutions")
issued by Vatican II, state that the church is called to be a sacrament of communion, which means that the church is to be a sign and an instrument of

union with God and unity among humanity.[23] In *Laudato Si'*, Pope Francis clarifies that nature is also a part of this communion, comprising along with God and our neighbor the "three fundamental and closely intertwined relationships" that ground human life.[24] By explicitly including nature, Francis's account is more adequate to key biblical texts envisioning God's will for harmony in all of creation while also affirming that environmental stewardship is integral to the mission of the church. The church's task in history is to live and to spread the union with God among humanity and with the rest of the natural world.

What may be even more surprising to many Catholics and other Christians is that Pope Francis specifies that the non-human natural world is part of God's plan not only for creation but also for redemption. Traditional Catholic teachings have often asserted that humans alone have souls and so only humans will be in heaven; indeed, this eternal destiny with God is still frequently cited as a reason for the dignity and worth of every human being. Francis, however, stipulates that *all* material creation has been taken up by Christ in the Incarnation and will return to God at the end of time. "The ultimate destiny of the universe is in the fullness of God," he declares.[25] Hence all of nature, and not only humanity, has intrinsic value: Francis insists that every part of creation is "willed in its own being" by God, so that its worth is not limited to the benefit it might provide to humanity.[26] This, too, is a development of Catholic doctrine, overturning the earlier teaching that the human person is "the only creature that God willed for itself."[27] Furthermore, Francis asserts that humanity has a vocation to "lead all creatures back to their Creator," thus assisting in the redemption of the universe in a manner that reverses the common Christian view that the natural world exists to serve humanity. Instead, Francis suggests that humans have a God-given responsibility to serve the rest of creation.[28]

Having determined that all of creation is intrinsically valuable and destined for redemption, Francis condemns "tyrannical anthropomorphism" and rejects evaluating any part of creation solely in terms of its use to humanity.[29] Every created being uniquely reflects the glory of God, Francis maintains, citing St. Francis of Assisi especially as one who recognized the beauty and goodness of God in all of creation and who demonstrated "how inseparable the bond is between concern for nature, justice for the poor, commitment to society, and interior peace."[30] Francis further concludes that, because all creatures have intrinsic worth and each praises God in its being, humanity "has no right" to drive any species into extinction.[31]

Integral Ecology

Building on this communion-oriented focus on the interrelatedness of humanity, nature, and God, Francis argues for an "integral ecology," a second major contribution of *Laudato Si'*. Because all is interrelated (even space and time), the health of all of our relationships increases or decreases together.[32] While identifying the climate crisis as one of the predominant moral issues of our day, Francis points to other forms of moral and spiritual breakdown that contribute to it: the rapaciousness of a profit-obsessed economy, the decay of political institutions, the disregard of local cultures, and even the (all too common!) lack of balance in our daily lives.[33] The instrumentalism that abuses the environment for economic advantage also instrumentalizes ourselves, other humans, and, it follows, God!

The Covid-19 pandemic demonstrates all too well the acuity of the Pope's analysis. At this point, it is clear that the SARS-CoV-2 virus passed to humans through their interactions with non-human animals, perhaps when humans captured and marketed wild animals as food sources.[34] The result has been the unleashing of a disease with enormous cost to human life and health, which in turn has devastated sectors of the economy, increased poverty and inequality, disrupted bonds of families and friends, and seriously stressed the entire social fabric. The image of a dominant humanity forcing nature to serve human purposes must be replaced with the more accurate concept of an interconnected humanity, inextricably part of a network of relations that work together to sustain life.

Pope Francis's defense of integral ecology is a call to recognize that we must combat the breakdown in the web of mutuality in all its dimensions. This approach, it should be noted, thus resists efforts to sideline the issue of climate change in favor of focusing on sexual matters that are so often given priority as "intrinsic evils" in Catholic political activism.[35] Nor can the abuse of the environment be justified on the basis of human economic needs. Instead, Francis proffers a deeper analysis emphasizing that just as reality is interrelated, so too are the many pressing problems of the contemporary world. *Laudato Si'* challenges readers to avoid any reductionism that might simplify matters by authorizing a narrow political focus—including the narrowing that withdraws into a sectarian church or in the individualistic "me-n-Jesus" faith that dominates contemporary American Christianity. Francis repeatedly reminds us that the broader Christian tradition upholds a relational, community-oriented anthropology that is incompatible with a circumscribed area of concern in politics or in any dimension of our lives.

Before we move on to the other contributions of this encyclical, I think a critical observation is in order. Even while Pope Francis's argument for an integral ecology aptly identifies the interconnections between abuse of nature, of the poor, and even of ourselves, he neglects the well-developed connection between these oppressions and the abuse of women. At least since Sherry Ortner's 1974 article "Is Female to Male as Nature Is to Culture?," scholars have pointed to the parallel between misogyny and the domination of nature.[36] Yet Francis scarcely mentions and certainly fails to explore the denigration of women; he seems insufficiently aware of the ways in which the context that he lives and works in as pope institutionalizes the neglect of women's contributions. Since women are half of the world's population, this is no small oversight. It undermines the holistic communion the pope advocates. Unfortunately, this oversight appeared again in the 2020 social encyclical, whose very title, *Fratelli Tutti* (literally "All Brothers"), intentionally or not, reinscribes neglect of women.[37] If the integral ecology that Francis describes is to counter the broken attitudes and institutions that treat nature, the poor, people of color, and women as instruments to benefit the powerful, then overcoming the devaluation of women must be a priority. Only then can the integral ecology that the pope has quite rightly defended as essential not only to Christianity, but also to a humane world, do its work.

The Reform of Politics and Political Discourse

In addition to emphasizing the inclusion of an intrinsically valued creation in the redemptive communion we seek and to defending an integral ecology recognizing the interrelation of all societal injustices, a third major contribution proffered in *Laudato Si'* is the call to reform politics and political discourse.[38] Moving beyond intra-ecclesial conversations, Francis identifies a need to develop what is often called "public theology" in the United States. David Tracy argued decades ago that American society is dominated by a technological reason that excels at figuring out how to achieve goals in the most efficient manner, but that cannot determine what those goals ought to be. Tracy insisted that public theology, with its attention to the ultimate goals of life, is a badly needed contribution to public reasoning about the direction of society.[39] Apparently, little has changed: Francis argues that "many problems of today's world stem from the tendency, at times unconscious, to make the method and aims of science and technology an epistemological paradigm which shapes the lives of individuals and the workings of society." Francis continues with his observation that "decisions which may seem purely instrumental are in reality decisions about the kind of society we want to build."[40]

This lack of attention to the values that ought to guide social development, as Francis rightly notes here and in his earlier apostolic exhortation *Evangelii Gaudium* (2013), reinforces the dominance of the economy and the widespread idolatry of money. Too often, the only clearly shared goal in public life is economic growth, regardless of the cost. The emphasis in capitalism on pursuing profits above all else is a major obstacle to action on climate change because citizens fear that climate regulations will disrupt the economy or, at least, will put the United States at an economic disadvantage. Moreover, a commonplace neoliberal ideology denies responsibility for directing the economy, instead maintaining that market dynamics will solve any significant problems without the need for political action. In this context, as Francis repeatedly warns, "whatever is fragile, like the environment, is defenceless before the interests of a deified market, which become the only rule."[41] Instead of ensuring that the economy serves the good of all, political debates and governmental actions are obsessed with serving the growth of the economy, with disastrous effects on both society and the environment.

Pope Francis further contributes to public theology by modeling a religiously based reasoning that takes science seriously. *Laudato Si'* acknowledges the scientific consensus on climate change, as do the American Catholic bishops in their 2001 statement, "Global Climate Change."[42] This should not be remarkable but, alas, it is: a vocal anti-science faction in the United States has been quite successful in popularizing the idea that the science on anthropogenic climate change is either not settled or is, in fact, a giant hoax perpetrated by scientists around the world. Not surprisingly, this anti-scientism is especially embraced by the Christian groups who also reject evolutionary science, thus strengthening the popular (mis)perception that religion and science are irreconcilably at odds. As the response to the Covid-19 pandemic and other political events has shown, serious public debate becomes impossible when people are free to make up their own "facts." It is doubtful that a democratic polis can be sustained without a shared commitment to the verifiable facts of our common reality, especially when those facts challenge religious or political preconceptions.

In addition to broadening public discourse in a manner that includes serious consideration of both religious values and scientific facts, Pope Francis also emphasizes the need to restore inclusive and respectful dialogue at all levels. It is certainly undeniable that American public life is highly polarized and that genuine listening across political differences is rare. There is a great deal of mutual suspicion today, with very little common ground on which to begin a conversation among opposing sides. Bishop Robert McElroy of San Diego argued that the most important task facing Christians—and indeed all Americans—after the 2016 presidential election is to reach across political divisions, listen respectfully to one another, and begin to rebuild public discourse.[43] With his integral ecology approach, Francis similarly calls for restoring public habits of mutual respect and fostering the relationships necessary for genuine dialogue to occur.[44] As the 2020 U.S. presidential election and its aftermath indicate, political healing remains an outstanding task. Yet Pope Francis and Bishop McElroy are right: It is only through recognizing our interrelatedness and rebuilding relationships of respectful dialogue that we will be able to heal not only the divisions, polarizations, and even abusive power relations in society, but also our distorted relation to nature.

Conversion to a Contemplative and Prophetic Spirituality

Finally, Francis astutely notes that the thoroughgoing change he envisions requires conversion to a spirituality that is contemplative as well as prophetic. Only by cultivating attention to the beauty and intrinsic goodness of God's creation can we sustain a truly alternative way of life, one that shifts from pursuing profits and power to a habit of appreciative enjoyment.[45] Intellectual arguments are not enough to inspire this radical transformation of attitude; what is needed is inner peace that is "reflected in a balanced lifestyle together with a capacity for wonder which takes us to a deeper understanding of life."[46] Ultimately, then, Francis calls Christians to a countercultural, healing way of being in the world, sustained by gratitude to God and appreciation of the beauty of creation and the web of interconnection that sustains us.

In *Laudato Si'*, Pope Francis is thus concerned with more than clarifying Christian doctrine. He summons his readers not only to think differently about nature, but also to reject the deification of the market, to engage in a values-oriented and respectful form of politics, and, even more fundamentally, to inhabit a more fulfilling and finally sacramental way of being in relation to all aspects of the world.

Playing a Long Game During a State of Emergency

Laudato Si' is a wise and timely document with rich insights that we may hope will bear considerable fruit within and beyond the Catholic community. Francis clarifies that care for the environment is an issue that is central to the life and faith of the church. He demonstrates that there are biblical as well as theological grounds for recognizing that God's redemptive plan for universal harmony includes nature as well as humanity. He also outlines a holistic form of discipleship predicated on the interconnectedness of all reality and oriented to healing this world through a spirituality that incorporates prayer, reduced consumption, respectful public discourse, and, especially, a grateful appreciation of the intrinsic value and beauty of all of creation. While it is true that the pope emphasizes the putatively progressive values of care and fairness in this encyclical, the allegation that he neglects supposedly conservative values of sanctity and loyalty is not true (though Francis does reject the unregulated, unbridled capitalism associated with conservatism in the United States).[47] Francis dedicates an entire chapter of *Laudato Si'* to describing a spirituality in which care for the environment is an expression of loyalty to God and integral to growth in holiness or sanctity.

Of course, if stopping the ravages of nature and society depends on all people achieving the holiness the pope envisions, despair is the only reasonable response. We know that complete holiness is not possible this side of the eschatological reign of God. While the world needs the witness that Pope Francis outlines, we must hope that a decent future does not depend on perfection but only on sufficient commitment to the good of others and of nature to make our lives, our cultures, our social institutions, and especially our public policies, saner and less rapacious.

Moreover, we must acknowledge that the pope's vision involves playing a long game, as public theology usually does. The changing of hearts and minds takes time. Spiritual conversion is a lengthy process, as is the restoration of a healthy political culture dedicated to directing, rather than be directed by, economic forces. Like Rome, civil public debate that values the truth, is founded on mutual care, seeks respectful dialogue, and affirms the intrinsic worth of all will not be built—or rebuilt—in a day.

Furthermore, in addition to its new teaching on the intrinsic value of nature, *Laudato Si'*'s emphasis on a communion-oriented spirituality requires a paradigm shift for many American Christians, including a good portion of Catholics, who embrace an individualistic Christianity at odds with the preponderance of traditional Catholic teaching. As long as Christianity is understood to be primarily about working out a personal salvation through one's own individual and largely solitary relationship with God, then all Catholic social teachings, including those concerning the environment, will continue to be relegated to the periphery of Christian life. This individualistic paradigm is, of course, a modern distortion that fails to do justice to the deeper wisdom of the Christian tradition, and Pope Francis joins other recent popes in striving to overcome this individualism and the concomitant tribalism (which is but a form of individualism writ large).[48]

Yet one might question whether the Catholic Church in the United States is able and willing to form people for the non-individualistic and countercultural mode of life that Francis rightly believes is necessary. With recent studies suggesting that political identity takes precedence over religious commitment, it is not surprising that some fear the church simply reflects broader social mores and has lost its particular ethos and identity. It is no wonder that sectarian or separationist Christian rhetoric continues to be popular, even though such a withdrawal from common life embraces a contemporary tribalism antithetical to the mission of the Christian church.[49]

The thesis that political identity takes priority over religious identity challenges the idea that religion is a direct force for social change, at least in the United States. Studies about the effect of *Laudato Si'* in the United States lend support to this contention, as statistics indicate that Catholics responded to the encyclical's message in accordance with their political affiliation: Democrat and Democrat-leaning Catholics embraced *Laudato Si'* and Republican and Republican-leaning Catholics rejected it.[50]

Nevertheless, I would caution against assuming that religious teaching makes little difference, or that religious commitments serve only to sacralize already settled political identities. Identity formation is a complex process, involving the alignment of multiple factors. Perhaps it is not surprising that polarization within religious communities mirrors the current polarization in U.S. politics, as people strive to construct coherent commitments in a complicated world. The fact that people exert so much effort in sermons, publications, talk shows, and other social media to persuade others that one or the other political stance is most consistent with Christianity indicates that faith remains an important element—one that, for many U.S. voters, must be integrated with their political commitments. Identification with a particular interpretation of Christianity may come after the determination of a theo-political vision of the world for many today, but the amount of energy invested in the topic suggests that a persuasive account of a religion's political implications remains a significant motivating factor in public life.

Of course, the extent of the industry devoted to persuading people about the proper politics of Christianity underscores the limits of papal pronouncements. The pope is far from the most dominant voice on the political implications of Christianity, even for Catholics. Besides, papal encyclicals are not often read outside of professional circles. Significant papal teachings generally have long-term impact in how Catholicism is taught, but in the short term may change little other than adding the ammunition of claiming papal authority for one's own side in the ongoing culture war between conservative and progressive U.S. Catholics. If *Laudato Si'* is to have the impact it should have on the life of the whole church now and in the future, faith leaders and teachers at all levels must disseminate the teachings of this encyclical, especially its commitment to an integral ecology, while clarifying the relation of these teachings to established principles of Catholic faith and practice.

U.S. Catholic Responses to *Laudato Si'*

It is fair to say that the work of the USCCB has not yet been adequate to this task. Consider, for example, the USCCB document, *Forming Consciences for Faithful Citizenship* (revised 2019), issued to provide guidance to Catholics on the relation between their faith and voting. The document starts well, acknowledging in its opening paragraphs that the various challenges to human life, human dignity, and the environment are "interrelated and inseparable." The document goes on to quote Pope Francis's statement from *Laudato Si'* that "We are faced . . . with one complex crisis which is both social and environmental. Strategies for a solution demand an integrated approach to combating poverty, restoring dignity to the excluded, and at the same time protecting nature."[51] Yet integral ecology is not discussed in this USCCB document, and care for the environment, which is often mentioned here only at the end of a long list of other political issues, is presented primarily as a matter of responsibility to the poor and to future generations.[52] Moreover, abortion is declared the "preeminent issue" of concern, with further emphasis on the importance of opposing "intrinsically evil" acts, which include abortion, redefining marriage (an odd fit here), and an undefined racism, but not, the reader is left to assume, contributing to the destruction of the conditions of life on this planet.[53]

Despite having acknowledged the interrelation of all issues, the discussion in *Forming Consciences for Faithful Citizenship* proceeds as though issues can, in fact, be separated and even ranked according to priority. Catholics who look to this document for guidance on the political implications of their faith will be hard-pressed not to conclude that the Republican Party's official opposition to abortion and gay marriage ultimately trumps any concern for climate change, immigrant rights, systemic racism, or economic inequality in the Catholic calculus, even though these are also urgent matters of life and death.

The USCCB's statements have not fully appropriated Pope Francis's affirmation of nature's intrinsic value, his advocacy of integral ecology, or his urgency about the ecological crisis. Nevertheless, I have no intention of detracting from the efforts of the many bishops and dioceses that have begun the hard and slow work of teaching, through words and deeds, that care for the environment is one element of Catholic practice today. For example, under the leadership of Bishop Wilton Gregory, the Catholic Diocese of Atlanta has developed—and shared with others—an extensive action plan to embody the principles of *Laudato Si'* in teaching, in sustainable practices in the parish as well as the home, and in political activism.[54] The USCCB has also sponsored the Catholic Climate Covenant, which works throughout the United States to organize Catholics to study and work on issues of the environment.[55]

But, in the meantime, the world is warming.

Given the importance of the environment for all life, the fact that we have already surpassed sustainable levels of greenhouse gases, and with a possible climate feedback loop threatening, we cannot rest content with laying the foundations for a Christian renewal that may make a difference decades from now. Current measurements indicate that the global average of CO_2 in the atmosphere exceeds 400 parts per million (ppm), far surpassing the pre-industrial high of 280 ppm and well above the 350 ppm that scientists identify as a reasonably "safe" and potentially sustainable CO_2 level.[56] With regard to the climate, we need immediate action, and even that may already be too late.

The most pressing question is: Will papal teaching, especially with the amplification of an encyclical, be able to reach and motivate enough people to make a difference in time? Or has the church (yet again) shown up with too little too late to help prevent an impending disaster?

Thus far, the measurable impact of the encyclical has been modest. A study of opinion surveys in the United States before and after *Laudato Si'* finds a small "Francis Effect." Serious concern about climate change increased overall in the years immediately following the release of the encyclical (despite the different reactions among Republicans and Democrats).[57] It is, of course, important to avoid the *post hoc ergo propter hoc* fallacy: This small shift in public opinion may have been due to other causes. Certainly, Catholics overall have not been galvanized to form a notable force for environmental activism even though some groups inspired by *Laudato Si'* have formed in Catholic schools and parishes not only to study but also to organize for climate action.

Three further observations are in order. First, we never know how long change will take. Struggles that appear to be hopeless can achieve unforeseen breakthroughs, with once radical ideas suddenly becoming mainstream, as we have seen recently with support for same-sex marriage and in growing dissatisfaction with the current form of capitalism in the United States. Since no one knows what the future will bring, we can never be certain what difference our actions will or will not make—and we cannot predict the tipping point that results in a paradigm shift (in religion or in politics). As the saints have long insisted, fidelity in discipleship is essential regardless of its effectiveness. It is especially critical to resist the paralysis-inducing presumption that it is too late for action on the climate; after all, this is a tactic used to support the status quo. So yes, American Catholics—and others—should continue to strive to embody *Laudato Si'*'s countercultural spirituality of reconciliation and harmony with society and the environment. They should resist the dominance of the economy and its consumerism by rebuilding public discourse and a public life oriented to values beyond the technocratic and by seeking in all ways possible to mend the world through increasing harmony with God, each other, and the natural world. The resources of Christian faith for clarifying and sustaining this countercultural spirituality merit ongoing study and clarification.

Secondly, and notwithstanding its tendency to think in centuries, the magisterium knows quite well how to exert its power on public issues that it deems sufficiently important. Consider the action taken by California Catholic bishops shortly before the vote on Proposition 8 to ban same-sex marriage in California. The bishops did not merely call for greater attention to the theological significance of sacramental marriage or a deepened witness of self-giving love in heterosexual marriage. They organized, raised money, and sent letters in support of Proposition 8 to be read in Catholic parishes before the vote.[58] Similarly, when Congress was debating the Affordable Care Act, the American Catholic bishops were not content to issue statements on Catholic teaching about the inherent link between marital sexuality and procreation. They lobbied collectively, publicly, and vociferously to influence the ACA's provisions on birth control with considerable success.[59] When the United Nations sponsored a conference on population issues in 1994, the Vatican expended considerable effort, publicly and privately, in an attempt to prevent the conference from supporting women's access not only to abortion but also to "artificial" contraception.[60] If the official leadership of the Catholic Church truly believes that care for the environment is central to Christian faith, they will do at least as much to mobilize the Catholic population and to energetically—and publicly—lobby governments to decrease the emission of greenhouse gases.[61]

Finally, the laity themselves have considerable power to affect public policy, especially in the United States. A large and mobilized body of Catholics dedicated to an integral ecology and committed to climate action could make all the difference in the next few years. As J. B. Metz argues, the laity must cease waiting for their bishops and priests to act, and instead recognize that they are themselves capable of living their Christian faith more fully and effectively.[62] This revival of lay witness is, in fact, a major focus of Francis's appeal in *Laudato Si'*; the pope envisions a transformation of the world through people living Christianity more fully in their personal lives, relationships, and politics. Catholics make up over twenty percent of the U.S. population, and approximately seventy percent of the U.S. population are non-Catholic Christians who share the Pope's beliefs about the Christian call to serve the communion of all creation. To be sure, good leadership from bishops and priests can contribute the institutional resources of the churches to this effort, but an informed and active laity could be quite effective in transforming national and international policies.[63]

Both climate science and Pope Francis maintain that the time to act is now. There is much that the pope, with the power of the Vatican, can do; there is perhaps more that the bishops in the United States and around the world can do. Yet the real difference will likely depend on the commitment of Catholic and other Christian laity. Ultimately, it is through the lives of the people of God that Christian beliefs can best effect long-term changes in society, politics, and the economy. Whether this encyclical contributes to the prevention of a climate catastrophe depends, finally, on the choices we all make in responding to it.

Notes

1. For climate information, see especially "Global Climate Change Evidence," NASA Global Climate Change and Global Warming: Vital Signs of the Planet, http://climate.nasa.gov/evidence. See also, Jeffrey Bennet, A *Global Warming Primer: Answering Your Questions About the Science, the Consequences, and the Solutions* (Boulder, Colo.: Big Kid Science, 2016).

2. In addition to Bennet, A *Global Warming Primer*, see also James Hansen et al., "Assessing 'Dangerous Climate Change': Required Reduction of Carbon Emissions to Protect Young People, Future Generations and Nature," PLOSONE 8, no. 12 (December 2013), http://journals.plos.org/plosone/article?id=10.1371/journal.pone .0081648.

3. Intergovernmental Panel on Climate Change, *Climate Change 2014: Mitigation of Climate Change* (Cambridge, UK: Cambridge University Press, 2015). See also Levi Tillemann et al., "Revolution Now: The Future Arrives for Four Clean Energy Technologies" (U.S. Department of Energy, September 2013), https://energy .gov/sites/prod/files/2013/09/f2/Revolution%20Now%20—%20The%20Future%20 Arrives%20for%20Four%20Clean%20Energy%20Technologies.pdf.

4. Michele Margolis, "When Politicians Determine Your Religious Beliefs," *New York Times*, July 11, 2018, https://www.nytimes.com/2018/07/11/opinion/religion -republican-democrat.html.

5. I address these issues at greater length and from a somewhat different angle in Mary Doak, A *Prophetic Public Church: Witness to Hope Amid the Global Crises of the Twenty-first Century* (Collegeville, Minn.: Liturgical Press, 2020), 151–83.

6. Lynn White, "The Historical Roots of Our Ecological Crisis," https://www.uvm .edu/~gflomenh/ENV-NGO-PA395/articles/Lynn-White.pdf.

7. Francis, *Laudato Si': On Care for Our Common Home*, especially 67, http://

w2.vatican.va/content/francesco/en/encyclicals/documents/papa-francesco_20150524
_enciclica-laudato-si.html.

8. Francis, *Laudato Si'*, 68.

9. See the visions also in Isaiah 2 and Micah 4.

10. See Vatican Council II, *Pastoral Constitution on the Church in the Modern World (Gaudium et spes)* 24, http://www.vatican.va/archive/hist_councils/ii_vatican _council/documents/vat-ii_const_19651207_gaudium-et-spes_en.html. See also John Paul II, *Redemptor Hominis* 13, http://w2.vatican.va/content/john-paul-ii/en /encyclicals/documents/hf_jp-ii_enc_04031979_redemptor-hominis.html.

11. See, for example, Ecumenical Patriarch Bartholomew, *On Earth as It Is in Heaven*, ed. John Chryssavgis (New York: Fordham University Press, 2011); and Lynne Whitney and Ellie Whitney, *Faith Based Statements on Climate Change* (CreateSpace Independent Publishing Platform, 2012).

12. See especially John Paul II, *Message for the Celebration of the World Day of Peace 1 January 1990*, http://w2.vatican.va/content/john-paul-ii/en/messages/peace /documents/hf_jp-ii_mes_19891208_xxiii-world-day-for-peace.html; and Benedict XVI, *Caritas in Veritate*, 48–51, http://w2.vatican.va/content/benedict-xvi/en/encyclicals /documents/hf_ben-xvi_enc_20090629_caritas-in-veritate.html.

13. United States Conference of Catholic Bishops, "Global Climate Change: A Plea for Dialogue, Prudence and the Common Good" (2001), http://www.usccb.org /issues-and-action/human-life-and-dignity/environment/global-climate-change-a-plea -for-dialogue-prudence-and-the-common-good.cfm.

14. A. Leiserowitz, E. Maibach, C. Roser-Renouf, G. Feinberg, and S. Rosenthal, *Climate Change in the American Christian Mind: March 2015* (New Haven: Yale Project on Climate Change Communication, 2015), esp. 7, 11, https:// climatecommunication.yale.edu/wp-content/uploads/2015/04/Global-Warming -Religion-March-2015.pdf. See also the similar conclusions of the Pew Research Center, "Religion and Views on Climate and Energy Issues" (October 22, 2015), https://www.pewresearch.org/science/2015/10/22/religion-and-views-on-climate-and -energy-issues/. Pew discovered that Hispanic Catholics in the United States were the group most likely to attribute global warming to human activity but concluded, "Political party identification and race and ethnicity are stronger predictors of views about climate change beliefs than are religious identity or observance."

15. For a discussion of Ratzinger's position along with an astute assessment of the issue overall, see Francis A. Sullivan, SJ, "The Teaching Authority of Episcopal Conferences," *Theological Studies* 63 (2002): 472–93, http://cdn.theologicalstudies .net/63/63.3/63.3.2.pdf.

16. Francis, *Laudato Si'*, esp. 93–95, 158–59.

17. USCCB, "Global Climate Change."

18. Francis, *Laudato Si'*, 61.

19. Francis, *Laudato Si'*, esp. 89–92.

20. John Paul II, *Message* 5.

21. In addition to USCCB, "Global Climate Change," see also USCCB, *Forming Consciences for Faithful Citizenship*, 86, http://www.usccb.org/issues-and-action /faithful-citizenship/forming-consciences-for-faithful-citizenship-title.cfm. For Pope Francis's treatment of communion, see especially *Laudato Si'*, 89–92.

22. Francis, *Laudato Si'*, esp. 66, 70.

23. See Vatican II, *Gaudium et spes*, 42; see also Vatican Council II, *Dogmatic Constitution on the Church (Lumen Gentium)*, 1, http://www.vatican.va/archive/hist _councils/ii_vatican_council/documents/vat-ii_const_19641121_lumen-gentium_en .html.

24. Francis, *Laudato Si'*, 66. See also 89–92.

25. Francis, *Laudato Si'*, 83. See also 99–100.

26. Francis, *Laudato Si'*, 69.

27. See especially *Gaudium et spes* 24 and *Redemptor Hominis* 13 for the earlier, more human-centered teaching.

28. Francis, *Laudato Si'*, 83.

29. Francis, *Laudato Si'*, 68; see also 107, 118–22.

30. Francis, *Laudato Si'*, 10.

31. Francis, *Laudato Si'*, 33, 69.

32. Francis, *Laudato Si'*, 137–62, esp. 138.

33. Francis, *Laudato Si'*, 137–62, esp. 142.

34. Smriti Mallapaty, "Where Did COVID Come From? WHO Investigation Begins but Faces Challenges," *Nature* 587, 342, https://www.nature.com/articles /d41586-020-03165-9.

35. See, for example, the discussion in USCCB, *Faithful Citizenship*, 34–37.

36. Sherry B. Ortner, "Is Female to Male as Nature Is to Culture?" in *Women, Culture, and Society*, ed. M. Z. Rosaldo and L. Lamphere (Stanford, Calif.: Stanford University Press, 1974), 68–87. See also Rosemary Radford Ruether, *New Woman, New Earth: Sexist Ideologies and Human Liberation* (New York: Seabury Press, 1975) and the more recent Elizabeth A. Johnson, *Women, Earth, and Creator Spirit* (New Jersey: Paulist Press, 1993).

37. Pope Francis, *Fratelli Tutti: On Fraternity and Social Friendship* (October 3, 2020), http://www.vatican.va/content/francesco/en/encyclicals/documents/papa -francesco_20201003_enciclica-fratelli-tutti.html.

38. This point is the subject of *Fratelli Tutti*.

39. David Tracy, *The Analogical Imagination: Christian Theology and the Culture of Pluralism* (New York, Crossroad, 1986), esp. 8.

40. Francis, *Laudato Si'*, 107.

41. Francis, *Laudato Si'*, 56. See also Francis, *Evangelii Gaudium* (November 24, 2013): 56, http://w2.vatican.va/content/francesco/en/apost_exhortations/documents /papa-francesco_esortazione-ap_20131124_evangelii-gaudium.html.

42. See Francis, *Laudato Si'*, 17–42; and USCCB, "Global Climate Change," esp. the section entitled "Sidebar: The Science of Global Climate Change."

43. Robert W. McElroy, "A Deeper Call to Citizenship," public address given at the University of San Diego, November 1, 2016.

44. Francis, *Laudato Si'*, 181.

45. Francis, *Laudato Si'*, 222, 215–16.

46. Francis, *Laudato Si'*, 225.

47. See the otherwise excellent analysis and overview provided by Asheley R. Landrum and Rosalynn Vasquez, "Polarized U.S. Publics, Pope Francis, and Climate Change: Reviewing the Studies and Data Collected Around the 2015 Papal Encyclical," *WIRES Climate Change*, August 10, 2020, https://doi.org/10.1002/wcc.674.

48. Vincent Miller notes that the further argument provided by Pope Francis in his later encyclical, *Fratelli Tutti*, may be the most sustained papal condemnation of nationalism and tribalist populism since the 1937 encyclical, *Mit Brenneder Sorge*. See Miller's contribution to "Five Theologians on the Biggest Takeaways from 'Fratelli Tutti' in *America: The Jesuit Review*, October 8, 2020, https://www.americamagazine.org/faith/2020/10/07/catholic-theologians-takeaways-fratelli-tutti-pope-francis.

49. See the excellent discussion in Vincent J. Miller, "Media Constructions of Space, the Disciplining of Religious Traditions, and the Hidden Threat of the Post-Secular," in *At the Limits of the Secular: Reflections on Faith and Public Life*, ed. William A. Barbieri, Jr. (Grand Rapids, Mich.: Eerdmans Publishing, 2014), 162–96.

50. In addition to Landrum and Vasquez, "Polarizing U.S. Politics," see also Michael Lipka and Gregory A. Smith, "Like Americans Overall, U.S. Catholics are Sharply Divided by Party," Pew Research Center, January 24, 2019, https://www.pewresearch.org/fact-tank/2019/01/24/like-americans-overall-u-s-catholics-are-sharply-divided-by-party/.

51. USCCB, *Faithful Citizenship*, 2. The quotation is from *Laudato Si'*, 139.

52. USCCB, *Faithful Citizenship*, esp. 29 and 51.

53. On abortion as the preeminent issue, see USCCB, *Faithful Citizenship*, esp. 40, 64, and 92. For the naming of intrinsic evils, see USCCB, *Faithful Citizenship*, 42, as well as 37.

54. "*Laudato Si'*, "On Care for Our Common Home: An Action Plan for the Roman Catholic Archdiocese of Atlanta," November 2015, https://2nix922u0v5c1unycf149lry-wpengine.netdna-ssl.com/wp-content/uploads/2019/11/laudato_si_actionplan.pdf. See also the "*Laudato Si'* Action Plan Fact Sheet," https://2nix922u0v5c1unycf149lry-wpengine.netdna-ssl.com/wp-content/uploads/2019/11/laudato-si-fact-sheet-web-082018.pdf.

55. For information about the Catholic Climate Covenant, see https://catholicclimatecovenant.org/about/story.

56. See, for example, "Another Climate Milestone Falls at Mauna Loa Observatory," Scripps Institution of Oceanography: The Keeling Curve," June 7, 2018, https://scripps.ucsd.edu/programs/keelingcurve/2018/06/07/another-climate

-milestone-falls-at-mauna-loa-observatory/. See also J. Hansen et al., "Target Atmospheric CO_2: Where Should Humanity Aim?" Cornell University Library: Atmospheric and Ocean Physics, October 15, 2008, https://arxiv.org/abs/0804.1126.

57. Landrum and Vasquez, "Polarizing U.S. Politics."

58. "Archbishop Niederauer Explains Catholic Involvement in Prop. 8," Catholic News Agency, December 4, 2008, https://www.catholicnewsagency.com/news /archbishop_niederauer_explains_catholic_involvement_in_prop._8; "Catholics United for California Marriage Vote: Knights Give $1 Million," *Catholic Review*, https://www.archbalt.org/catholics-unite-for-california-marriage-vote-knights-give -1-million/; and Joe Garofoli, "Salvatore Cordileone's Key Prop. 8 Role," *SFGate*, https://www.sfgate.com/politics/joegarofoli/article/Salvatore-Cordileone-s-key-Prop-8-role-3742409.php.

59. Leslie Griffin, "The Catholic Bishops vs. the Contraceptive Mandate," *Religions* 6, 1411–32, https://www.researchgate.net/publication/290786577_The _Catholic_Bishops_vs_the_Contraceptive_Mandate. See also "The USCCB and Health Care Reform," https://www.usccb.org/issues-and-action/human-life-and -dignity/health-care/upload/health-care-reform-summary-2010.pdf.

60. See "Vatican Fights U.N. Draft on Women's Rights," *New York Times*, June 15, 1994, http://www.nytimes.com/1994/06/15/world/vatican-fights-un-draft-on -women-s-rights.html, and "U.N. Population Meeting Adopts Program of Action," *New York Times*, September 14, 1994, http://www.nytimes.com/1994/06/15/world /vatican-fights-un-draft-on-women-s-rights.html.

61. The USCCB has issued statements and written letters to Congress and federal agencies regarding various actions the U.S. government was and was not taking with regard to decreasing climate change and protecting the environment. However, these statements fall far short of the public, energetic, and concerted organizational efforts the bishops have exerted on issues of abortion, so-called artificial contraception, and same-sex marriage. For a list of episcopal action on the environment, see https://www.usccb.org/issues-and-action/human-life-and-dignity /environment/index.cfm#tab—_018.

62. Johann Baptist Metz, *Faith in History and Society: Toward a Practical Fundamental Theology* (New York: Crossroad, 2007).

63. See "Religious Landscape Study," Pew Research Center, 2018, http://www .pewforum.org/religious-landscape-study/.

PART II

Race, Aesthetics, and Religion

4

Whiteness and Civilization

Shame, Race, and the Rhetoric of Donald Trump

Donovan O. Schaefer

And can anyone suppose that we'll ever figure out what happened around political correctness if we don't see it as, among other things, a highly politicized chain reaction of shame dynamics?

— EVE KOSOFSKY SEDGWICK, *Touching Feeling*[1]

Feels Good, Man

If you wade through the Twitter subtweets of flashpoint political figures such as Donald Trump, Hillary Clinton, or Barack Obama, you might find yourself surrounded by avatars of cartoon frogs.[2] They come dressed in SS uniforms, clown wigs, MAGA hats, sunglasses, trench coats, balaclavas, yarmulkes, fedoras, and other accessories. Some of them have Trump's signature platinum combover. They're smirking. The users lurking behind them speak in a sort of woozy dialect, flush with irony, bursting with internet-based inside jokes, memes spliced into memes, skillfully riding the line (or not) between offensive and innocuous.

They're the grimy offspring of Pepe the Frog, a human-bodied frog character created by the cartoonist Matt Furie in 2005. Pepe is a sort of sad-clown figure who finds himself in embarrassing situations, like being caught urinating with his trousers around his ankles. Unflappable when confronted, he waves off all embarrassment with a stoner smile and his breezy catchphrase, *Feels good, man*. An upload of Furie's comic, *Boy's Club*, to his Myspace page around 2005 led to Pepe becoming a hugely popular internet meme in the late 2000s through the mid-2010s, spawning a baroque gallery of magnificently absurd cartoon concept art.[3]

But with the emergence of what has been called the alt-right, Pepe has turned into something much more sinister. Irish journalist Angela Nagle offers an extensive profile of this movement in her book *Kill All Normies* (cover image: a photograph of a live frog).[4] Nagle's argument is that the alt-right, which she defines as including both newer "white preservationists" and old guard white supremacist groups, emerged from right-wing "chan culture," short for 4chan, a freewheeling internet forum where disturbing images and teenagerish humor are the stock in trade. The custom Pepes with their Nazi and Trump paraphernalia commandeered the character, turning the smirking amphibian into an immediately recognizable mascot for right-wing racial provocation. In 2016, Pepe was designated as a hate symbol by the Anti-Defamation League.[5] After several frustrated years working to rehabilitate the character (including by drawing anti-Trump Pepe cartoons), Furie killed him off.[6]

I suggest that it is no accident that the alt-right would be attracted to Pepe—and eventually resolutely claim him as their own. The alt-right ethos is built around shock—the tactical transgression of cultural taboos. Nagle argues that the *épater les bourgeoisie* mindset of the alt-right does not materialize out of thin air. A feature of her analysis is that the online alt-right is, in part, a reaction against increasingly precious left-wing identity politics. One of the flashpoints she identifies, for instance, is the "Gamergate" controversy of 2015, which triggered an anti-feminist backlash and "politicized a broad group of young people, mostly boys, who organized tactics around the idea of fighting back against the culture war being waged by the cultural left."[7] Pepe's smug but goofy hangdog routine evolved into the perfect emblem for the alt-right's approach to politics—a refusal to be shamed. Pepe's shtick is to deflect every attack with a shrug. His grinning defiance of every effort to shame him became theirs.

This chapter emerges from a conviction that understanding Donald Trump's political effectiveness requires a sophisticated attention to the dynamics of shame. Specifically, I argue here that the success of Trump's rhetoric emerges in part from his mastery of a circuit of shame and dignity, in which supporters who feel ashamed find, in his verbal and visual style, a repudiation of that shame and so mobilize behind him. This requires an attention to both sides of the equation—some of the channels by which shame circulates within contemporary American culture *and* the way Trump has developed a compelling set of techniques for capturing this pressure and harnessing it for his own political purposes.

My line of analysis builds on the work of scholars of media, rhetoric, and communication who have considered affect theory and their home fields as a conjoined exploration of the dynamic between communication and motivation.[8] These thinkers and others have also expressed particular interest in

Trump's communication techniques.[9] This scholarship maps the affective dimension of Trump's communication to emotions like rage or disgust.[10] Without contradicting this, my suggestion is that we need a vocabulary for thinking about Trump's rhetorical techniques that includes attention to dynamics of shame and dignity. Rage and disgust may be closely bonded to this terrain, but without a consideration of shame, we lose a register of specificity in how Trump's rhetoric *works*.

As Lauren Berlant has proposed, "The Trump Emotion Machine is delivering feeling ok, acting free."[11] This chapter builds a comprehensive theory of shame, dignity, and political rhetoric around this insight. It contends that Trump responded to a situation in which the fever of white shame was boiling over—a racial formation that, as Anthea Butler has pointed out, is also powerfully bonded to conservative forms of Christianity[12]—and was able to exploit that for political power through rhetorical techniques that converted shame into a felt sense of dignity. After diagraming the affect theory perspective and its usefulness in building a model of how shame shapes a landscape of political communication, the chapter will closely examine Trump's techniques for circulating shame and dignity.

Affect Theory and Political Communication

Affect theory is a field of conversations emerging from queer theory, post-structuralism, feminism, and antiracist theory. Following a loose typology developed by thinkers such as Sara Ahmed, Ann Cvetkovich, Mel Chen, Elspeth Probyn, and myself,[13] affect theory can be divided into two branches. In the one stream, thinkers inspired by the philosopher Gilles Deleuze, such as Patricia Ticineto Clough, Erin Manning, and Brian Massumi, identify affect as a radically pre-cognitive, pre-conscious, and non-conceptual force that shapes subjectivity upstream of self-awareness.[14] The dominant move in communication theory has been to emphasize this Deleuzian mode.[15]

Although I will draw on the Deleuzian interpretation, my suggestion is that it is not sufficient for the purposes of an analysis of Trump's rhetoric. I find affect theory in the second mode, what Ahmed calls "feminist cultural studies of emotion and affect" and I have called the "phenomenological strain" of affect theory, to be more versatile for mapping the landscape of feeling, emotion, experience, and communication.[16] Where the Deleuzian approach stresses that politics *can be* affective, I would follow Berlant in affirming that political communication is *always* affectively organized: "*All* the messages are emotional."[17] Because Deleuzian vocabulary cannot go much farther than positing an on-off switch (affect either *is* or *is not* present), it forecloses the development of a sophisticated vocabulary of multiple *formations of affect* with distinct rhetorical and political effects for specific audiences. For this reason, I will not only move into detailed discussion of what some Deleuzian theorists would dismiss as *emotions*, but also use the words "affect" and "emotion" roughly interchangeably.[18]

What all affect theories share is a commitment to looking at subjects not as self-ruled calculating machines, but as bodies mobilized by the unruly matrix of dense affects working their way through us. Bodies, in the affect theory picture, are coalitions of affective drivers pulling us in different directions, but loosely affiliated into a single social organism. Spinoza, one of the key background figures of affect theory, wrote that the "human body is composed of a great many individuals of different natures, each of which is highly composite."[19] Lawrence Grossberg writes that affect "encompasses a variety of ways in which we 'feel' the world in our experience, including moods, emotions, maps of what matters and of what one cares about, pleasures and desires, passions, sentiments, etc."[20] Affect theory focuses on the messy felt composites of experience that sediment to become macro-level political subjectivities.

This has been a particularly appealing framework for scholars working on political communication. The convergence point, for these scholars, lies in affect theory's model of self and political subjectivity. In the affect theory picture, the self is constituted not by a sovereign, top-down, reasoning I, but by a tangle of forces. The forces run through us, we are made by them, and our decisions reflect the priorities of those forces rather than an abstract assessment of the world around us according to a standard of detached calculation. This resonates with the fundamental insight of rhetorical studies, namely, that communication is not (necessarily) effective because it appeals to the machinery of rational persuasion. Instead, rhetoric works on listeners through a range of devices that are not necessarily thoughtful—nor even necessarily discursive.

Jenny Edbauer Rice proposes that, rather than a "conversational" model of communication in which the public sphere is constituted by a rationally organized stock exchange of ideas, "what underscores civic or rhetorical deliberation is arguably an affective element."[21] Joshua Gunn goes so far as to suggest that rhetorical genres "are the names of forms that are repeatedly felt, or instances of the linguistic sedimentation of an affective recurrence into code and meaning."[22] Rhetoric does not land on a flat plain. It seeks out the desires of an audience. These desires are ultimately a configuration of affects. As Brian L. Ott and Greg Dickinson write, "Affective aesthetics links the sensual, immediate, and prediscursive responses of bodies to specific environmental energies with historically situated discursive processes and practices."[23] All of these scholars point out that studies of rhetoric almost always import a theory of affect and that theories of affect that examine communication end up leaning on ideas about rhetoric.

Shame, Pedagogy, Politics

From the time of Trump's campaign announcement in 2015 to the present, scholars of political communication have devised a number of avenues for applying affect theory to his rhetoric. Most prominent among these are two book-length studies of Trump and affect published by scholars of political communication. Lawrence Grossberg's *Under the Cover of Chaos* is a sprawling, multi-dimensional exploration of Trump's relationships with predecessor movements in American conservatism.[24] Grossberg suggests that Trump has managed to pleasurize disruption. "The most obvious and pervasive feature of Trump's highly visible and almost entertaining . . . if also terrifying performance," he writes, "is the normalization of a frenetic chaos and hyperactivism."[25] Grossberg suggests that it is the reveling in motion, spontaneity, and the Deleuzian concept of *becoming* that consolidates Trump's command of his political constituencies. However, this is only the main axle of this wide-ranging book, which ends up also speculating on the importance of shame, anxiety, narcissism, and alienation for mapping Trump's appeal to his followers.[26]

The most focused study of Trump, affect, and communication to date comes in Ott and Dickinson's *The Twitter Presidency*, which expressly argues that the aesthetic dimensions of Trump's style are designed to resonate with what they refer to as *white rage*.[27] They locate white rage in "the fear and anxiety surrounding the social decentering of white privilege and hegemonic masculinity."[28] Trump, they propose, is an effective communicator precisely by virtue of his ability to ignite this latent fund of frustration. They further suggest that Twitter is a uniquely effective tool for Trump by virtue of its medium-specific affordances in favor of simplicity, impulsivity, and incivility.[29] These features allow Trump to match the rhythm of white rage—and to become its conductor.

My project here is to build on these approaches by expanding the vocabulary of affective elements used to assess Trump's communication strategy. Specifically, I want to make an argument for including *shame* and, by extension, *dignity* as inflection points in this field. This interlocks with Joshua Gunn's emphasis on perversion as pleasurable rules-breaking and Ott and Dickinson's proposal that Trump appealed to his followers' "memories of a bygone era in which they, too, viscerally enjoyed the unearned assets of [white, male] privilege."[30] But I propose here that shame needs to be *specifically* named in order to increase the precision of this analysis. This requires returning to affect theory to develop a more detailed account of shame.

Silvan Tomkins—one of the background figures of contemporary affect theory—defines shame by first abandoning the traditional psychoanalytic distinction between shame and guilt. Instead, he proposes that both share a common currency, "the affect of indignity, of defeat, of transgression, and of alienation."[31] Tomkins then assigns shame a role that is asymmetric with the other affects in his nine-piece inventory. Shame, for Tomkins, is a sort of meta-affect that conditions and positions all other emotional states. "Though terror speaks to life and death and distress makes of the world a vale of tears," he writes, "yet shame strikes deepest into the heart of man."[32] As Tomkins's student Donald Nathanson writes, "Shame is the dominant negative affect of everyday life. . . . Just as each of us longs for pleasurable excitement and reasonable amounts of joy, the ubiquity of situations that interfere with the experience of positive affect makes shame—no matter how disguised—our constant companion."[33]

The reason for this extraordinary meta-status is that shame is a sort of master switch responsible for suppressing other affective responses, like joy or excitement. Shame is best understood as a hyper-dense distillation of disappointment that has been injected into a particular object in mind. It resurfaces when we re-encounter that object, extinguishing the joy that once attached to it and leaving a radioactive residue behind. "The innate activator of shame," Tomkins writes, "is the incomplete reduction of interest or joy. Hence any barrier to further exploration which partially reduces interest or the smile of enjoyment will activate the lowering of the head and eyes in shame and reduce further exploration or self-exposure powered by excitement or joy."[34]

The head bowed, eyes lowered, is the visual motif of Tomkins's writing on shame—both a metaphor for its political effects and an actual physiognomy. For Tomkins, the face reticulates us into a social body. When we lower our head and eyes, we disconnect from pleasure. We fall backwards into alienation. In this way, shame is resolutely political. "Whenever an individual, a class, or a nation wishes to maintain a hierarchical relationship, or to maintain aloofness," he writes, "it will have resort to contempt of the other. Contempt is the mark of the oppressor. The hierarchical relationship is maintained either when the oppressed one assumes the attitude of contempt for himself or hangs his head in shame."[35] Social beings, inasmuch as they stratify themselves internally, use shame as the currency of elevation and degradation.

Elspeth Probyn writes that rather than seeing shame as a toxin to purge from the social body, we should think of it as a necessary element of embodied interliving. In particular, I would add, shame is a necessary component of pedagogy. Many scholars, including Probyn, Eve Kosofsky Sedgwick, and Megan Watkins have commented on the affective dimensions of pedagogy.[36] The question of the role of shame in pedagogy tends not to be a salient theme of this research, but Tomkins makes the link in his work on child development.[37] Tomkins proposes that parents form their children's behaviors by shaming them around particular actions and allowing others to flourish.[38] Shame is the chisel that sculpts civilized subjects, chipping away at some desires and producing disciplined bodies.

This is where the communication field of politics loops back in. Pedagogy is not just something that happens to kids. We are always being taught. Progressive politics—in particular, the politics of antiracism, gender emancipation, queer emancipation, and of new horizons of political enfranchisement— is organized around a retraining and a reteaching of bodies. Therefore, progressive politics is a project intimately associated with shame. As critical race theorist Sharon Patricia Holland argues, racism is not simply a neutral exercise of opinion. It is maintained by a formation of pleasure, what Tomkins might identify as the thrill of contempt.[39] In contrast to those who see cruelty as an expression of emotional deadness, Marina Levina writes:

> as I think back to my childhood tormentors, I do not think of them as sad, or disempowered, or ugly in any sense of that word. I know that being cruel brought them joy—the glint in the eyes, the straightening of the posture, the smirk—the joy of the oppressor is what makes cruelty so effective as a tool of oppression.[40]

Holland calls this racism's "own erotic life," and I have referred to it as the "hedonicity of hate."[41] It is precisely because racism (and other forms of racialization) is pleasurable that the effort to unravel it is so perilous. Yet this is exactly what left politics sets out to do. It blocks the circuit of desire for debased others by adding shame.

In fact, we might even say that this orientation to shame is one of the cardinal principles of progressivism. Shame on the move—an openness to shame, a trafficking in shame—is how left-wing politics feels. Leftists use shame to challenge not only the politics of others, but also themselves, grinding away their own sense of comfort in a relentless project to become more sensitive, more thoughtful, more moral. The modern American progressive political project is heavily keyed to this internal disciplinary apparatus. "I've been shamed by feminism," Probyn confesses. "[W]hat feminist hasn't?"[42] This reflects an openness to—maybe even a pleasure in—using shame as a technique of the self to tailor one's own body as a more versatile and sophisticated political subject.[43] The tension between left and right political orientations is,

I propose, generated in part through divergent affective tastes at the level of bodies, which then scale up into different priorities, different political platforms, and different rhetorical mechanisms.

Shame saturates contemporary politics. Bodies that once felt like the unchallenged masters of their space—white bodies, male bodies, Christian bodies, cis bodies, straight bodies, rich bodies, citizen bodies—are being confronted, more and more, with a demand to respond to the violence trailing in the wake of the comforts and pleasures they enjoy. This effect is amplified by the increasing mediation of society, that is, the way in which the density of social interactions is steadily increasing, underwritten by technological shifts. The pedagogical sphere is condensing. More interactions with more people equals more chances to be shamed. We live in an increasingly saturated shame panopticon. This has led some of the former masters to a state of shame-exhaustion, in which it becomes easier to repudiate shame altogether than respond to the moral demands placed on them.[44]

Eve Sedgwick asks: "Can anyone suppose that we'll ever figure out what happened around political correctness if we don't see it as, among other things, a highly politicized chain reaction of shame dynamics?"[45] The insight of this framing lies in the way it stages political correctness as a pedagogy, a sweeping masterwork of shame designed to topple residual structures of degradation from speech. It is to be expected then, that this chain of shame would provoke a shame response, a furious refusal of culpability. This is where Trump comes in.

Lauren Berlant has proposed that the political appeal of Trump does not rest in an ideological posture. "Trump's people," they write,

> want fairness of a sort, but mainly they seek freedom from shame. Civil rights and feminism aren't just about the law after all, they are about manners, and emotions too: those "interest groups" get right in there and reject *what feels like* people's spontaneous, ingrained responses. People get shamed, or lose their jobs, for example, when they're just having a little fun making fun. Anti-PC means "I feel unfree."[46]

Making a consonant point, Grossberg says that rather than focusing, as some pundits do, on "resentment" as a root of Trump's appeal, we should examine "the terror of the humiliation of being a victim. One avoids the humiliation of loss and victimage by humiliating the other, by diminishing their status and capacity, destroying their sense of pride, reducing them to a lower state of being."[47] Affect theory anchors the analysis of Trump's rhetorical efficacy not in economic opportunism, but in a particular affective configuration—the thrust and counter-thrust of shame and humiliation—leading to the rhetorical power of white defiance.

White Defiance and the Rhetoric of Trump

Trump's presidential campaign announcement on June 16, 2015, is an early indicator of the driving dynamic of Trump's rhetoric. It offers a dyad of shame and dignity, often organized around race. "Our country is in serious trouble," Trump says, as he begins his prepared remarks. "We don't have victories anymore. We used to have victories, but we don't have them. When was the last time anybody saw us beating, let's say, China in a trade deal? They kill us. I beat China all the time. All the time."[48] This is not simply a promise of an economic turnaround. It also suggests an affective state shift. *We are humiliated. Yet I deliver dignity.* "When do we beat Mexico at the border?" Trump continued. "They're laughing at us, at our stupidity. . . . The U.S. has become a dumping ground for everybody else's problems."[49]

This leads into Trump's notorious "they're rapists" line about Mexicans, in which he simultaneously slurs immigrants and then allows that some, perhaps, are "good people." Trump also makes his first mention of his infamous wall project: "I will build a great, great wall on our southern border. And I will have Mexico pay for that wall."[50] It needs to be noted here that in an otherwise precise and unusually well-constructed speech, Trump doesn't offer any explanation for *why* Mexico must pay for the wall. In no other scenario does a poorer nation pay for the defense of a stronger, richer nation. But this line, notoriously, becomes a linchpin of Trump's campaign. Why do they have to pay for it? Once again, the issue isn't the economics. It's the degradation. Mexico has to be humiliated in retaliation for "laughing at us."

Less often noted about this speech is the fact that it is not only non-Americans who get hit by Trump.[51] He segues into a story about how he will beat down not only other countries, but also corporate lobbyists and CEOs. This narrative line builds up to his imagined back-and-forth with the CEO of Ford, in which the CEO "begs" him to let him build a factory in Mexico. Trump archly refuses, using his superior negotiating clout, which he wields because he is "really rich" and has no need to rely on lobbyists to fund his campaign.[52] Again, Trump is the vindicator, a scion of defiance. When Trump debuts his slogan at this event—*Make America Great Again*—it represents a perfect encapsulation of the affective dynamic that animates his entire campaign—a transition from a state of ignominy to a state of glory.

One of Trump's primary weapons during the primary and general election campaigns was the catchy binomial insult, such as Lyin' Ted [Cruz], Crooked Hillary [Clinton], or Little Marco [Rubio]. This was, needless to say, a way of tearing down his opponents. But it is important to highlight how it also functioned to consolidate Trump's status as a hub of degradation. The insult coincided with his frequent reminders that his opponents have, at various times, asked him for money or support. His announcement speech reminds us that his Republican opponents "all want me to support them. They don't know how to bring it about. They come up to my office. I'm meeting with three of them in the next week. And they don't know— 'Are you running? Are you not running? Could we have your support?'"[53] Ott and Dickinson call our attention to Trump's pantomime, in a later speech, of a conversation with Obama in which he tells him *You're fired*, "at which point the crowd erupted, their bodies instantaneously responding to a white man putting a black man in his place."[54] Media and affect theorist Michael Richardson points out that Trump has a tendency to amplify the charge of these insults by applying liberal dollops of disgust—at John Kasich's eating habits, Marco Rubio's sweat, or Hillary Clinton taking a restroom break.[55] Through these techniques, Trump consolidates his status as the ringmaster of shame and dignity.

Trump develops this same repertoire of themes in the speeches he gives as president. In his inaugural address, Trump paints a dreary picture of the U.S.'s many embarrassments and failures, before pivoting to the promise of his presidency. "We stand at the birth of a new millennium," he declares, "ready to unlock the mysteries of space, to free the Earth from the miseries of disease, and to harness the energies, industries and technologies of tomorrow. A new national pride will stir our souls, lift our sights, and heal our divisions."[56]

But the unifying (if still angry) rhetoric of the inaugural speech is short-lived. Trump's rhetorical signature remains strongly marked by a programmatic division of the world into in-groups and out-groups. This is particularly the case in speeches written by his white nationalist advisor, Stephen Miller. In his speech to the Values Voters Summit in October 2017, for instance, Trump builds up a strong cushion of applause lines reaffirming the nobility of the conservative political platform.

> We believe in strong families and safe communities. We honor the dignity of work. (Applause.) We defend our Constitution. We protect religious liberty. (Applause.) We treasure our freedom. We are proud of our history. We support the rule of law and the incredible men and women of law enforcement. (Applause.) We celebrate our heroes, and we salute every American who wears the uniform. (Applause.) We respect our great American flag. (Applause.) Thank you. Thank you. Thank you. And we stand united behind the customs, beliefs and traditions that define who we are as a nation and as a people.[57]

This leads into a programmatic mingling of white nationalism and Christian supremacism, in which Trump insists, "We are stopping cold the attacks on Judeo-Christian values," before continuing. "You know, we're getting near that beautiful Christmas season that people don't talk about anymore. (Laughter.) They don't use the word 'Christmas' because it's not politically correct. . . . Well, guess what? We're saying 'Merry Christmas' again. (Applause.)"[58] Trump's move here is to constitute his rhetorical sphere as a culture war battlefield. He reconstructs the trajectory through which religious and political conservatives have been shamed—by progressives calling them to account for exclusivism and hypocrisy—and reverses the tide. Ott and Dickinson quote a supporter who gushes: "Donald Trump is not politically correct, and I love that about him."[59]

For Trump's audience, there is a strong hit of dignity carried in the affective charge of words like *salute, respect, stand up, stand united, the flag, men and women in uniform, law enforcement, Judeo-Christian values*—and *dignity* itself. This dictionary of dignity reflects a set of swelling ideas and images, which resonate for conservatives as material manifestations of pride. This is what leaves Trump's rhetoric, for this audience, pregnant with a hovering sense of *felt* glory. It is why Trump is able to trigger a cascade of applause among the values voters after every line.

A few months later, in his commencement address to the U.S. Naval Academy in May of 2018, Trump sounded the same defiant tones:

> Together, there is nothing that Americans can't do. In recent years, and even decades, too many people have forgotten that truth. They've forgotten that our ancestors trounced an empire, tamed a continent, and triumphed over the worst evils in history. In every generation there have been cynics and critics who tried to tear down America. It's not working too well lately. But in recent years the problem grew worse. A growing number used their platforms to denigrate America's incredible heritage, challenge America's sovereignty, and weaken America's pride.[60]

This is a sneering *How dare they?*—Trump explicitly defining America's enemies as an internal fifth column, intent on sabotaging national dignity.

Trump's response is to reiterate the glory of the American nation as well as the cravenness of its critics:

> But we know the truth, we will speak the truth, and we will defend that truth. America is the greatest fighting force for peace, justice, and freedom, in the history of the world. And in case you haven't noticed we have become a lot stronger lately. A lot. We are not going to apologize for America. We are going to stand up for America. No more apologies. We are going to stand up for our citizens. We are going to stand up for our values. And we are going to stand up for our men

and women in uniform. . . . We trekked the mountains, explored the oceans, and settled the vast frontier. We won two world wars, defeated communism and fascism, and put a man on the face of the moon. We cured disease, pioneered science, and produced timeless works of art that inspire the human soul.[61]

Here, Trump etches even more brightly the contest between those who wish to shame and those who refuse to be shamed, in part by refusing to "apologize." This relates to Ott and Dickinson's note that Trump is unbendable in his rule of never using the *apologia*, or self-justification.[62] Trump never admits fault: "The fact that he exhibits no self-questioning is appealing to his supporters, many of whom feel powerless."[63] This all interlocks with his rhetorical repudiation of never allowing oneself to be called to account. No apology and no *apologia* run very close together here.

Trump's attacks on athletes protesting racial injustice are another specimen of this technique. In the wake of the ongoing protests in solidarity with the Black Lives Matter movement—for instance, by players such as Colin Kaepernick, who began a practice of taking a knee during the national anthem as a response against anti-Black police brutality—Trump has frequently flung scorn during his rallies and interviews. At a September 2017 rally, Trump proposed that a team owner's response to a protesting player should be, "Get that son of a bitch off the field right now, he's fired!" "For a week," Trump continued, the owner would "be the most popular person in this country. Because that's a total disrespect of our heritage. That's a total disrespect for everything we stand for."[64] In an interview with *Fox and Friends* eight months later, immediately after a new NFL policy banning all players who engaged in protest, Trump escalated his claims: "You have to stand proudly for the national anthem or you shouldn't be playing, you shouldn't be there. Maybe you shouldn't be in the country."[65] This rhetorical mechanism is the epitome of Trump's method. Taking the side of whites who have been confronted with their complicity in a system of racial disparity, he assures them that rather than feeling ashamed, they should take revenge on those who challenge their sense of ease. Trump skillfully converts a racialized dynamic into an affective battlefield, mobilizing political power.

However, it is important to look at the affective dimensions of Trump's communication even outside of discourse. As Ott and Dickinson observe, not only is it the case that "[w]ords can appeal to the body and can be structured rhetorically for the purpose of this embodied aesthetic appeal," but also that "the non-symbolic parts of rhetorical performances—the grain of the voice, the order of the words and their rhythms, the form of the gestures—are organized invitations to pre-cognitive affect."[66] According to the journalist Chuck Todd, Trump is acutely sensitive to these aspects of communication to the extent that Trump will, after taping a television interview, re-watch the tape in the studio with the sound off, studying his own face.[67] The Trump script—the ticker tape of words coming out of his mouth—is an important part of the Trump emotion machine, but is not actually sufficient for his political purposes. Ideological grenades are only part of Trump's arsenal. He is able to mobilize a very particular suite of affects that amplify the anti-shame salvos of his political profile external to the words he says.

Trump's face, I would suggest, is a major component of his ability to orchestrate shame. Tomkins's refrain, "Head bowed, eyes lowered," is exactly what Trump *never does*. He rarely looks down during speeches, instead staring evenly at the horizon or flicking his gaze up and to the side when he needs to pause. One gets a strange vertigo effect in paying close attention to Trump's face while he speaks. Although Obama, for instance—like most speakers—would frequently glance down to collect his thoughts, Trump is conspicuously out of sync with one's expectation of when someone would naturally lower their gaze. It's also not a coincidence, I would suggest, that Trump frequently refused to wear a mask in public during the COVID-19 pandemic. Trump wanted his face to be seen. The opportunity to project an aura of defiance and invincibility sweetened the deal.

When Trump was caught on tape practicing a speech on his way to address Congress in March 2017, pundits were surprised that he seemed to be rehearsing the facial expressions he would use to amplify the impact of his words. In between reading the lines on the freshly printed pages in his hands, he exercised the specific affects he wanted to convey. We see Trump cycle through three practiced expressions: a sneer; an almost-ecstatic, ferocious pietà in which Trump stares upward with an open-mouth grimace; and a sort of triptych in which Trump mimes three glares in rapid succession, bobbing his head and sharpening his stare with each beat. Trump knows that the root of his power is his face and tunes his instrument accordingly. The visual rhetoric of Trump's body—"controlling, coercive, and conceited, a combination of traits that embody white privilege and hypermasculinity"—is a necessary augmentation to the Trump script. It consolidates his status as the humiliator-in-chief.[68]

Conclusion: The Labyrinth of Attitudes

J. D. Vance, the Silicon Valley entrepreneur from rural Ohio and self-appointed apostle of conservative values to coastal liberals, sees the same shame dynamics in Trump's rhetoric that I do. In a 2016 essay on how Trump's "antiwar" message resonated with rural whites, he proposed that "Americans today look to a Middle East that is humiliatingly worse off than the way we found it. The burden of this humiliation fell hardest on Republican strongholds . . . [such as] the South, rural areas and the working and middle class."[69] Each time Trump lashes the Republican establishment for their failure to win in the Middle East, Vance writes, "each time he shrieks about our country no longer winning, I can hear Mamaw cheering."[70] It is exactly Trump's repudiation of shame that establishes his power base.

But Vance totally sidesteps the issue of race, disingenuously implying that Trump's (fickle) antiwar stance was the driver of his campaign, ignoring Trump's library of techniques for humiliation—especially racial humiliation. Trump's supporters (and, to a lesser degree, Trump himself) aim to refute the accusation of racism by pointing to the racial diversity among Trump's associates and employees. As Imani Perry notes, the classical understanding of racism as *prejudicial intent* layered on top of *articulate, hierarchical beliefs* is not adequate for thinking about the twenty-first-century political field. Perry's *post-intentional* definition of racism proposes that racism percolates through us, often outside of our field of awareness.[71] As scholars such as Holland and Levina propose, racism is better thought of as an effect of a field of desire, as something that bodies want, often without realizing that they want it.[72] In the twilight of overt racism, a massive shadow apparatus of instrumentalized racialization—used to elevate oneself by enveloping others in shame—thrives.

James Baldwin's *The Fire Next Time* is in many ways a meditation on the relationship between race and dignity—an existential necessity he claims white liberals have largely missed.[73] But Baldwin goes further. In studying anti-Black racism, he attributes it to a pathology *within American whiteness itself*. A deeply carved white self-loathing thirsts for a distraction, a conduit for its own tangled energy. "[I]t is this individual uncertainty on the part of white American men and women, this inability to renew themselves at the fountain of their own lives," Baldwin suggests,

> that makes the discussion, let alone elucidation, of any conundrum— that is, any reality—so supremely difficult. The person who distrusts himself has no touchstone for reality—for this touchstone can be only oneself. Such a person interposes between himself and reality nothing less than a labyrinth of attitudes.[74]

The labyrinth of attitudes—the racialized citadel they called "civilization"—is passing away. As the old economy of dignity collapses, white shame seeps to the surface leading to an urgent desire for the shame of others as recompense. This produces a rhetorical field ripe for exploitation.

This proposal to install white shame in the lexicon of analytical terms for understanding the rhetorical field Trump commands is only a starting point. We still need a more textured account of how shame *works* as a resource for rhetoric. What is the alchemical relationship between shame and rage, for instance? Does shame potentiate rage, producing a psychic system in tension—more liable to explode? Are these affects more closely related than Tomkins suggests? When does shame prompt retreat and when does it prompt retaliation? Is there a political difference between the shame of those who have been systemically marginalized and the shame of those who have been schooled out of their racism by the stern lessons of political correctness? And—most perplexingly—why does nationalist rhetoric so often look like a sort of *structured (self) subordination*—usually under a masculine leader? Think of alt-right early adopter Milo Yiannopolis referring to Trump as "Daddy." The rhetorical dynamic between self, group, and leader is part of a recipe for repudiating shame, but we need a more sophisticated attunement to how it also involves a specific *canalizing* of shame.

Shame, Tomkins writes, "is an affect of relatively high toxicity . . . it strikes deepest into the heart of man . . . it is felt as a sickness of the soul which leaves man naked, defeated, alienated, and lacking in dignity."[75] Indexing shame as a foundational stratum of the way bodies become societies helps to make sense of the twisted landscape of our politics today. Where pundits puzzle over an invisible war over resources and why anyone would vote against their economic interests, cynical politicians have long since realized that they can weaponize the identitarian logic of whiteness into an electrifying rhetorical machine for overruling shame.

Notes

1. Eve Kosofsky Sedgwick, *Touching Feeling: Affect, Pedagogy, Performativity* (Durham: Duke University Press, 2003), 64.

2. Many thanks are due to several people who have encouraged this project. First and foremost, thanks to Gregory Seigworth, who invited me to speak as one of the plenaries at the "Capacious: Affect Inquiry/Making Space" conference in Lancaster, Pa., in 2018, then helped me workshop the paper for publication. Thanks also to my colleague Anthea Butler for reading the paper and urging its publication. I also thank Tat-Siong Benny Liew for the invitation to present this work at the "Religion, Protest, and Social Upheaval" conference at the College of the Holy Cross, and to Kevin O'Neill for an invitation to the Centre for Diaspora and Transnational Studies at the University of Toronto. Participants and audiences at these events provided invaluable feedback. Thanks to Rob Spicer for calling my attention to the Chuck Todd interview. This chapter is a modified excerpt from an article of the same name published in the *Communication and Critical/Cultural Studies*, and I'm very grateful

to the journal and editors not only for permission to reprint, but to two anonymous reviewers who provided generous and focused reports that significantly shaped the final version.

3. Jessica Roy, "How Pepe the Frog Went from Harmless to Hate Symbol," *Los Angeles Times*, October 11, 2016, https://www.latimes.com/politics/la-na-pol-pepe-the -frog-hate-symbol-20161011-snap-htmlstory.html.

4. Angela Nagle, *Kill All Normies: The Online Culture Wars from Tumblr and 4chan to the Alt-Right and Trump* (Winchester, UK: Zero Books, 2017). Nagle's own conclusions bear passing similarity to my own in this piece, but she is ultimately sympathetic to the alt-right's ardent refusal of shame.

5. Roy, "Pepe the Frog."

6. James Vincent, "Pepe the Frog Is Officially Dead," theverge.com, May 18, 2017, https://www.theverge.com/2017/5/8/15577340/pepe-the-frog-is-dead-matt-furie.

7. Nagle, *Kill All Normies*, 24.

8. Lawrence Grossberg, *Cultural Studies in the Future Tense* (Durham: Duke University Press, 2010); Joshua Gunn, "On Speech and Public Release," *Rhetoric and Public Affairs* 13, no. 2 (Summer 2010): 1–41; Zizi Papacharissi, *Affective Publics: Sentiment, Technology, and Politics* (Oxford: Oxford University Press, 2015); Jenny Edbauer Rice, "The New 'New': Making a Case for Critical Affect Studies," *Quarterly Journal of Speech* 94, no. 2 (2008): 200–12; Melissa Gregg and Gregory J. Seigworth, "An Inventory of Shimmers," in *The Affect Theory Reader*, ed. Melissa Gregg and Gregory J. Seigworth (Durham: Duke University Press, 2010): 1–28; Brian L. Ott and Greg Dickinson, *The Twitter Presidency: Donald J. Trump and the Politics of White Rage* (New York: Routledge, 2019). For an excellent introductory survey of the interrelationships between affect theory and communications and rhetorical studies, see Brian L. Ott, "Affect in Critical Studies," in *Oxford Research Encyclopedia of Communication*, ed. J. F. Nussbaum (Oxford: Oxford University Press, 2017).

9. In addition to those listed previously, see Lawrence Grossberg, *Under the Cover of Chaos: Trump and the Battle for the American Right* (London: Pluto Press, 2018); Joshua Gunn, "On Political Perversion," *Rhetoric Society Quarterly* 48, no. 2 (2018): 161–86; Robert L. Ivie, "Rhetorical Aftershocks of Trump's Ascendency," *Res Rhetorica* 2 (2017): 61–80; Robert J. Ivie, "Trump's Unwitting Prophecy," *Rhetoric and Public Affairs* 20, no. 4 (Winter 2017): 707–17; Kumarini Silva, "Having the Time of Our Lives: Love-Cruelty as Patriotic Impulse," *Communication and Critical/Cultural Studies* 15, no. 1 (2018): 79–84; Marina Levina, "Whiteness and the Joys of Cruelty," *Communication and Critical/Cultural Studies* 15, no. 1 (2018): 73–78; Michael Richardson, "The Disgust of Donald Trump," *Journal of Media and Cultural Studies* 31, no. 6 (2017): 747–56.

10. On rage, see, for instance, Ott and Dickinson, *The Twitter Presidency*. On disgust, see, for instance, Richardson, "Disgust of Donald Trump."

11. Lauren Berlant, "Trump, or Political Emotions," *The New Inquiry*, August 5, 2016, https://thenewinquiry.com/trump-or-political-emotions/.

12. Anthea Butler, *White Evangelical Racism: The Politics of Morality in America* (Chapel Hill: University of North Carolina Press, 2021). Butler argues that white evangelicalism is deeply in thrall to an implicit understanding of American citizenship as both white and Christian.

13. Sara Ahmed, *The Promise of Happiness* (Durham: Duke University Press, 2010); Mel Y. Chen, *Animacies: Biopolitics, Racial Mattering, and Queer Affect* (Durham: Duke University Press, 2012); Ann Cvetkovich, *Depression: A Public Feeling* (Durham: Duke University Press, 2012); Elspeth Probyn, "Affect: Let Her RIP," *Media/Culture Journal* 8, no. 6 (December 2005), http://journal.media-culture .org.au/0512/13-probyn.php; Donovan O. Schaefer, *Religious Affects: Animality, Evolution, and Power* (Durham: Duke University Press, 2015).

14. Patricia Ticineto Clough, Introduction to *The Affective Turn: Theorizing the Social*, ed. Patricia Ticineto Clough and Jean Halley (Durham: Duke University Press, 2007): 1–33; Erin Manning, *Always More Than One: Individuation's Dance* (Durham: Duke University Press, 2013); Brian Massumi, *Parables for the Virtual: Movement, Affect, Sensation* (Durham: Duke University Press, 2002). See also Gilles Deleuze, *Spinoza: Practical Philosophy* (San Francisco: City Lights Books, 1988).

15. See, for instance, Grossberg, *Cultural Studies*; Papacharissi, *Affective Publics*; Rice, "The New 'New.'" For a discussion, see the oft-cited definitional framework put forward by Eric Shouse: "feelings" are seen as "personal," "emotions" as social expressions that can be deceitful, and "affects" as pre-personal, pre-conscious, and fundamentally exterior to awareness, which is what makes them transmissible between bodies. Eric Shouse, "Feeling, Emotion, Affect," *Media/Culture Journal* 8, no. 6 (December 2005), http://journal.media-culture.org.au/0512/03-shouse.php.

16. Ahmed, *Promise of Happiness*, 13; Schaefer, *Religious Affects*, 37.

17. Berlant, "Trump, or Political Emotions."

18. See, for instance, Rice, "The New 'New,'" 201. See Donovan Schaefer, *The Evolution of Affect Theory: The Humanities, the Sciences, and the Study of Power* (Cambridge: Cambridge University Press, 2019) for a sustained criticism of the Deleuzian mode of affect theory as an account of power.

19. Benedict Spinoza, *Ethics*, ed. and trans. Edwin Curley (New York: Penguin Books, 1996), 44.

20. Grossberg, *Cover of Chaos*, 11.

21. Rice, "The New 'New,'" 211.

22. Gunn, "Political Perversion," 173.

23. Ott and Dickinson, *Twitter Presidency*, 31.

24. Grossberg, *Cover of Chaos*, xi.

25. Ibid., 3.

26. Ibid., 98–107.

27. Ott and Dickinson, *Twitter Presidency*, 3.

28. Ibid., 29.

29. Ibid., 61.

30. Ibid., 41.

31. Silvan S. Tomkins, *Shame and Its Sisters: A Silvan Tomkins Reader*, ed. Eve Kosofsky Sedgwick and Adam Frank (Durham: Duke University Press, 1995), 133.

32. Ibid., 133.

33. Donald L. Nathanson, "Prologue: Affect Imagery Consciousness," in Silvan S. Tomkins, *Affect Imagery Consciousness: The Complete Edition*, ed. Bertram P. Karon (New York: Springer Publishing Company, 2008), xix.

34. Tomkins, *Shame and Its Sisters*, 134–35.

35. Ibid., 139.

36. Elspeth Probyn, "Teaching Bodies: Affects in the Classroom," *Body & Society* 10, no. 4 (2004): 21–43; Eve Kosofsky Sedgwick, "Teaching/Depression," *The Scholar and Feminist Online* 4, no. 2 (2006), http://sfonline.barnard.edu/heilbrun/sedgwick_01.htm; Megan Watkins, "Desiring Recognition, Accumulating Affect," in *The Affect Theory Reader*, ed. Melissa Gregg and Gregory J. Seigworth (Durham: Duke University Press, 2010), 269–85; Megan Watkins, "Pedagogic Affect/Effect: Embodying a Desire to Learn," *Pedagogies: An International Journal* 1, no. 4 (2006): 269–82; Megan Watkins, "Thwarting Desire: Discursive Constraint and Pedagogic Practice," *International Journal of Qualitative Studies in Education* 20, no. 3 (May–June 2007): 301–18.

37. Silvan S. Tomkins, *Affect Imagery Consciousness: The Complete Edition*, ed. Bertram P. Karon (New York: Springer Publishing Company, 2008), xxxvii.

38. Tomkins, *Shame and Its Sisters*, 153.

39. Sharon Patricia Holland, *The Erotic Life of Racism* (Durham: Duke University Press, 2012).

40. Levina, "Whiteness and the Joys of Cruelty," 75.

41. Holland, *Erotic Life of Racism*, 107; Schaefer, *Religious Affects*, 123.

42. Elspeth Probyn, *Blush: Faces of Shame* (Minneapolis: University of Minnesota Press, 2005), 75.

43. Michel Foucault, *The History of Sexuality*, volume 2 (New York: Vintage Books, 1990), 10.

44. This is not to claim that shame should be expunged from politics. But it does indicate that left progressivism has become increasingly sophisticated in its understanding of politics *without* a meta-reflection on the invisible affect/labor economies underwriting this process of sophistication.

45. Sedgwick, *Touching Feeling*, 64.

46. Berlant, "Trump, or Political Emotions."

47. Grossberg, *Cover of Chaos*, 98.

48. "Here's Donald Trump's Presidential Announcement Speech," *Time*, June 16, 2015, http://time.com/3923128/donald-trump-announcement-speech/.

49. Ibid.

50. Ibid.

51. Ivie's commentaries in "Rhetorical Aftershocks" and "Trump's Unwitting Prophecy" do not mention this feature, for instance.

52. "Trump's Presidential Announcement Speech."

53. Ibid.

54. Ott and Dickinson, *Twitter Presidency*, 35.

55. Richardson, "Disgust of Donald Trump," 747.

56. "The Inaugural Address," *The White House*, January 20, 2017, https://www.whitehouse.gov/briefings-statements/the-inaugural-address/.

57. "Remarks by President Trump at the 2017 Values Voter Summit," The White House, October 13, 2017, https://www.whitehouse.gov/briefings-statements/remarks-president-trump-2017-values-voter-summit/.

58. Ibid.

59. Ott and Dickinson, *Twitter Presidency*, 49.

60. ABC News, "Pres. Donald Trump Gives Commencement Speech at U.S. Naval Academy, ABC News," YouTube video, 3:02:04, May 25, 2018, https://www.youtube.com/watch?v=z2lmMm47wJo.

61. Ibid.

62. Ott and Dickinson, *Twitter Presidency*, 8.

63. Ibid., 46.

64. Sophie Tatum, "Trump: NFL Owners Should Fire Players Who Protest the National Anthem," CNN, September 23, 2017, https://www.cnn.com/2017/09/22/politics/donald-trump-alabama-nfl/index.html.

65. "Fox and Friends," Fox News Network, May 24, 2018, https://insider.foxnews.com/2018/05/23/president-donald-trump-fox-friends-thursday-ms-13-north-korea.

66. Ott and Dickinson, *Twitter Presidency*, 31.

67. Glenn Thrush, "What Chuck Todd Gets about Trump," *Politico*, December 30, 2016, https://www.politico.com/story/2016/12/chuck-todd-donald-trump-off-message-podcast-233066.

68. Ott and Dickinson, *Twitter Presidency*, 36.

69. J. D. Vance, "Why Trump's Antiwar Message Resonates with White America," *New York Times*, April 4, 2016, https://www.nytimes.com/2016/04/04/opinion/campaign-stops/why-trumps-antiwar-message-resonates-with-white-america.html.

70. Ibid.

71. Imani Perry, *More Beautiful and More Terrible: The Embrace and Transcendence of Racial Inequality in the United States* (New York: New York University Press, 2011), 42.

72. Holland, *Erotic Life of Racism*; Levina, "Whiteness and the Joy of Cruelty," 75.

73. James Baldwin, *The Fire Next Time* (New York: Penguin Books, 1963), 54.

74. Ibid., 43.

75. Tomkins, *Shame and Its Sisters*, 148.

5

Rootedness on the Slippery Earth

Migration in a Time of Social Upheaval

Nichole M. Flores

The situation of immigrants and refugees in the United States became increasingly unstable after the 2016 elections. These elections yielded a president and a congress whose political, policy, and cultural goals were openly hostile to the safety and flourishing of migrant populations. The Trump administration enacted "zero tolerance" policies and promoted an anti-immigrant culture that exacerbated fear in Latine immigrant communities that already live in the economic, political, and social shadows of society.[1] Fear is a feature, not a bug, of a global capitalist system that exploits migrant vulnerability as an engine for profit. Accordingly, the Trump administration's policy and political goals simultaneously satisfied the desire to demonize immigrant groups for the sake of preserving so-called "American" identity predicated on whiteness and a veneer of national security while reaping the economic benefits of exploiting these vulnerable populations.

This social upheaval exacerbated the conditions of contingency and indeterminacy that are enduring features of migrant life in the United States. Even so, Latine communities are organizing to pursue immigration justice. The history of Latine resistance against immigration injustice is an uneven one, with some Latine organizations resisting immigration on the grounds of economic and political interests.[2] Still, twenty-first-century Latine organizations in the United States have reached a consensus about the necessity of advocacy for immigration justice for the survival of Latine communities and the thriving of all people. These movements employ discursive means (making arguments) to make the case for immigrant justice and practical means (taking actions) to enact it. But these movements also engage aesthetic experience in advocacy for migrant justice. *La Virgen de Guadalupe* has been the aesthetic heart of several Latine movements for social justice both within and outside of the Catholic Church, including the United Farm Workers movement and Just Immigration Reform movement. Recently, Guadalupe has become a symbol of Latine Catholics struggling to keep their churches and parishes open against dioceses seeking to close them.[3] While Guadalupe is often narrowly associated with popular religious devotion among Mexican Catholics, her image takes on an explicitly public and political role in justice advocacy.[4] Invocation of Guadalupe's encounter with Juan Diego reveals the aesthetic significance of this expression of popular religious devotion for the public struggle for justice.

Aesthetic experience is concerned with the sensory dimensions, or the *felt* qualities, of everyday encounters and how such encounters may shape human action.[5] Christopher Tirres describes aesthetic meaning as emerging organically within everyday experience. Interlacing John Dewey's argument for the everyday character of the aesthetic with Ada Maria Isasi-Diaz's *mujerista* theological account of the ethical significance of *lo cotidiano* (or everyday reality), Tirres argues for the essential role of aesthetic experience in the struggle for justice.[6] The aesthetic quality of everyday experiences, Tirres argues, can empower communities for political and social change by allowing them to express their desire for liberation.[7] The movement for immigration justice thus engages the "everydayness" of aesthetic experience—stories, music, poetry, dancing, art, religious images—toward both consoling and empowering those who live amid conditions of indeterminacy and upheaval while also cultivating a rich imaginative space for recognizing human dignity and the common good.

Tirres's delineation of the ethical significance of everyday aesthetics demonstrates the need for a more adequate account of the relationship between aesthetic experience and the pursuit of social justice. The Aztec (or, more properly, Nahua) idea of *neltiliztli*, which L. Sebastian Purcell translates as "rootedness," helps to articulate this relationship.[8] *Neltiliztli* describes the power of the poetic (flowers and song) to offer roots or grounding to human beings amid the "slipperiness" of life. Writes Purcell: "The word nelli is related to nelhuayotl, which is a root or base. The metaphorical idea behind the Nahua understanding of 'truth,' then, is that it is a matter of being rooted like a tree, as opposed to sliding about on our slippery earth. The goal, the solution to our human problems, then, is to find rootedness, which as an abstract substantive would be expressed in Nahuatl as *neltiliztli*."[9] This concept illustrates the capacity of aesthetic experience to give roots to human beings amid circumstance of indeterminacy. This rooting offers balance, harmony, and even stability that is crucial to the struggle for justice under conditions of constant social and political contingency. Beyond the ability of the aesthetic to console, however, *neltiliztli* as rootedness demonstrates the ability of the aesthetic to empower those whom society has rendered powerless. I will use the narrative of Juan Diego's encounter with La Virgen de Guadalupe to illustrate both the consoling and empowering capacity of aesthetic experience.

Rootedness, interpreted through the account of Guadalupe's encounter with Juan Diego on Tepeyac, offers a fresh philosophical framework for articulating the role of aesthetic experience in the pursuit of justice for migrant populations. The first part of this essay offers a brief description of the significance of aesthetic experience in Latine social justice movements, including an elaboration of Guadalupe's particular importance to aesthetic experience in Latine protest tradition. The second part examines accounts of the relationship between beauty and justice in Latine theological aesthetics before introducing rootedness as a philosophical grounding for the relationship between aesthetic experience and social justice. The third part applies the framework of rootedness to the case of Guadalupe devotees advocating for immigration justice in New York City, demonstrating how aesthetic experience offers stability and political empowerment amid contingency and insecurity.

Latine Social Movements

Latine-led immigrant justice advocacy is pursued within the broader context of Latine justice movements. These movements have often engaged in public argumentation on issues pertaining to justice, offering what political liberalism calls "public reasons" for these causes. According to John Rawls, political stability of a democratic society requires a freestanding conception of justice that can be affirmed from different comprehensive doctrines.[10] Particular religious, philosophical, or moral views can offer support for justice in a pluralistic and democratic society, but must not be the basis for society's basic structures. Reasons from particular comprehensive doctrines must be translated into public reasons that can support a freestanding conception of justice. Accordingly, the immigration justice movement has employed publicly accessible reasons and rhetoric to make its case.

The discursive act of exchanging arguments is crucial in a pluralistic and democratic society where not all citizens share the same religious or philosophical commitments. Exchanging arguments fosters intellectual solidarity in pursuit of the common good.[11] Further, public reason is bulwark against public factions increasingly enticed by "alternative facts."[12] It requires communication through common terms that give arguments the necessary traction to contribute to the improvement of our common life.

Further, immigration advocates have a keen awareness of the necessity of direct action (boycotts and civil disobedience, for example) in making a moral appeal to a broader public. Jeffrey Stout, while arguing that the life of democracy principally resides in its discursive practices, nonetheless highlights its practical dimensions: "Democracy isn't all talk. Now and then there is a lot of marching involved, for example."[13] While Stout concedes the importance of practices, Lisa Cahill argues for their centrality in the pursuit of justice. She highlights the political power of practical actions to enact justice. Justice-oriented practices give life to the virtue of hope: "Not only do human solidarity and practical action to change conditions of violence express hope," she writes, "they nourish hope and make hope for a better future possible."[14] Hopeful action is the adhesive of these justice movements, leveraging the economic and political power of Latine communities toward attaining concrete objectives.

Beyond these discursive and practical dimensions of advocacy, Latine social justice advocacy employs aesthetic experience for illustrating the vision of human flourishing and justice that is at the heart of these movements. This priority has strong resonance with the Latin American Catholic ritual context, which influences many of these movements.[15] The role of aesthetic experience is especially apparent in the Latine processional tradition. For example, Latine popular religious processions such as Via Cruses, Las Posadas, and Mañanitas each remember specific sacred texts and events but also often function as forms of political and social resistance. In 2018, for example, members of the Denver-area Latine parish Our Lady of Visitation celebrated Las Posadas, a re-enactment of Mary and Joseph's search for a place to stay in Bethlehem. Celebrated during Advent, this procession is a linchpin of Latine popular Catholicism. But it has also served as a protest against political, economic, and ecclesial forms of exclusion, including as a critique of the United States' unjust immigration policies and, in this case, as a critique of the Archdiocese of Denver's decision to close its thriving church in 2017. For Latine justice movements, protest is more than mere practice; it is liturgy that expresses a vision of justice through movement, image, music, and poetry.

The Latine protest tradition is shaped, in part, by the aesthetic power of Latine religious processions. These protests employ/leverage narratives, sounds and images in "ritualized physical action" that moves its participants on both the intellectual and emotional levels.[16] This layering of sights, sounds, and smells within the context of the procession offers dimensions of meaning that would be inaccessible through strictly discursive means. The liturgical character of protest thus augments the discursive and practical aspects of justice work by inviting the community to imagine a just society in which fundamental human dignity is acknowledged and valued.

The most conspicuous of these Latine justice movements is the United Farm Workers (UFW) led by César Chavez and Dolores Huerta. The UFW's protests reflected the Latine aesthetic and processional tradition. Chavez and his cohorts, David Gutierrez writes, utilized, "emotionally charged ethnic symbols, such as the union's stylized black Aztec eagle insignia and banners of Mexico's patron saint, the Virgin of Guadalupe, to attract members and garner publicity."[17] The use of these symbols allowed Chavez to capture the Mexican American imagination, situating the plight of the workers at the heart of Mexican American religious and cultural identity.

Devotees believe that Guadalupe appeared to Juan Diego, an indigenous man, in 1531 on a hill called Tepeyac on the outskirts of Mexico City. Guadalupe exhorted Juan Diego to ask the local bishop to build a basilica in her honor there. Juan Diego initially demurred, feeling unworthy and incapable of this task due to his marginal status in society. Guadalupe persisted, convincing Juan Diego to appear before the bishop. After several unsuccessful attempts to persuade the bishop to build the basilica, Juan Diego appeared before him one final time, bearing a cloak full of roses from Guadalupe, grown in the frozen December earth. When Juan Diego unfolded his cloak to offer the roses to the bishop, an image of Guadalupe's exquisite image, brilliantly colored, appeared there. Her image was remarkable in that it had both Spanish and Nahua elements, mapping these conflicting identities onto the same canvas. Overwhelmed by the image, the bishop granted Guadalupe's request to build the basilica. Today, the cloak is kept at *Basílica de Nuestra Señora de Guadalupe* where it receives millions of visitors each year.

The narrative of this encounter assisted the UFW movement in articulating its aims. In the Plan of Delano, the UFW workers declare: "We seek, and have, the support of the Church in what we do. At the head of the pilgrimage we carry La Virgen de Guadalupe because she is ours, all ours, Patroness of the Mexican People."[18] By including the Guadalupe banner in its protest and invoking her in its central documents, the UFW effectively incorporated the aesthetic constellation of Guadalupe's encounter with Juan Diego—narrative, images, hymns, prayers, poems, plays—into the political fabric of the UFW's movement.

By including Guadalupe in the vision and practices of the movement, the UFW also demonstrated the public and democratic meanings of this religious image. Guadalupe's inclusion in this social justice movement is not simply a matter of style; her symbol substantively contributes to the UFW's democratic message. The narrative of empowerment associated with her symbol—along with her association with the political goals of participation, equality, and justice via Mexican American, Chicanx, and Latine activism—is crucial to the contemporary public voice of these communities. For these reasons, an adequate understanding of the movement, in both its means and ends, must attend to the aesthetic dimensions of incorporating this significant religious and cultural symbol.

The importance of Guadalupe to the UFW movement indicates the relationship between aesthetic experience and social justice advocacy in Latine-led movements. But why is this so? The next section briefly addresses the attempt to articulate this relationship between aesthetics and justice in Latine theology before suggesting a fresh philosophical angle for grounding this relationship.

Rootedness on the Slippery Earth

Latine-led justice movements can teach us much about the relationship between aesthetics and the pursuit of justice, including the important connection between everydayness (*lo cotidiano*) and the pursuit of social justice. Latine theological aesthetics, pioneered by Latino theologians Alejandro Garcia-Rivera and Roberto Goizueta and elaborated by a second generation of Latine theologians, has reflected on this connection.[19] Still, this literature requires further elaboration in order to account for contingency of lived experience as manifest in the lives of migrants living in the United States today.

Both Garcia-Rivera and Goizueta are interested in developing accounts of theological aesthetics that are grounded in the particularities of lived experience—stories, histories, experiences, practices, artistic forms, and the like. This experiential turn resonates with the contextual method privileged in Latine theology and ethics. At the same time, their works are also influenced by pragmatic semiotics as articulated by Charles Sanders Peirce and Josiah Royce; their thought informs both Garcia-Rivera's and Goizueta's turns toward transcendental categories of truth, goodness, and beauty in Latine theological aesthetics. These categories allow for engagement with Catholic accounts of virtue ethics inflected by Aristotle's teleological and eudaemonist ethics. Virtue ethics are at the heart of Catholic social thought, allowing the tradition to assert the priority of human flourishing and make persuasive claims about the role of human action in attaining justice and the common good. At the same time, the virtue perspective has often struggled to grapple with the realities of contingency and indeterminacy that characterize human experience in general, and especially of migrant life.[20]

Latine theological aesthetics needs to articulate a positive account of justice, one that comprehends the transitory and contingent character of lived experience. This is especially important for reflection upon the political contexts that shape our everyday reality (*lo cotidiano*). Amid conditions of insecurity and instability, it is essential to formulate an ethic that can respond to that which is beyond one's control while avoiding a slide into passive resignation or political despair.

Engagement with a new set of philosophical resources, especially sources beyond western philosophy that offer alternative visions of the connection between aesthetics and human flourishing, can help connect aesthetic experience to personal and communal struggles for justice. In his article "*Eudaimonia* and *Neltiliztli*: Aristotle and the Aztecs on the Good Life," L. Sebastian Purcell offers a comparative study of the meaning of the good life for pre-Colombian Nahuas, on the one hand, and Aristotle, on the other. Purcell argues that the Nahuas, in fact, held a similar (if still distinct in significant ways) view of the good life as Aristotle. Purcell defends this claim with a comparative analysis of *eudaimonia* and *neltiliztli*, the latter of which he translates as "rootedness."[21] Whereas *eudamonia* is based on a teleological understanding of human flourishing, rootedness is concerned with how one might live life on a "slippery earth," or amid circumstances that are transitory and can be difficult, if not impossible, to control. Rootedness seeks stability in a life characterized by manifest instability. This grounding was found not in the pursuit of human perfection, which was seen as impossible in light of the transitory and "slippery" character of life. Rather, rootedness was found in encounters with *xochitl in cuicatl*, or flower and song, which can best be understood as poetry or beauty. It is in flower and song that one can find stability in the midst of highly contingent circumstances.[22]

An ethics of rootedness, with its assertion of flower and song as a way of pursuing goodness amid conditions of instability, enriches analysis of the Guadalupe–Juan Diego relationship. Juan Diego, enticed to the peak of Tepeyac by flower and song, is invited to an encounter with Guadalupe that generates deep delight and joy. It is in his encounter with Guadalupe's beauty that he learns of his own goodness. The *Nican Mopahua* (one of the four major accounts of the Guadalupe–Juan Diego encounter, notable for its composition in Nahuatl instead of Spanish) testifies that Juan Diego is dignified and is her beloved child. This affirmation, encountered through the aesthetic experience of flower and song, convicts Juan Diego of his own worth and capacity. Through his relationship with Guadalupe, Juan Diego comes to see himself as worthy of confronting the colonial ecclesial authorities and thus worthy of a place in a society in which his status is profoundly unstable. In other words, Guadalupe helps Juan Diego find his roots.

Guadalupe and an Ethic of Rootedness

What does an ethics of rootedness look like for Latine communities working for social justice today? This final section demonstrates how an ethics of rootedness is reflected in the just immigration reform movement which was led by the *Comités Guadalupanos* in the Archdiocese of New York.

Guadalupe continues to be a crucial image in Latine social movements, including the just immigration movement. In New York City, undocumented Mexican immigrants anchor their own public efforts for just immigration reform in the Guadalupe image and narrative through performance of both devotion and public practices.

Alyshia Gálvez demonstrates that Guadalupan devotion anchors the work of parish-based *comités Guadalupanos* (Guadalupe Committees) that are united at the diocesan level in the *Asociation de Tepyac* (Tepeyac Association). The parish-based committees preserve devotional practices such as the display of Guadalupe's image in homes and church sanctuaries and the maintenance of parish Guadalupe shrines. Beyond these rituals, however, the *comités* collaborate as the *asociation* to organize an annual Guadalupe feast day procession. This procession is rich with religious ritual, but also serves the explicit political purpose of protesting for immigrant justice. Gálvez describes this event:

> Every year on December 12, thousands of Mexican immigrants gather
> for the mass at Saint Patrick's Cathedral in honor of Our Lady of
> Guadalupe's feast day. They kiss images of the Virgin, carry costumes
> associated with the story of the Virgin's apparition; and they also carry
> signs asking for immigration reform, chant "¡Si se puede!" [Yes, we
> can!] just like protesters do at marches, and display Mexican and U.S.
> flags.[23]

Additionally, the *Asociation de Tepeyac* organizes *La Antorcha Guadalupana*, a torch run in which a flame is carried by relay runners from the Basilica of Our Lady of Guadalupe on the outskirts of Mexico City over land to Saint Patrick's Cathedral in New York, arriving at the cathedral during the feast day procession.

While these practices are essentially acts of devotion, each one aims to raise public awareness about the struggle for dignity and participation among Guadalupe's devotees in New York City. "While the devotional practices centered on Our Lady of Guadalupe engaged in by Mexican immigrants in New York City may seem familiar to some observers," writes Galvez, "they occur in a

unique historical moment of massive and accelerated migration, militariza-
tion of the border, stagnation of immigration laws, and worldwide struggles
for rights by those displaced by globalization."[24] Hence, these practices adopt
both devotional and political meanings. For example, although the binational
relay is a religious pilgrimage, it also possesses a politically transgressive quality, serving as a public demonstration against the separation of families and
communities by unjust immigration policies. Guadalupan devotional practices thus enter the public square, articulating rights claims in the idiom of
U.S. Latine popular religious devotion.

Guadalupe's devotional-political character offers rootedness in a profoundly "slippery" and transitory situation of undocumented life in the United
States. In accord with Purcell's analysis, we see the creation of flower and song
as a rooting activity that allows these religious and political activists to encounter beauty, experience joy, and come to acknowledge their own dignity and
the dignity of those in their communities, even under conditions of profound
insecurity. Just as Juan Diego's encounter with flower and song through his
relationship with Guadalupe empowered him to confront the bishop with
Guadalupe's request, so does the encounter with flower and song in Guadalupan devotion empower her devotees in New York to continue their struggle
for justice.

This experience of rootedness has implications for political participation
and definitions of citizenship. According to Galvez:

> Mexican immigrants are engaging in political, activist activities which
> enhance their sense of well-being in material, lived and symbolic ways
> even while their juridical status remains unchanged . . . This kind
> of citizenship—broader, more performative, and more agential than
> the strictly juridical classification of citizens—is necessary to all other
> rights projects, both in the realm of formal citizenship and in other
> areas of social life.[25]

This exercise of citizenship, inspired by Juan Diego's empowerment and participation in colonial society, stresses the necessity of political participation
for all members of society, including alternately documented people. By an-
choring their activism in this narrative, these protesters model the relationship
between dignity and political participation while also challenging laws and
policies that limit their incorporation into political society. It would be coun-
terproductive to assert this vision of practice-oriented citizenship in the place
of juridical or legal definitions of citizenship (after all, one of the goals of the
movement is to make attainment of U.S. permanent residency and legal citizenship possible); however, this movement demonstrates the priority of more

inclusive citizenship laws while also illustrating the necessity of active and participatory citizenship practices for society in general.

The just immigration reform movement in New York City models an ethics of rootedness in the midst of an increasingly "slippery" situation, with aesthetic experience offering balance in the midst of instability. These movements foreground the themes of dignity and participation in service of its larger goals of inclusion, citizenship, and the common good.

Through Guadalupan devotional and political practices, says Gálvez, "many undocumented Mexican immigrants are finding the will and the vocabulary to demand rights, immigration reform, and respect."[26] The reality of religious aesthetics in public as illustrated by these movements demonstrates the necessity of further developing frameworks for constructive engagement in civil life. Public conversations that foster solidarity rely on participants coming together across difference in acts of communication and interpretation. It is crucial that Guadalupe's message of dignity and empowerment be engaged in a pluralistic and democratic public square, especially in conversations surrounding policy measures that directly influence Latine communities.

Conclusion

Latine social movements are instructive for thinking about the relationship between aesthetic experience and social justice. Attending to the lived experience of migrant communities reveals the necessity of an account of this relationship that grapples with the indeterminacy of migrant life, especially the instability and insecurity of this situation.

Rootedness offers a helpful framework for constructing this relationship. Aesthetic experience, which resonates with the Nahua description of flower and song, is essential for achieving balance on the slippery earth, or grounding in the face of social upheaval. Whereas virtue ethics aims for a particular *telos*, rootedness gestures to the role of aesthetic experience for surviving and thriving amid life's contingencies. Its ability to connect aesthetic experience with life's struggle makes it particularly well suited for articulating the empowering potential of aesthetic experience that is crucial to sustaining the ongoing struggle for immigrant justice.

Notes

1. See Nichole M. Flores, *The Aesthetics of Solidarity: Our Lady of Guadalupe and American Democracy* (Washington, D.C.: Georgetown University Press, 2021), 15. As I explain in *The Aesthetics of Solidarity*, I prefer the term "Latine" to other

options (including Latinx and Latina/o) due to its ability to convey the broad scope of Latinx/a/o identity while still being able to be readily incorporated into spoken Spanish and English.

2. David Gutiérrez, *Walls and Mirrors: Mexican Americans, Mexican Immigrants, and the Politics of Ethnicity* (Berkeley: University of California Press, 1995).

3. Nichole M. Flores, "The Heart of the Neighborhood: Why Dioceses Need to Support Struggling Latino Parishes," *America: The Jesuit Review of Faith and Culture*, December 24, 2018.

4. Luís D. León, "César Chávez and Mexican American Civil Religion," in *Latino Religions and Civic Activism in the United States*, ed. Gastón Espinosa, Virgilio Elizondo, and Jesse Miranda (New York: Oxford University Press, 2005), 60.

5. Frank Burch Brown, *Religious Aesthetics: A Theological Study of Making and Meaning* (Princeton, N.J.: Princeton University Press, 1989), 22; Christopher D. Tirres, *The Aesthetics and Ethics of Faith: A Dialogue Between Liberationist and Pragmatic Thought* (New York: Oxford University Press, 2014), 57. Frank Burch Brown highlights the sensory dimension of religious aesthetics: "In point of fact, aesthetics should perhaps be nothing less than basic theoretical reflection regarding all aesthetic phenomena, including modes of significant interrelation with, and mediation of, what is not inherently aesthetic: abstract ideas, useful objects, moral convictions, class conflicts, religious doctrines and so forth. The coherence of the field of aesthetics so conceived would derive its central interest in *aesthetica* — a term we can use technically to denote not perceptibles (as in Greek) or beautiful objects alone, *but all those things employing a medium in such a way that its perceptible form and 'felt' qualities become essential to what is appreciable and meaningful*" (emphasis added).

6. Ada María Isasi-Díaz, *La Lucha Continues: Mujerista Theology* (Maryknoll, N.Y.: Orbis Books, 2004), 48.

7. Tirres, *The Aesthetics and Ethics of Faith*, 72, 76–77.

8. L. Sebastian Purcell, "Eudaimonia and Neltiliztli: Aristotle and the Aztecs on the Good Life," *Hispanic/Latino Issues in Philosophy* 16, no. 2 (2017): 10–21. Purcell explains his translation: "Should one like to form a new word in Nahuatl, the language is well equipped with the capacity for compounding, much as ancient Greek was. Yet one may also make use of what Angel Maria Garibay has called '*difrasismo*,' which is the expression of one idea in two words. Examples in English might be 'with blood and fire,' or 'against wind and tide.' This sort of expression was extremely common in Nahuatl, and one must be careful to catch the metaphorical meaning at work. For if taken literally, the meaning of a *difrasismo* is almost totally lost." While Purcell's elaboration helps clarify his principle for the translation and use of *neltilitzli*, it is important to note that Nahuatl is still a living, spoken language.

9. Purcell, "Eudaimonia and Neltiliztli," 13.

10. John Rawls, A *Theory of Justice*, 1st ed. (Cambridge: Belknap Press, 1971).

11. David Hollenbach, *The Common Good and Christian Ethics* (Cambridge: Cambridge University Press, 2002).

12. Rebecca Sinderbrand, "How Kellyanne Conway Ushered in the Era of 'Alternative Facts,'" *Washington Post*, January 22, 2017, https://www.washingtonpost.com/news/the-fix/wp/2017/01/22/how-kellyanne-conway-ushered-in-the-era-of-alternative-facts/.

13. Jeffrey Stout, *Democracy and Tradition* (Princeton, N.J.: Princeton University Press, 2004), 6.

14. Lisa Sowle Cahill, *Global Justice, Christology and Christian Ethics* (New York: Cambridge University Press, 2013), 290.

15. Jaime Lara, *Christian Texts for Aztecs: Art and Liturgy in Colonial Mexico* (Notre Dame, Ind.: University of Notre Dame Press, 2008).

16. Lara, *Christian Texts for Aztecs*, 172.

17. David Gutiérrez, *Walls and Mirrors*, 196.

18. Luís D. León, "César Chávez and Mexican American Civil Religion," in *Latino Religions and Civic Activism in the United States*, ed. Gastón Espinosa, Virgilio Elizondo, and Jesse Miranda (New York: Oxford University Press, 2005), 60.

19. For examples of the second-generation works in Latine aesthetics, see Michelle A. González, *Sor Juana: Beauty and Justice in the Americas* (Maryknoll, N.Y.: Orbis Books, 2003); Nancy Pineda-Madrid, *Suffering and Salvation in Ciudad Juarez* (Minneapolis: Fortress Press, 2011); Cecilia González-Andrieu, *Bridge to Wonder: Art as a Gospel of Beauty* (Waco, Tex.: Baylor University Press, 2012); Tirres, *The Aesthetics and Ethics of Faith*.

20. See Lisa Tessman, *Burdened Virtues: Virtue Ethics for Liberatory Struggles*, Studies in Feminist Philosophy (New York: Oxford University Press, 2005). Tessman's work is a notable exception to this tendency.

21. L. Sebastian Purcell, "Eudaimonia and Neltiliztli," 10.

22. Purcell, "Eudaimonia and Neltiliztli," 13.

23. Alyshia Gálvez, *Guadalupe in New York: Devotion and the Struggle for Citizenship Rights among Mexican Immigrants* (New York: New York University Press, 2010), 3.

24. Gálvez, *Guadalupe in New York*, 3.

25. Gálvez, *Guadalupe in New York*, 4.

26. Gálvez, *Guadalupe in New York*, 3.

6

Christian Responses to the "Revolutionary Aesthetic" of Black Lives Matter

Jermaine M. McDonald

On July 13, 2013, a six-person jury found George Zimmerman not guilty of a second-degree murder charge in the shooting death of Trayvon Martin, a seventeen-year-old African American teen who was in the neighborhood visiting his father at the time. Zimmerman, a neighborhood watch participant, initiated the fatal encounter after spotting Martin walking in the neighborhood, racially profiling Martin as a "real suspicious guy . . . up to no good . . . on drugs or something,"[1] and pursuing Martin against the verbal instructions of the 911 dispatcher, whom Zimmerman had called to report the presence of Martin in his neighborhood. The not guilty verdict was a crushing blow for those hoping to see justice done in this case. As Ta-Nehisi Coates wrote, "It is painful to say this: [the verdict] is not a miscarriage of American justice, but American justice itself. This is not our system malfunctioning. It is our system working as intended."[2]

That anguish inspired activist Alicia Garza to lament on social media "how little Black lives matter" in the United States. Her friend, Patrisse Cullors, distilled Garza's lament into a hashtag, #BlackLivesMatter, and their friend, Opal Tometi, offered to help build social media presence and platform to allow activists to better connect with one another.[3] Thus was born the activist organization Black Lives Matter. From lament to hashtag to activist organization to social justice movement, Black Lives Matter has become a force to be reckoned with in the U.S. socio-political arena. But, what exactly is it and where are the fractures that allow some Christians to embrace it fully, some to keep it at arm's length with reservation, and still others to reject it as incompatible with Christianity altogether?

Black Lives Matter did not gain traction as a political force until the tragic second half of 2014, when a wave of killings of unarmed African Americans at the hands of law enforcement and white supremacists caused a social reckoning in U.S. society. In a one-year span, we experienced the deaths of Michael Brown in Ferguson (August 2014), Tamir Rice in Cleveland (November 2014), Freddie Gray in Baltimore (April 2015), nine Bible study attendees at a historic African Methodist Episcopal church in Charleston (June 2015), and Sandra Bland (July 2015). Each incident sparked dramatic increases in the use of the hashtag #BlackLivesMatter on social media, just one indicator of the rise in the saliency of Black Lives Matter as a political and organizing principle.[4]

To be clear, a single calendar year and an exclusive focus on the specifics of tragic one-off injustices form an arbitrary delineation of the movement. Other names such as Philando Castile, Breonna Taylor, Eric Gardner, Rekia Boyd, George Floyd, and so many more warrant inclusion in the narrative. Broadening the scope to include the public discourse, public protests, state responses, and mostly unsatisfying (and unjust) outcomes to these incidents further sheds light on how Black Lives Matter as an organizing principle seeks to explicitly name the injustices facing Black people in the United States and strategize on how to overcome these injustices. Sharpening the analytical tools at our disposal reveals underlying systemic issues and interconnected causes that fit under a general rubric of Black Lives Matter while inspiring their own specific calls to action, even if most of those causes (prison abolition, for one) predate the Black Lives Matter movement.

Thus, when someone either supports or criticizes Black Lives Matter, it is often difficult to determine whether they are referring to the general principle, the public protests and actions that have been labeled as BLM activity, one of the wide-ranging causes that fit within a BLM rubric, or the "official" organization founded by Garza, Cullors, and Tometi. The amorphous nature of Black Lives Matter inspires a variety of Christian responses. To better contextualize these responses, one must understand the varying shades of Black Lives Matter.

Black Lives Matter Global Network Foundation, Inc.

In 2013, Alicia Garza, Patrisse Cullors, and Opal Tometi created the "Black-centered political will and movement building project" in response to the acquittal of George Zimmerman. They acknowledge, however, that their vision began to take shape during the activism in Ferguson, Missouri after the killing of eighteen-year-old Mike Brown by officer Darren Wilson. Cullors explained years later:

Every generation of Black resistance is launched by an uprising; Ferguson was ours and we are forever indebted to every single Black person (and all the allies) who decided to fight for their dignity, and to challenge one of the smallest police forces in the state of Missouri, expose it for its corruption and collusion with white supremacist officers. The Ferguson Police Department had access to military grade weaponry that was used against the people who were grieving the death of their child, son, brother and friend. The Ferguson uprising gave birth to a Black resistance movement that continues to thrive today [in 2020].[5]

It was not happenstance that Cullors, Garza, and Tometi would be prepared to initiate what would become a generational movement. Cullors grew up in Section 8 apartments in California, lived through the repeated incarcerations of her father and brother, became a community activist in high school, and used those skills to advocate for her brother to ease his harsh treatment by the prison system and help him with his personal struggle against mental illness.[6] Before Black Lives Matter, Cullors had already learned "how to launch, execute, and win campaigns by building power among those the world considers powerless,"[7] including founding the organization Dignity and Power Now, which helped to establish the first civilian oversight board of the L.A. County Sheriff's Department, the source of her brother's trauma. Garza grew up as a Black girl in a predominantly white environment, experiencing "all the ways that Blackness was penalized."[8] Studying Black feminist thought in college helped her name the alienation she felt growing up and taught her about how "relationships of power were shaped by race, class, gender, and sexuality."[9] After college, she worked for AmeriCorps, volunteered for an organization dedicated to ending sexual violence, and stumbled into a training program for community-based organizing, where she found her life's passion. Garza cut her teeth as an organizer for People Organized to Win Employment Rights (POWER) in the Bayview Hunters Point section of San Francisco. There she learned that the "mission and purpose of organizing is to build power" necessary to "change conditions in our communities that hurt us."[10] Tometi grew up in Phoenix, Arizona with undocumented Nigerian parents. Her parents' successful battle against deportation "galvanized Tometi to become involved in the larger immigrants' rights movement."[11] Tometi's experience led her to volunteer with the ACLU as a legal observer at the U.S.-Mexico border on the way to working for the Black Alliance for Just Immigration (BAJI), becoming the executive director of that organization at the age of 27.[12] She had been working for BAJI for eight years when she connected with Garza and Cullors to envision Black Lives Matter. All three women had ample experience in activism and community organizing on issues directly relevant to the causes engaged by the Black Lives Matter movement. Those experiences would inform the work, structure, and philosophy of their specific organization, as well as the character of the entire mutually aligned network of activists, volunteers, and organizations.

Cullors and activist Darnell L. Moore started organizing the Black Lives Matters Ride to Ferguson, just ten days after Mike Brown's death. Modeled after the 1960s Freedom Rides to Mississippi, the BLM Ride, with endorsements from over 50 activist organizations nationally, brought like-minded people from across the United States to reinforce the burgeoning movement seeking justice for Mike Brown. The group of freedom riders stayed in Ferguson for four days, participating in street protests and strategy meetings, planning activities for further engagement in their home communities, and even attending church service.[13] That church, St. John's United Church of Christ, hosted the activists for their strategy sessions and would continue to play a crucial supporting role for movement activities in Ferguson. They model how churches can play a role in the movement for Black lives without centering the church, or its sometimes harmful theologies, in the work.

One of the tenets of the successful BLM Freedom Ride was to reflect on how Michael Brown's death demonstrated the need for an intersectional framework to specify and address the social injustices that make Black lives matter a point of inquiry rather than statement of fact. This commitment led Moore to frequently express to participants the need to include *all* Black lives, including Black queer and Black trans lives, in a racial justice framework.[14] This is one way in which the Black Lives Matter Movement distinguishes itself as different from the 1960s civil rights movement. In its original "What we believe" statement, the BLM Global Network would make clear its commitment to a decentralized, inclusive movement that would center the lives of people traditionally ignored in Black freedom struggles:

> We are guided by the fact that all Black lives matter, regardless of actual or perceived sexual identity, gender identity, gender expression, economic status, ability, disability, religious beliefs or disbeliefs, immigration status, or location.
>
> We make space for transgender brothers and sisters to participate and lead.
>
> We are self-reflexive and do the work required to dismantle cisgender privilege and uplift Black trans folk, especially Black trans women

who continue to be disproportionately impacted by trans-antagonistic violence.

. . .

We disrupt the Western-prescribed nuclear family structure require-ment by supporting each other as extended families and "villages" that collectively care for one another, especially our children, to the degree that mothers, parents, and children are comfortable.[15]

That last statement became a source of controversy not only from op-ponents of the very idea of Black Lives Matter, but from some movement participants who did not accept some of the more radical premises of the organization. This speaks to the differences between the organization and the movement, as well as the contested nature of the meaning of the phrase "Black Lives Matter" in general.

The organization founded by Garza, Cullors, and Tometi has evolved, di-viding its work into three partnering entities: the Black Lives Global Network Foundation, the BLM Political Action Committee, and BLM Grassroots. Led by Executive Director Patrisse Cullors, the Foundation raised $90 million in 2020, distributing to its grassroots chapters and thirty additional, nonaffiliated local organizations more than $21 million, leading to a reserve of $60 million. The BLM PAC partnered with other political organizations to impact Black voter turnout in the battleground states of the 2020 U.S. presidential election (particularly in Georgia). Individual chapters affiliated with BLM Grassroots continue to engage in activity that pertains to their local situations.[16] For ex-ample, Black Lives Matter South Bend disrupted the presidential candidacy of then–South Bend, Indiana Mayor Pete Buttigieg by questioning Buttigieg's handling of the police shooting of a 54-year-old Black man, Eric Logan.[17] Black Lives Matter Louisville partnered with other local activist organizations to participate in one hundred days of protest in Louisville over the police kill-ing of Breonna Taylor. Furthermore, in the wake of the grand jury's decision not to indict the officer who killed Taylor, the group called for a Louisville Community Bail Fund,[18] demanded the resignation of Louisville Mayor Greg Fischer, and advocated for divesting funding from police and the dismissal of all officers involved in the incident.[19]

The Black Lives Matter Global Network is one of the most recognizable organizations in the Black Lives Matter movement, but by no means does it represent the entirety of the movement. As with any social justice movement, particularly one that resists being organized by hierarchy and centralization, disagreements about credit, status, tactics, and goals abound. In the next section, I discuss the ambiguity that arises when we broaden the lens to the movement itself.

Black Lives Matter as a Movement

If the killing of Trayvon Martin was the spark that ignited the idea of Black Lives Matters, the killing of Michael Brown by a Ferguson, Missouri police officer one year later was the accelerant that caused that idea to burn as a full-fledged, wildfire movement. Seemingly overnight, the phrase "Black Lives Matter" became the most prominent slogan used during the Ferguson protests. It has since become the preferred shorthand for labeling protests, community actions, groups, and supporters who seek racial justice for Black people in the United States, regardless of the official connections, or lack thereof, the invocators of the phrase may have to one another.

The Ferguson uprising included a variety of actors: religious leaders, local civic and elected officials, national mainstream activist and civil rights organizations, neophyte protesters, grassroots organizations local to the area, and an influx of already engaged activists from around the country. The uprising was often chaotic, in part due to the militaristic response of the police department who brought in tanks and armored vehicles and fired tear gas and rubber bullets at protestors. The outsized response actually inspired young locals to abandon jobs in the pursuit of justice in Ferguson.[20] The uprising also connected Brown's killing to larger systemic issues facing the Black communities in the St. Louis metropolitan area, so much so that it pressured the United States Department of Justice to conduct an investigation into the city of Ferguson and its police department. That investigation found that "the combination of Ferguson's focus on generating revenue over public safety, along with racial bias, has a profound effect on the FPD's police and court practices, resulting in conduct that routinely violates the Constitution and federal law . . . [and] create[s] a lack of trust between the FPD and significant portions of Ferguson's residents, especially African Americans."[21] The report makes plain many of the specific issues that Black Lives Matter has come to confront.

One initiative to emerge out of the Ferguson protests was the call to address and end police violence in the United States. To that end, three activists who each established a national profile due to their work and social media presence in the wake of Ferguson co-founded We The Protesters, featuring a signature initiative called Campaign Zero. Originally detailed in August 2015, Campaign Zero proposed ten policy solutions to limit police interventions, improve community interactions, and ensure police accountability to the public. This data-focused, police reform-minded campaign is rooted in a politics of redemption that "regards its targets of criticism as capable of rehabilitation, potential future allies whose moral commitments should be taken seriously."[22]

Another organization that has emerged out of the Ferguson protests is the Movement for Black Lives (M4BL). About fifteen hundred people from the coalition of over fifty Black-led organizations (including BLMGN) gathered on the campus of Cleveland State University in July 2015 (one year after Michael Brown's death) to strategize about the future of the burgeoning movement. At this meeting as well as in follow-up smaller retreats and sessions, the coalition navigated sometimes conflicting philosophies and contentious ideas to develop a comprehensive mission statement to guide the work of the coalition. Released in August 2016, the M4BL's platform, "Vision 4 Black Lives," lays out six core planks around criminal justice, reparations, investment and divestment, economic justice, community control, and political power.[23] The wide-ranging, ambitious platform contains radical provisions that do not have mainstream political support. In particular, its call to divest funds from policing, incarceration, and the military and divert the money to education, employment, universal health care, mental health services, and the like are a stark contrast from the police reform measures advocated by Campaign Zero. Overall, M4BL's vision reflects the inherent political tension in the Black Lives Matter movement, articulated by Charles Olney as a struggle to balance a politics of redemption against a politics of distrust. The tension lies in the desire for an inclusive, universal political application of justice against the tragic sense that the reimagining of justice will simply exclude the already excluded parties in a novel way.[24] The overarching fear is that people who do not share the radical commitments of M4BL's vision will coopt the language of Black Lives Matter into their own political discourse, resulting in lukewarm societal reformations that do not bring about the radical change that the principles of Black Lives Matters demand

Barbara Ransby observes that Black feminist politics have been the bedrock of the Black Lives Matter movement.[25] Many of the activist organizations that have embraced the call for Black Lives Matter feature Black women in leadership positions, reject a politics of respectability, and use an intersectional lens to broaden the scope of Black liberation beyond a focus on Black, cisgender, heterosexual men. BYP100, for one, is quite explicit about this, declaring that the organization "works through a Black queer feminist lens, meaning that we are radically inclusive and strive to move those of us who are marginalized (e.g. Black women, girls, and LGBTQ folks) to the center."[26] This commitment has led to a push for a wider recognition of the injustices facing Black queer and transgender lives as well as intentional direct action focused on valuing Black trans lives.[27]

Another representative feature of Black Lives Matter activists and organizations is a call for racial economic justice that often embraces strong criticisms of capitalism. For example, M4BL's platform on economic justice demands a radical and sustainable redistribution of wealth, the breakup of large banks, a jobs program to support a living wage, and the financing of Black community-based institutions.[28] Movement actors and organizations have supported ancillary actions such as the 2021 effort to unionize Amazon workers in Alabama[29] and the Fight for $15, a national campaign to raise the minimum wage in the United States to $15 per hour.[30] BYP100 created the *Agenda to Build Black Futures* to "articulate a set of economic goals and structural changes that could improve the lives of Black people living in America."[31] The *Agenda* demands structural changes such as the defunding of police and systems of punishment, cancellation of all student debt, redress for predatory lending practices against Black communities across the United States, universal child care, and more. Keeanga-Yamahtta Taylor views such efforts as necessary for the future viability of the Black Lives Matter movement, arguing, "The long-term strength of the movement will depend on its ability to reach large numbers of people by connecting the issue of police violence to the other ways that Black people are oppressed."[32] For Taylor, a key area of solidarity for Black Lives Matter is with low-wage workers' campaigns, especially considering that Blacks are overrepresented in the ranks of the American poor and working classes.

The Black Lives Matter movement has prioritized justice over peace, disruption over comfort, inclusivity over respectability, and democracy over charisma. These prioritizations present challenges to many forms of Christianity attempting to respond to the demands of justice in the present day.

White Evangelicalism and Black Lives Matter

> Evangelicalism is synonymous with whiteness. It is not only a cultural whiteness but also a political whiteness. The presupposition of the whiteness of evangelicalism has come to define evangelicalism, and it is the definition that the media, the general public, and politicians agree on.
>
> —ANTHEA BUTLER[33]

If Anthea Butler is correct about the racism baked into white evangelicalism, then white evangelical churches and their leaders would be natural foils to the Black Lives Matter movement. After all, if they could make theological arguments in support of slavery, advocate for the continuation (or slow devolution) of Jim Crow segregation, or blame discrepancies between white and Black economic flourishing, education, and incarceration rates on individual choice and Black culture, how could white evangelicalism possibly be open to concerns raised by Black Lives Matter? The very premise of Black Lives Matter is the need for social justice, an idea that is often anathema to white evangelicals.

Consider the "Statement on Social Justice and the Gospel" (https://statement onsocialjustice.com/) produced by a coalition of pastors led by John MacArthur, pastor of Grace Community Church in Southern California. The authors are more determined to defend their specific interpretations of Scripture regarding race and ethnicity, manhood and womanhood, and human sexuality against the "nebulous rubric of concern for 'social justice,'"[34] pitting social justice as an adversary of the gospel. The group denies that "intersectionality, radical feminism, and critical race theory are consistent with biblical teaching."[35] Their definition of sin is individualistic to the point of affirming that "subsequent generations [only] share the collective guilt of their ancestors if they approve and embrace (or attempt to justify) those sins."[36] They resist the notion that political or social activism is "primary to the mission of the church."[37] Other aspects that reveal a natural opposition to Black Lives Matter are the denial of the legitimacy of same-sex attraction or gender fluidity,[38] the denial of white privilege or the preferential option of the poor and oppressed,[39] and the reduction of racism to pride, malice, partiality, and prejudice rather than wrestling with systemic racism.[40]

Every now and then critical events force the nation to have discourse about race and racism in a way that even white evangelicals cannot ignore. The same touchpoints that sparked Black Lives Matter, the unjustified killings of unarmed Black people by police, have provoked conversations in evangelical spaces. Black leaders in white evangelical spaces can often mark the conversations they have had with some of their white pastor colleagues by news cycle of racial violence in the United States.[41] The murder of George Floyd by Officer Derrick Chauvin proved to be one such touchpoint, provoking Southern Baptist Convention president, J. D. Greear to implore his denomination to "say it clearly as a gospel issue, 'Black Lives Matter.'"[42] It would also inspire Joel Osteen, the prosperity gospel preaching senior pastor of the Lakewood Church, to participate in both a protest march seeking justice for Floyd and the #BlackOutTuesday social media hashtag movement. Osteen would confess that although he tends to stay away from political issues in the pulpit, the Floyd murder is "a human issue. Wrong is wrong and we want to lend our voice . . . to stand with our Black brothers and sisters and stand against injustice."[43] Critical cultural flashpoints, particularly of racial violence, indeed force conversations about race within white evangelical spaces. Yet those conversations tend to be truncated by the desire to assuage white discomfort and defend the current social power structures. Avoiding "political issues" is a privilege afforded to those who are not meaningfully impacted by whether or not those issues are addressed.

In his address to the Southern Baptist Convention mentioned earlier, J. D. Greear would indeed affirm the idea the Black Lives Matter because Black people, like all people, are made in the image of God. He empathized with the stories of injustice told to him by many of his Black friends and provided a colorful parable explaining why "All lives matter" is not a helpful retort. Nevertheless, Greear disassociated the Black Lives Matter movement from his sentiment of Black Lives Matter, accusing the movement of having been "hijacked by some political operatives whose worldview and policy prescriptions would be deeply at odds with my own."[44] Richard Land, president of Southern Evangelical Seminary, expressed a similar wariness of the Black Lives Matter movement's worldview and goals. In an op-ed, he affirmed that Black lives matter as a subset of the idea that all human lives are sacred. Yet, he declared that Evangelicals "should not mouth the mantra 'black lives matter,' lest we be misunderstood as supporting their godless agenda."[45] For Lind, the movement's anti-biblical definition of love, freedom, justice, and family, and commitment to LGBTQ ideologies and Marxism, render it incompatible with Christianity.

Resistance to the notion that pursuing social justice is commiserate and a function of the Gospel has manifested in a tension within white evangelical spaces that becomes a barrier for these entities to make lasting commitments to race and economic-based social change. Even more than the oppositional philosophical frameworks between the Black Lives Matter movement and Evangelicalism, which suggests that it would be difficult at best for both sides to work together to bring about racial justice, the two sides have radically different goals. While Black Lives Matter oscillates between a politics of redemption and distrust, white Evangelicalism is primarily interested in a politics of reconciliation, and perhaps only mildly so. As Michelle Oyakawa observes, white evangelicals tend to approach racial issues from an individualistic standpoint, believing that a shared commitment to Christian identity over racial identity will bring about racial harmony.[46] Their interest in everyone getting along ends up discouraging discourse that questions the validity of white cultural dominance and thus helps to preserve the status quo.[47] Racial justice for white evangelicals is the colorblind riff from Martin Luther King Jr.'s "dream," when all (meaning white evangelicals) can be judged by character, not color. Justice for the Black Lives Matter movement is more a matter of equity, a fairer distribution of social goods, and the elimination of white cultural dominance. Social justice–minded Christians do not share all the same barriers to the Black Lives Matter movement as evangelicals, but they do have their own challenges to overcome.

Progressive Christians and Black Lives Matter

Our collective memory of the civil rights movement of the 1950s and '60s is that the fight for racial equality was birthed out of and driven by Black churches. This romanticized narrative tends to erase movement actors, leaders, and organizations who were not religious, not to mention the number of Black churches that did not participate in movement activity at all.[48] Nevertheless, out of the Black church emerged a multitude of key figures and leaders in the civil rights movement. The Black Lives Matter movement is certainly different in that regard. First, as a result of various social factors and cultural change, Black churches in the United States have a less prominent role in influencing Black life today, a trend that is not unique to Black people in the United States. Black social networks are more varied and expansive. Black churches are no longer the primary means for reaching potential volunteers for activist work. Second, the Black Lives Matter movement intentionally avoids a top-down hierarchy of leadership in favor of a decentralized structure that empowers local activism. Taking their cue from Ella Baker, the movement intends to be "leaderful" and cultivate a multitude of people who can contribute and lead as opposed to uplifting or supporting singular charismatic leaders.[49] Black churches, for the most part, continue to operate under a top-down model, where the guidance, strategy, direction, and agenda flow from the pastor. Clergy are used to assuming positions of authority, but such deference to clergy is not likely to be found within the movement. Third, the Black radical feminism that serves as the foundation of Black Lives Matter presents challenges to many Black churches who remain committed to respectability and traditional notions of family and human sexuality.

One moment from a Ferguson town hall meeting encapsulates the divide well. On Sunday, October 12, 2014, activists staged a mass rally at Saint Louis University's Chaifetz Arena, in part to encourage more supporters to join the activities on the street. NAACP President Cornell Brooks, himself an ordained minister in the African Methodist Episcopal Church, was preaching his address to the audience when people in the crowd began to chant "Let them speak" and "This is what democracy looks like!" The chants turned into shouts, forcing Brooks to stop mid-address. The event's emcee, Pastor Traci

Blackmon, shifted gears and invited the young protesters up to speak. Those who spoke wondered if the large attendance at the safe and respectable rally would translate into more protestors in the streets, shook their heads regarding the repetitive "political talking points" that pointed to the desire for a charismatic leader, and questioned local clergy for not being reliable and failing to join the demonstrations.[50]

Leah Gunning Francis was among the clergy in the St. Louis area who participated in the pursuit of justice for Mike Brown as an expression of her faith. In her book, *Ferguson and Faith*, Francis interviews clergypersons local to St. Louis who participated in the Ferguson protests as clergy, as well as a few of the young activists who interacted with them. A consistent theme that resonated with Francis's clergy cohort was the feeling that God was calling each of them to use their skills, experiences, and resources for the benefit of the demonstrations.[51] As clergy, they were able to mediate between protestors and police, leveraging their status in the community to facilitate conversations in the heat of the moment between the two opposing groups. Some opened their churches up to protestors as safe spaces to recuperate, regroup, strategize, and plan. They facilitated town hall sessions where members of the community could voice their concerns to those in the seat of power, including to the governor of Missouri. They prayed with and for the protestors, girding them up to go into the streets. In some of the more intense moments of street protest, they formed a prayer wall between protestors and police. They talked about the meaning of Black Lives Matter from their pulpits and invited their congregations to march to the police station and demand justice. They provided training on nonviolent civil disobedience. All of this was done in a supporting role.

The clergy who participated in Ferguson understood that this movement was not going to resemble our popular conception of the civil rights movement. As Reverend Osagyefo Sekou observed, "The leadership is Black, poor, queer, women. It presents in a different way. It's a revolutionary aesthetic. . . . These folks embody intersectionality."[52] To truly be a part of the Black Lives Matter movement beyond hashtags and lawn signs, clergy and churches must be willing to follow Sekou's example and take their orders from "23-year-old queer women."

Ferguson was not the only place where the church would play a supportive role in movement activity. In the wake of the decision of a Kentucky grand jury to not indict the officers responsible for killing Breonna Taylor, demonstrators took to the streets in Louisville.[53] A small group already had a consistent presence in Jefferson Square Park, maintaining a memorial to Taylor for months after her tragic death. The First Unitarian Church had been supporting the Jefferson Square Park protestors for months, providing medical care, food, and supplies, and simply engaging and listening to the protestors. When protest activity spiked in response to the grand jury's decision, First Unitarian Church, located a few blocks from Jefferson Square Park, was already in a position to give aid. Church leaders had already informed the protestors that they could seek refuge there as needed, but the need for refuge exploded as police in riot gear enforced a 9:00 PM curfew set by local officials. First Unitarian declared itself a sanctuary space and allowed marching protestors to cram into its courtyard and front lawn, and inside its building while police set up a perimeter and helicopters circled overhead. Inside, congregants would tend to the wounds, physical, emotional, and spiritual, of the protestors—a scene that would repeat every day until the curfew was lifted.[54] First Unitarian provided a crucial supportive function during a crisis moment that would prove to be another flashpoint in the struggle to affirm the value of Black lives. In doing so, they risked their property, their reputations, and even their lives. Churches have engaged in similar actions to support Black Lives Matter protests in other areas of the United States as well.

Conclusion

The Black Lives Matter movement's decentralized structure, commitment to radical feminist politics, and vision of justice that seeks to overturn the existing structures of power make a sustained cooperation between it and Christianity a difficult task. If Christian institutions remain committed to defending the status quo and a limited vision of justice that has room only for racial reconciliation, the movement and the church will always be at odds. If Christian institutions can at least move toward a politics of redemption where they are able to confess and atone for the systemic oppression wrought by its historic sanction, then perhaps there will be common ground to build something anew. When the church is able to channel a vision of Jesus as a radical revolutionary and preach the Gospel as God desiring justice for the oppressed, then there will be a consistent, substantial Christian effort to ensure that Black Lives Matter. In the meantime, perhaps more of us can humble ourselves and follow the orders of 23-year-old queer Black women.

Notes

1. Transcript of the first 911 call by George Zimmerman on February 26, 2012.

2. Ta-Nehisi Coates, "Trayvon Martin and the Irony of American Justice," *The Atlantic*, July 2013, https://www.theatlantic.com/national/archive/2013/07/trayvon -martin-and-the-irony-of-american-justice/277782/.

3. Jelani Cobb, "The Matter of Black Lives: A new kind of movement found its moment. What will its future be?" *The New Yorker*, March 6, 2016, https://www.newyorker.com/magazine/2016/03/14/where-is-black-lives-matter-headed.

4. Monica Anderson, "The hashtag #BlackLivesMatter emerges: Social activism on Twitter," Pew Research Center, August 15, 2016, https://www.pewresearch.org/internet/2016/08/15/the-hashtag-blacklivesmatter-emerges-social-activism-on-twitter/. This is part of a larger Pew study on "Social Media Conversations about Race" produced by Monica Anderson and Paul Hitlin in August 2016, published at https://www.pewresearch.org/internet/2016/08/15/social-media-conversations-about-race/.

5. Patrisse Cullors, "Black Lives Matter began after Trayvon Martin's death. Ferguson showed us its staying power," NBC News, January 1, 2020, https://www.nbcnews.com/think/opinion/black-lives-matter-began-after-trayvon-martin-s-death-ferguson-ncna1106651.

6. Patrisse Khan-Cullors and Asha Bandele, *When They Call You a Terrorist: A Black Lives Matter Memoir* (New York: St. Martin's Griffin, 2018).

7. Ibid., 164.

8. Alicia Garza, *The Purpose of Power: How we come together when we fall apart* (New York: One World, 2020), 48.

9. Ibid., 50.

10. Ibid., 56.

11. Ella Alexander, "Black Lives Matter Co-Founder Opal Tometi: Black People Can't Catch a Break, Even in a Global Pandemic," *Harper's Bazaar*, December 22, 2020, https://www.harpersbazaar.com/uk/culture/a35034879/black-lives-matter-co-founder-opal-tometi-interview/.

12. "Biography," AyoTometi.org, https://ayotometi.org/biography/.

13. See the eyewitness account from journalist Akiba Solomon who took a more than twenty-hour bus ride with volunteers to cover the Freedom Ride and in doing so, became, not just a journalist covering the movement, but a volunteer. Akiba Solomon, "Get on the Bus: Inside the Black Life Matters 'Freedom Ride' to Ferguson," *Colorlines*, September 4, 2014, https://www.colorlines.com/articles/get-bus-inside-black-life-matters-freedom-ride-ferguson.

14. Ibid.

15. The "What We Believe" section of the Black Lives Global Network was deleted and reworked after controversy arose regarding phrases such as "disrupt the Western-prescribed nuclear family structure." One can read the entire original statement in the internet archives. See http://web-old.archive.org/web/20200914205003/https://blacklivesmatter.com/what-we-believe/, archived on September 14, 2020.

16. See "Black Lives Matter 2020 Impact Report," https://blacklivesmatter.com/2020-impact-report/.

17. Trip Gabriel. "Buttigieg's Debate Remarks on Police Shooting Don't Satisfy Some Back Home," *New York Times*, June 28, 2019, https://www.nytimes.com/2019/06/28/us/politics/pete-buttigieg-debate-south-bend.html. Jordan Gieger is an activist involved with Black Lives Matter South Bend. His affiliation is denoted only as

"nonprofit group" in the article. See also, Roge Karma, "The millennial left's case against Pete Buttigieg, explained," *Vox*, February 11, 2020.

18. "Louisville Community Bail Fund, *The Action Network*, https://actionnetwork .org/fundraising/louisville-community-bail-fund/.

19. Meghan Roos, "BLM Louisville Calls for Mayor Fischer to Resign, Lists 5 Other Demands After Breonna Taylor Decision," *Newsweek*, September 23, 2020, https://www.newsweek.com/blm-louisville-calls-mayor-fischer-resign-lists-5-other -demands-after-breonna-taylor-decision-1533962.

20. See Barbara Ransby, *Making All Black Lives Matter: Reimagining Freedom in the 21st Century* (Oakland: University of California Press, 2018 [Kindle version]). In Chapter 3, Ransby profiles several such women.

21. "Justice Department Announces Findings of Two Civil Rights Investigations in Ferguson, Missouri," U.S. Department of Justice, Office of Public Affairs. Press release issued March 4, 2015, https://www.justice.gov/opa/pr/justice-department -announces-findings-two-civil-rights-investigations-ferguson-missouri.

22. Charles Olney, "Black Lives Matter and the Politics of Redemption," *Philosophy & Social Criticism* (April 2021): 7.

23. Vann R. Newkirk II, "The Permanence of Black Lives Matter: A new policy platform from a coalition of activists signals a new stage in the protest movement," *The Atlantic*, August 3, 2016, https://www.theatlantic.com/politics/archive/2016/08 /movement-black-lives-platform/494309/.

24. Olney, "Black Lives Matter and the Politics of Redemption," 8.

25. Ransby, Introduction, *Making All Black Lives Matter*.

26. "Agenda to Build Black Futures," *Black Youth Project (BYP100)*, https://www .agendatobuildblackfutures.com/view-agenda, p. 4.

27. Sony Salzman, "From the start, Black Lives Matter has been about LGBTQ lives," ABC News, June 21, 2020, https://abcnews.go.com/US/start-black-lives-matter -lgbtq-lives/story?id=71320450.

28. M4BL, "Economic Justice," https://m4bl.org/policy-platforms/economic -justice/.

29. Joseph Pisani, "Black Lives Matter backs Amazon union push in Alabama," *PBS News Hour*, March 12, 2021, https://www.pbs.org/newshour/economy/black-lives -matter-backs-amazon-union-push-in-alabama.

30. Errin Haines Whack, "Black Lives Matter joining forces with minimum wage activists for nationwide protests," *Chicago Tribune*, March 24, 2017, https://www .chicagotribune.com/nation-world/ct-black-lives-matter-minimum-wage-activists -20170324-story.html.

31. "Agenda to Build Black Futures," 2.

32. Keeanga-Yamahtta Taylor, *From #BlackLivesMatter to Black Liberation* (Chicago: Haymarket Books, 2016), 183.

33. Anthea Butler, *White Evangelical Racism: The Politics of Morality in America* (Chapel Hill: University of North Carolina Press, 2021), 11.

34. John MacArthur et al., "The Statement on Social Justice & the Gospel,"

https://statementonsocialjustice.com/, produced in 2018. The quotation is from the introduction of the statement.

35. Ibid., Section I, Scripture.

36. Ibid., Section V, Sin.

37. Ibid., Section VIII, The Church.

38. Ibid., Section X, Sexuality and Marriage.

39. Ibid., Section XII, Race/Ethnicity.

40. Ibid., Section XIV, Racism.

41. Emma Green, "The Unofficial Racism Consultants to the White Evangelical World," *The Atlantic*, July 5, 2020. Pastor Philip Pinckney reflects on white evangelical resistance to racial equality and wariness of social justice.

42. J. D. Greear (June 11, 2020). "A portion of my SBC address was clipped and taken out of context. Watch the full comment below. To be clear, The Summit Church and I do not endorse the BLM organization though we proudly say Black lives MATTER. Because they do, and our gospel demands we acknowledge that." (Facebook update). Retrieved from https://www.facebook.com/pastorgreear/videos /292847851843579.

43. Samuel Smith, "Joel Osteen: George Floyd's death was a 'turning point,' 'ignited something in me.'" *The Christian Post*, June 9, 2020, https://www .christianpost.com/news/joel-osteen-george-floyds-death-was-a-turning-point-ignited -something-in-me.html.

44. Ibid., 1:43.

45. Richard Land, "A Southern Baptist leader's response to the Black Lives Matter movement," *The Tennessean*, August 20, 2020, https://www.tennessean.com/story /opinion/2020/08/20/southern-baptist-leader-richard-land-response-black-lives-matter -movement/5616017002/.

46. Michelle Oyakawa, "Racial Reconciliation as a Suppressive Frame in Evangelical Multiracial Churches," *Sociology of Religion* 80, no. 4 (Winter 2019): 496–517.

47. Ibid., 498.

48. One consequence of this divide in Black church participation in direct action during the civil rights movement was the failed takeover attempt by Martin Luther King Jr., Gardner Taylor, and others of the National Baptist Convention, led by president J. H. Jackson, in 1961. See Taylor Branch, *Parting the Waters: America in the King Years 1954–63* (New York: Simon and Schuster, 1988), 500–7.

49. Kandia Johnson, "Co-Founder of Black Lives Matter Talks Misconceptions and Plans for 2018," *Black Enterprise*, February 12, 2018, https://www.blackenterprise .com/co-founder-black-lives-matter-talks-blm-misconceptions-plans-2018/. See also Barbara Ransby's reflection on the false charge of Black Lives Matter being leaderless. "Ella Taught Me: Shattering the Myth of the Leaderless Movement," *Colorlines*, June 12, 2015, https://www.colorlines.com/articles/ella-taught-me -shattering-myth-leaderless-movement.

50. Tim Lloyd, "Young Demonstrators Demand To Be Heard; Monday Begins

with Early-Morning Games and Silent March," *St. Luis Public Radio*, October 13, 2014, https://news.stlpublicradio.org/government-politics-issues/2014–10–13/young-demonstrators-demand-to-be-heard-monday-begins-with-early-morning-games-and-silent-march. The disruption was also featured in a documentary about the Ferguson uprising. See *Whose Streets?*, directed by Sabaah Foylayan and Damon Davis (New York: Magnolia Pictures, 2017). The moment discussed starts at the 49:40 mark.

51. Francis, Chapter 2, loc 459.

52. Sarah Van Gelder, "Rev. Sekou on Today's Civil Rights Leaders: 'I Take My Orders From 23-Year-Old Queer Women.'" *Yes! Magazine*, July 22, 2015, https://www.yesmagazine.org/social-justice/2015/07/22/black-lives-matter-s-favorite-minister-reverend-sekou-young-queer.

53. Bill Hutchinson, Stephanie Walsh, and Sabina Ghebremedhin, "Breonna Taylor shooting case: Hankison indicted on wanton endangerment of neighbors," ABC News, September 23, 2020, https://abcnews.go.com/US/grand-jury-set-announce-decision-breonna-taylor-police/story?id=73165512. One officer was indicted for firing his gun without a line of sight, but no one was held accountable for killing Taylor.

54. Claire Galofaro, "Inside the church at the heart of the Louisville's Breonna Taylor protests," Religion News Service, October 22, 2020, https://religionnews.com/2020/10/22/inside-the-church-at-the-heart-of-the-louisvilles-breonna-taylor-protests/.

PART III

Migration, Labor Movements, and Islam

7
Caught in the Crosshairs

Muslims and Migration

Zayn Kassam

In a response to the rise of Trumpism in the United States prior to the 2016 election, during which time Donald Trump made a campaign promise to ban all Muslim migration to the United States,[1] journalist Rhonda Roumani (qtd. by Uri Friedman, 2016 in *The Atlantic*) wrote:

> If Donald Trump's ban had been in effect over the last several decades, America would have missed out on Steve Jobs, whose biological father, Andulfattah Jandali, hailed from Syria. Also Farooq Kathwari, the CEO of Ethan Allen, Mohamed El-Erian, the former head of the investment company Pimco, and Tariq Farid, the founder of Edible Arrangements. Fazlur Khan, a Bangladeshi American architect and structural engineer who helped develop the technology for skyscrapers, would never have made it to the United States. The same goes for Ayub Khan Ommaya, a Pakistani American doctor who created the Ommaya reservoir, a catheter that drains fluid from the head and spine, and Ahmed Zewail, an Egyptian American Nobel Prize winner in chemistry who pioneered the field of "femtochemistry," which enables the study of chemical reactions in real time. Sabri Ben-Achour of Marketplace recently estimated that banning Muslims could cost the U.S. economy roughly $24 billion.[2]

She could also have mentioned a Turkish immigrant named Hamdi Ulukaya who created Chobani yogurt. Ulukaya recently gave his employees ten percent of his company's stock, translating into $150,000 for the average employee, and over a million dollars for the longest serving employees.[3] More recently, Murad Ajani from Houston was awarded The Points of Light award created by five former U.S. presidents for recruiting more than 2,500 volunteers from the Ismaili Muslim community to volunteer a total of 13,000 hours of service evacuating and restoring the greater Houston area devastated by Hurricane Harvey.[4] The positive difference Muslim migrants have made in their host societies is often forgotten in the climate of fear surrounding immigrants that has become the norm in Europe and North America.

Rather than focusing on the many contributions of migrants to their host societies, the dominant narrative around migrants is exemplified by Donald Trump, who began his campaign against migrants and Muslims in his pre-election campaign promises, when he called for surveillance of Muslim migrants and warned about "the 'horrendous' results of Syrian refugees flowing into Europe."[5] Such comments have been followed by a series of policy initiatives: a tightening of U.S. borders through several initiatives including but not limited to the construction of a wall between the U.S. and Mexican border; the refusal of entry, detention, and criminalization of asylum seekers that has led to the heart-wrenching separation of children from their parents; and a severe reduction in the numbers of refugees allowed to enter the United States each year, the lowest in almost thirty years.[6]

Factors Driving Migration

It is essential to consider larger global factors that drive migration in order to understand what pushes migrants to come to our countries and develop a better understanding of the struggles they face. The first factor is economic globalization. The current global economic regime of market neoliberalism can perhaps be traced back to the post–World War II Bretton Woods conference in which representatives of the forty-four Allied nations agreed to open markets and remove obstacles to international trade. This neoliberal form of capitalism was further strengthened by the Washington Consensus, consisting of ten policy recommendations promoted by Washington-based institutions such as the International Monetary Fund, the World Bank, and the U.S. Department of Treasury. These recommendations promote wealth creation through a global economic system that is predicated on dismantling barriers to corporate activity and free trade, the search for and control over finite resources including those that are essential for life, the relentless search for markets and consumers to fill those markets, and the insatiable pursuit of energy sources that will allow the global capitalist machine to continue to function.

Despite the promises made by neoliberal capitalism to raise the standard of living for all through privatization, open markets, reduced trade barriers, and the free flow of goods into ever-consumptive markets, the reality is that a few already wealthy people around the globe have become even wealthier. A 2019 study notes that in the world as a whole, "the bottom half of adults account for less than 1 percent of total global wealth in mid-2019, while the richest decile (top 10 percent of adults) possesses 82 percent of global wealth and top percentile alone owns nearly half (45 percent) of all household assets."[7]

In relation to globalization, a variety of factors or "drivers" lead to migration. For instance, *preexisting* factors create a context in which migration is more likely, such as globalization, environmental changes, urbanization, and demographic transformation. *Proximate* factors include downturns related to economics, security, human rights, and climate change. As Van Hear, Bakewell, and Long note, there are certain *precipitating* factors that trigger departure such as financial collapse, unemployment, or a downturn in social services including health, education, and welfare. Persecution, disputed citizenship, or outbreak of war, as well as environmental disasters can also be precipitating factors, while *mediating* factors comprise available transport and resources in order to make the migration. All these factors "shape the conditions, circumstances, or environment within which people make choices whether to move or stay put, or have such decisions thrust upon them."[8] In considering how we treat migrants, understanding such factors can help us consider the contexts from which migrants are led to leave their places of origin—rarely an easy decision—to come to areas of the world where they may not be readily welcomed. Additionally, each of these factors identifies economics as a component in driving migration, suggesting that economic globalization is a key element in facilitating the growth of wealth for a few, but a climate of insecurity for far more. Migrants may not understand the larger global economic forces at work that cause economic and social injustice for them, but they certainly feel their effects.

Returning to the larger issue of neoliberal market capitalism, incessant economic growth, considered to be the benchmark of a thriving economy, is predicated on availability and unimpeded access to energy resources upon which many forms of production depend.

Thus, our interest in the oil-bearing regions of the world, an interest now shared by China and India, is directly tied to the economic growth and the wealth creation promised by neoliberal economic globalization. Without access to energy resources, corporations could not continue their path of economic growth. However, oil is not an infinite resource. The American scientist and Shell oil geologist, Dr. Marion King Hubbert, predicted that U.S. oil would peak in 1972, and global oil supplies would peak in about 2000.[9] This would have been true had the oil embargo of the 1970s not extended global oil reserves for a few more years. The noted Princeton geologist Kenneth

Deffeyes declared that we would reach the peak in 2005,[10] meaning that we would extract conventional oil in increasingly diminishing quantities. The Association for the Study of Peak Oil and Gas (ASPO) moved the peak to 2010. Peak oil anxieties have abated due to the increase in production from non-conventional oil sources, leading the United States to lower its petroleum imports and increase its exports in the decade between 2009 and 2019.[11] Despite this, the United States continues to import close to ten million barrels per day, of which about 45 percent comes from OPEC and Persian Gulf countries. In addition, China and India, two countries whose elites have benefited immensely from globalization, have joined the industrialized world in their consumption of energy to fuel their economic growth. As Michael Klare notes, competition for energy resources means that the United States increasingly expends American military, political, and economic resources to preserve its access to worldwide energy supplies, which "will require an ever-increasing payment in American blood."[12]

Thus, the political, military, and foreign policy interventions stemming in part from concerns about energy security all have a role to play in fueling migration instigated by the wars and conflicts in the last four decades: the Iran-Iraq war; the Gulf Wars; the interventions in Afghanistan and Iraq; and the conflicts in Chechnya, Xinjiang, the Sudan, and Nigeria, to name just a few. However, there is another factor: military action. Along with the pursuit of energy resources to fuel neoliberal economic growth, Schwartz argues, with others, that military interventions are extensions of neoliberal economic globalization aimed at "'opening' otherwise resistant economies to multinational trade and capital investment."[13] He further argues that in the Iraq and Afghanistan wars, the role of the military enacted neoliberal reforms. To this we might add that the unintended consequences of wars driven in part by neoliberal economic imperatives are dislocation and increased migration for migrants, refugees, and asylum seekers. Some would argue that the politics around the pursuit of energy resources plays a role in creating and fueling militant movements. The claim is that such groups seek to capitalize upon the political and economic destabilization brought about by conflict, thereby consolidating their power over resource-rich territories on the one hand, and on attacks in Western countries aimed at striking terror at the heart of the new global economic empire on the other.[14] Indeed, very few media analysts have focused on ISIS/ISIL/Daesh's capture of oil fields and hydroelectric power plants in Iraq and Syria in 2014. Dubbed the "black gold feeding the black flag," the captures of these fields and plants, along with the civil war in Syria, have led and continue to lead to the displacement of over half of Syria's population. Many of these people are internally displaced, and as many who have fled its borders to seek refuge elsewhere. A UNHCR report notes that Syrians are the largest forcibly displaced population today, with 13 million Syrians displaced, of whom just over 6.5 million are refugees, 6 million are internally displaced, and 140,000 are asylum seekers.[15]

Construction of the Muslim Other

Concomitant with the militant activity that arises from both Western and Muslim-majority societies in trying to establish control over and/or guaranteed access to energy resources (and opening markets for capitalist intervention) is the alarming rhetoric—and policy enactments—that echoes a colonial-era discourse on and governance of the Other. During the colonial era, as has been explored and argued so compellingly by Edward Said and others, a narrative of the Islamic Other was generated. This narrative put forth the idea of a civilizing mission on the part of British and European colonial powers, coupled with a sense of noblesse oblige, that largely masked the massive transfer of wealth taking place from the colonized nations to the center of empire. Perhaps this narrative is best illustrated in the words of Lord Cromer, British consul-general to Egypt during the British occupation, who stated in the early 1900s that Egyptians should "be persuaded or forced into imbibing the true spirit of western civilization," and, therefore, "it was essential to change the position of women in Islam, for it was Islam's degradation of women, expressed in the practices of veiling and seclusion, that was 'the fatal obstacle' to the Egyptian's 'attainment of that elevation of thought and character which should accompany the introduction of Western civilization'; only by abandoning those practices might they attain 'the mental and moral development that he [Cromer] desired for them.'"[16] Cromer advanced these views while he cut back on schooling for both boys and girls, thereby curtailing the very advancement of civilization he desired for both Egyptian men and women. Ironically, while he blamed Islam for degrading women, he also was the founding member and onetime president of the Men's League for Opposing the Suffrage of Women in England, suggesting that the advancement of women was not among the list of his priorities. This little bit of history demonstrates that what we today call "Islamophobia" actually has a long history going back to colonization, and before that to the Crusades, and before that to the Greco-Peloponnesian wars, predating the terrible events of September 11, 2001, on American soil that ostensibly gave rise to what has been called the Global War on Terror. What is to be noted for our purposes is that Islamophobia has created a rhetoric of the Other in need of civilization in the colonial era, and in need of democracy in the current era, and that the evidence offered to justify the need to civilize the Other is most readily found in how Muslims treat women. And because Muslims are portrayed as inherently violent, military interventions are rendered essential in order to keep the world safe from Muslim violent extremism. Thus, one may ask whether an analogy can be made between the pursuit of resources during the colonial era and its accompanying construction of a rhetoric of the Other, and the pursuit of energy resources in our contemporary era and the accompanying construction of a rhetoric of fear and suspicion of the Muslim Other.

Compounding the generation of Islamophobia in the United States, a 2013 report titled *Fear, Inc.*, published by the Center for American Progress Action Fund, argues that there is a small but influential group of misinformation experts influencing Americans to believe that Muslims are terrorists; that people who practice Islam are a threat to national security; and that Sharia law is a threat to Americans and to democracy in general. The hate and fear of Muslims peddled by such organizations is undergirded by funding to the tune of some $42 million received between 2001 and 2009.[17] A report from *The Guardian* names seventy-four core groups contributing to generating prejudice or hatred of Islam and Muslims in the United States. "The core group, which includes the Abstraction Fund, Clarion Project, David Horowitz Freedom Center, Middle East Forum, American Freedom Law Center, Center for Security Policy, Investigative Project on Terrorism, Jihad Watch and Act! for America, had access to almost $206m of funding between 2008 and 2013" (para. 3) and their efforts have real consequences, seen most readily in attacks on Muslims, whether victims were mistaken to be Muslim or not, and attacks on mosques, with seventy-eight attacks on mosques recorded in 2015 alone (para. 13). One organization has gone so far as to create the Thin Blue Line Project—a database of all Muslim student associations, mosques, and Islamic institutions—labeling them as "suspected national security concerns" (para. 12).[18] They have been able to generate reports that are read by politicians and security experts, while their blogs and TV appearances expose the public to such misinformation. For instance, Newt Gingrich, in a speech made to the American Enterprise Institute, having read one of these reports, noted that Islamic or Sharia law was "a mortal threat to the survival of freedom in the United States and in the world as we know it."[19] He was basing his comments on a report written by Andrew McCarthy at the Center for Security Policy, who called sharia "the preeminent security threat of our time."[20]

Rabbi Bruce Warshal, in a piece directed at rabbis published in the *Sun Sentinel* on January 23, 2013, reports that "78 bills or amendments aimed at interfering with Islamic religious practices were considered in 31 states and the U.S. Congress. Of these, 73 bills were introduced by Republicans . . .

Most of these bills were aimed at outlawing Sharia law (comparable to Jewish Halacha), a non-existent problem. . . . Yet six states actually passed anti-Sharia laws—Arizona, Kansas, South Dakota, Tennessee, Oklahoma and Louisiana" (1, para. 6). Warshal continued: "Sixty-two of the above 78 referenced anti-Muslim laws were based on David Yerushalmi's American Laws for American Courts (ALAC) model legislation" (1, para. 9). In a courageous call-out of his fellow Jews, Warshal names Pamela Geller, Steven Emerson, Daniel Pipes, and David Horowitz, citing their mistaken belief that "delegitimizing Islam somehow helps Israel in its conflict with Palestinians" (1, para. 3) and exhorts rabbinic and lay leaders to break out of their silence and preach "against anti-Muslim hatred from the pulpit" (2, para. 5).[21] The Southern Poverty Law Center claims that "Since 2010, 201 anti-Sharia law bills have been introduced in 43 states. In 2017 alone, 14 states introduced an anti-Sharia law bill, with Texas and Arkansas enacting the legislation."[22] These efforts supplement the larger process of "othering" Muslims in relation to the global economy's search for energy resources by amplifying political Zionist concerns about Muslim presence in the United States, and Christian Zionists who see their efforts to Christianize the Middle East and to return all Jews to Israel as a necessary part of their premillennial teleology.[23]

The Racialization of Muslims

Thus far, I have described some of the structural dynamics that cause migration and analyzed some of the rhetoric surrounding Muslims in order to indicate what kind of reception Muslim migrants can expect in their Western host countries. In addition to deliberate efforts to "delegitimize Islam," Cainkar examines the larger question of racial ideologies in the United States to argue that racism is not simply an ideological phenomenon. Rather, it is accompanied by racial structures that "are identified through laws, policies, and concrete micro and macro level practices."[24] Cainkar traces the increased racialization of Arab Americans, once considered marginally white, back to the 1967 Israeli conquest of parts of Palestine, Egypt, Lebanon, and Syria and the subsequent activism on the part of Arab Americans to counter U.S. policies in the region and Israeli dispossession of Palestinian lands and residency rights. This resulted in both governmental and civil society efforts "to actively silence Arab Americans, censor information, curtail their organizing efforts, and deny them a political voice. These actors intentionally deployed racialized constructions of Arabs as the ideological component of their strategy, constructing a race-making narrative of inherent threat and barbarism in a 'process of "othering"' to justify the coercive structural components of the project."[25]

Such "racialization" of Arab Americans, Cainkar argues, was then extended to Muslims/Middle Easterners following the Iranian Revolution of 1979 and the hostage situation at the site of the U.S. Embassy in Tehran. At the same time, "the Reagan Administration was bankrolling the idea of jihad, paying hundreds of millions for the recruitment of tens of thousands of foot soldiers, especially low-wage workers from the Arab world, to be armed and trained in Pakistan to fight the Soviets in Afghanistan."[26] Significantly, the ideological constructions in media coverage about Muslims/Middle Easterners were now extended to Iranians, while at the same time the structural policies of the administration instrumentalized such ideological constructions for its own war against the Soviets within the framework of the Cold War. The racialization of such "brown" bodies—which now included South Asians—dovetails with the white nationalist project for whom the threat represented by non-white and Muslim bodies justifies the ongoing surveillance of such bodies through the ideological frameworks and structural practices that were generated by the post–9/11 War on Terror.

The tactics of surveillance and classification and the production of racial difference are woven into the fabric of capitalism and the nation state. In coining the concept of racial capitalism, Cedric J. Robinson argued that the production of racial difference was essential to allow capitalism to survive through the exploitation of slave labor.[27] Michel Foucault takes this concept a step further in positing the view that the modern nation state deploys bio-power to identify and place under surveillance those parts of itself that it considers healthy, and those that it considers unhealthy and thus a threat to the common good. Couched as liberalism, in order for the nation state to generate and accumulate wealth, it has to produce delinquency, or racialization, for "The first function of racism: [is] to fragment, to create caesuras within the biological continuum addressed by bio-power"[28] so as to separate the useful from those who are useless or dangerous—or lacking in human capital. The neoliberal discourse of the Chicago School elevated the market as the foundation and regulating mechanism for the state and social relations. Consequently, race becomes primarily an economic category, and "gets increasingly associated with a normative economic deficiency—an unwillingness to work and properly reap the fruits of labor as becoming one's human capital,"[29] the failure of which is punished. Once a population, such as Muslims, is racialized and viewed as potentially posing a threat, then, as Clough and Willse note, the "deployment of a population racism in neoliberalism functions in a field of many populations, all of which are differently targeted for manipulation through technical solutions . . . Technical solutions have been made ordinary practice in neoliberalism, where economy and governance together have had as their primary function the evaluation and management of risk through processes of technically supported calculation, digitization especially. . . . Here population racism also plays an important part in producing affect, as, for example, it circulates fear along with statistical profiles of populations, providing neoliberalism with a rhetoric of motive in the process of political branding."[30]

Refugee and Migration Policies

Considered the worst humanitarian crisis in this past decade, the Syrian civil war has subjected a little over half of Syria's pre-war population, about 12.5 million people, to forced dislocation or death, according to humanitarian organizations and the United Nations.

On September 11, 2015, news broke that President Obama had cleared the way for 10,000 Syrian refugees to be admitted to the United States.[31] Under President Obama, the quota for refugees was set at 110,000 refugees. Syrian refugees living in refugee camps are registered by the U.N. High Commissioner for Refugees, which then refers them to countries such as the United States for resettlement. The U.S. State Department then prescreens each case file for eligibility for refugee status, after which the officials from the Department of Homeland Security fly to refugee camps to conduct interviews with candidates. Each case file is also "reviewed by the National Counterterrorism Center, the FBI's terrorist screening center, the DHS, the Department of Defense and 'other agencies' . . . (r)efugees are subject to the highest level of security checks of any category of traveler to the United States. . . ."[32]

Once approved, the United States pays the International Organization for Migration to fly refugees to the United States. They are then met by non-government resettlement agencies contracted by the State Department and flown to one of 180 resettlement centers around the country connected to one of the nine national resettlement agencies. After 90 days the refugees are no longer eligible for State Department–funded support disbursed through the resettlement agencies, and local groups work with resettlement agencies to continue the effort in resettling refugees.

Under the Trump administration, the ceiling for refugees to be admitted to the United States was lowered from the 110,000 set by the Obama administration for 2016 to 50,000 in 2017, 45,000 in 2018, and 30,000 in 2019. The real number for those admitted in 2017 was 53,716, while in 2018 the number fell to 22,491, well short of the ceiling, and in 2019, 29,916 refugees were admitted.[33] The ceiling for 2020 was set at 18,000, even as the number of refugees in the world is the highest it has been since World War II. Eleven of the twenty-eight agencies that receive federal funding to resettle refugees have been shuttered as a result. As noted by the Migration Policy Institute,

> the Trump administration has significantly lowered the admissions ceiling each year and suspended the resettlement program for 120 days in 2017 to review and strengthen vetting procedures. The Department of Homeland Security (DHS) announced additional screening for nationals of 11 high-risk countries in January 2018. These countries were never officially delineated but are believed to be Egypt, Iran, Iraq, Libya, Mali, North Korea, Somalia, South Sudan, Sudan, Syria, and Yemen. Refugee admissions from these countries fell from 43 percent of all refugee resettlement in FY 2017 to 3 percent in FY 2018.[34]

In addition, the Trump administration instituted "the Muslim Ban," beginning with Executive Order 13780, dated March 6, 2017, in which entry into the United States by nationals of Iran, Libya, Somalia, Sudan, Syria, and Yemen was suspended.[35]

After two Presidential Proclamations, the first of which removed Sudan from the list and added Chad, North Korea, and Venezuela, and the second of which removed Chad, the Supreme Court upheld the Executive Order and allowed the travel ban to go into effect on December 4, 2017. Despite multiple challenges, the Supreme Court sided with the government in a ruling handed down on June 26, 2018, allowing what has been termed Travel Ban 3.0 to remain indefinitely.[36] Such language clearly follows the logic of population racism. First, it identifies terrorism as a threat to the security of the nation. Second, it identifies the citizens of several Muslim-majority nations as embodying such a threat. Third, it raises fears among the U.S. population that members of these nations, even if already in the United States, are always a threat to the safety of the United States. In addition to the additional scrutiny of migrants from the countries named in the Executive Order and the two subsequent Presidential Proclamations, the Pew Research Center reports that there has also been a drop-off in Muslim migrants admitted to the United States. As further evidence of population racism, 79 percent or 23,800 of the refugees admitted in 2019, were Christian, with the remaining 4,900 comprising Muslims and other groups. This is in comparison to 2016, when 38,900 Muslims were admitted, along with 37,500 Christians.[37]

Faith and Civic Community Responses

The question that follows is: How are faith and civic communities to respond? Is it possible to espouse a politics of compassion and empathy to address the politics of fear that are currently holding our societies in their grasp?

As a case in point, I would now like to turn to efforts in my area to help with refugee resettlement. A local pastor of the Presbyterian church in Pomona, California, asked the question, "What does it mean to love my neighbor?" and he reached out to someone in the Claremont Presbyterian Church. Together, they decided to form a refugee resettlement team, later known as RR1, drawn from members of both churches. They contacted IRIS, the Interfaith Refugee and Immigration Service in Los Angeles, a local affiliate of Episcopal Migration Ministries, which is one of the nine national resettlement agencies. IRIS called RR1 and told them a Syrian refugee family was on its way, and after a 4–5 hour wait at Los Angeles International airport on August 10, 2016, the refugee family emerged: a man, his wife, and their four children, ranging in age from 20 to 4. Then began the hard work of finding housing for them. The Pomona church loaned them an apartment attached to the church in the short term, enrolled the kids in school, and signed up the parents and the eldest son (who was no longer at school) for ESL classes. They also took them to medical appointments to fulfill all the health check and vaccination requirements for all refugees, got them social security numbers, and applied for Refugee Cash Assistance, CalWORKs aid for families, food stamps, and health insurance. An apartment was found with great difficulty, as landlords will not rent to people who cannot show evidence of income, utilities, and other services. The local mosque got them a car, but then there was the issue of procuring a driver's license for both the son and the father: easier for the son with his rudimentary English, but harder for the father who speaks but cannot read Arabic and has no knowledge of English.

The volunteers who spent countless hours sorting out all these issues and driving them and the school-age children to school, their multiple medical appointments, and grocery shopping said that their work was a response to the question of how do we love our neighbor. It was also a way to address the Syrian humanitarian crisis, helping a migrant to find their way into a welcoming community, and doing something to address Islamophobia. The Claremont Presbyterian Church held a musical fundraiser featuring a Christian Palestinian musician and a West African musician, with several Syrian refugee families present. Out of that event, several other community members got together to form RR2, or refugee resettlement team 2, and they have taken on the task of welcoming and settling several families, partnering with other resettlement groups in the area. A member of a group in Riverside who teaches ESL classes came up with the idea of starting friendship circles for refugee women and children and local women to facilitate the building of friendships while also learning English. Doing so humanizes the refugees in the eyes of those who come to know them and goes a long way in combatting Islamophobia as they share stories of their life experiences and struggles and joys. Another local group of women founded Claremont Canopy: Helping Refugees Thrive. They connected with Miry's List in Los Angeles, founded by Miry Whitehall who organizes the New Arrival Supper Club, aimed at empowering "newly settled refugees with unique opportunities to earn money, meet their new communities and share their culture through food."[38] One of the families that cooked for Miry's list was none other than the one welcomed by RR1 fifteen months before in August 2016. This family was asked to cater a traditional Syrian breakfast for the Los Angeles screening of Ai Weiwei's documentary on the global refugee crisis, *Human Flow*—a film whose intent was captured by the reporter, Deborah Vankin, as being "to humanize refugees."[39] Through the efforts of those who have laid aside their fear and suspicion to exercise an ethic of compassion, this family and others are finding their way, and yet challenges remain in the medium and long term.

Such work has continued in the years since 2016 when the pastor in Pomona, California, found himself asking the question that led to the formation of RR1. However, several developments in the securitization of borders have greatly exacerbated the challenges faced by migrants and helping organizations alike.

Along with such cuts came the detention of asylum seekers, and the separation of families. The National Immigrant Justice Center notes, "Since 2017, the federal government has unleashed relentless attacks on the U.S. asylum system and against the people who seek safety within our borders. Internal memos have revealed these efforts to be concerted, organized, and implemented toward the goal of ending asylum in the United States."[40]

Although initially announced in 2017, Attorney General Jeff Sessions formally authorized the "zero-tolerance" policy in April 2018. In essence, the policy treated all attempts to cross the border other than at checkpoints not as a civil case (as was most often the case under 8 USC Section 1182, which housed those caught crossing illegally in Customs and Border Protection [CPB] Facilities, into which minors were allowed), but as a criminal case under 8 USC Section 1325A, which housed those caught in a Bureau of Prisons (BP) Detention Facility, at which minors were not allowed.[41] This change has led to the separation of 5,460 children from their families since July 2017, according to some estimates.[42] In addition, Migrant Protection Protocols (MPP) were put into effect on January 24, 2019, couched as a "humanitarian approach,"[43] and have thus far forced over 60,000 asylum seekers to wait in Mexico.[44]

As asylum seekers were put into detention camps and separated from their families, a group of people from Pilgrim Place traveled some fifty-seven miles from Claremont to Adelanto Detention Facility to assess the needs of the detainees and find ways to help. The detention facility, a privately owned center in the high desert contracted by Immigration and Customs Enforcement (ICE), has the capacity to hold approximately 2000 detainees. "A surprise government inspection" there "found nooses hanging in cells, misuse of solitary confinement, and delayed medical care . . . findings that inspectors warn pose significant health and safety risks for immigrants held there."[45] Although California's Assembly Bill No. 32 states that after January 1, 2020, ICE may not renew an existing contract with a private, for-profit prison facility, and that no for-profit prison facilities may continue to operate in the state after 2028, "GEO and the Trump administration effectively circumvented the state of California until 2034"[46] by renewing its contract with Adelanto for 15 years on December 20, 2019.[47]

Concerns about the current climate are evident among key activists in Claremont. A student leader of 5C RAN (Refugee Assistance Network), a student-founded and student-run organization at the Claremont Colleges, observed, "I had always felt a strong connection to the history of migration in my family, even though I didn't experience it myself, and I think I saw the plight of refugees as the same thing that my great-grandparents, grandparents, and parents had been through in fleeing anti-Semitism over generations."[48] Such historical memories led Jewish students to give of their time, energy, and knowledge to help others making that journey, creating a bridge across social privilege and the passage of time and generations. And in so doing, how they are viewed changes also:

> One little side effect of the program has been improved interfaith understanding between many of the people we work with and Jews. A lot of our tutors are Jewish, and many of them were the first Jewish people that the people we worked with met. 5C RAN has no religious affiliation, but we end up talking a lot about religious beliefs, mostly because many people who are around the mosque have a special interest in religion. Several of the people we've worked with have had negative opinions about Jews and have changed their minds when faced with Jewish tutors. A man told me once that he used to believe that all Jews were evil, and that meeting me changed his mind, and that was a really powerful moment for me.[49]

One of the people working with the Newcomers Access Center, established when a second Refugee Resettlement group was formed in 2017, reflected on the current climate:

> I worry more about how this situation affects new immigrants, refugees, and asylum seekers. Stoking up racism and xenophobia in the

United States has been done many times throughout our history. It is evil, wrong and hurtful to all in that it creates division between people and weakens our society. This is one of those times in our history. We can work and pray for a change in national leadership that will move us away from this hatred and toward healing of our nation.[50]

One of the members of RR1, when asked about her involvement, had this to say:

I have been working with Syrian refugees since summer 2016. I became interested in refugee resettlement when I learned that a group from Pomona First Presbyterian Church was organizing a team of people to help resettle a Syrian family of 6 who were arriving to Pomona in August. My husband and I have hosted international students from The Claremont Colleges and other international visitors in our home for 40 years so I am always open to interacting with people from other places in the world. However, my primary motivation regarding refugee resettlement was that I was deeply disturbed by the tone and content of the presidential campaign in the spring/summer of 2016, specifically with then-candidate Donald Trump. My soul ached to think that a candidate such as he could actually gain traction in this wonderful nation of ours. I was aware that I needed an antidote to the hatred, lies, bullying, willful ignorance, reprehensible character, etc. that he presented to this country. The chance to do something good, kind and helpful for others who have suffered greatly through no fault of their own was and remains tremendously appealing.[51]

When asked, those who work to resettle such families invariably break down and say how enriched their own lives have become through the encounter, so much so that they are not sure who is being helped.

Concluding Remarks

This chapter has attempted to show that immigrants, refugees, and asylum seekers do not come to the United States to undermine its civil society, institutions, or its democracy. Rather, the larger systemic logics of instability wrought by climate change, environmental degradation, privations brought about by economic globalization, resource wars, as well as hopes for a better future, drive migrants to our borders. This chapter also shows that the climate of fear and suspicion of migrants, especially Muslim migrants, is constructed rather than supported by the actual cases of those who have sought to make America their home and contributed to its flourishing. Alongside the racialization and surveillance of Muslims is the creation of policies intended to keep America white, which is a failing proposition given the multicultural diversity of the nation. More importantly, though, the humanitarian crisis of migration has called forth faith and civic responses that privilege compassion and empathy in embracing pluralism and difference in order to help settle migrants in their new and unfamiliar home. Such responses are part and parcel of the democratic project. They foster inter-communal collaboration as well as civic organization and resistance to injustices that are contrary to American values.

Notes

1. Miriam Valverde, "Trump's travel restrictions survive Supreme Court, fall short of promised Muslim ban," November 14, 2018, https://www.politifact.com/truth-o -meter/promises/trumpometer/promise/1401/establish-ban-muslims-entering-us/.

2. For the *Marketplace* calculation, see Marketplace, "The Cost of Banning All Muslims," http://www.marketplace.org/2016/06/14/world/cost-banning-all-muslims.

3. Stephanie Strom, "At Chobani, Now It's Not Just the Yogurt That's Rich," *New York Times*, April 26, 2016, https://www.nytimes.com/2016/04/27/business/a-windfall -for-chobani-employees-stakes-in-the-company.html?_r=0.

4. See Points of Light press release, "Five Daily Point of Light Awardees to be Honored by Five Former Presidents for Disaster Relief Work," October 17, 2017, https://www.pointsoflight.org/press-releases/five-daily-point-of-light-awardees-to-be -honored-by-five-former-presidents-for-disaster-relief-work/.

5. J. Diamond, "Trump doubles down on calls for mosque surveillance," June 15, 2016, http://www.cnn.com/2016/06/15/politics/donald-trump-muslims-mosque -surveillance/index.html.

6. Natasha Frost, "Not a single refugee was resettled in the U.S. last month," November 3, 2019, https://qz.com/1741113/no-refugees-were-resettled-in-the-us-in -october-2019/.

7. See https://www.credit-suisse.com/about-us/en/reports-research/global-wealth -report.html, 13.

8. Nicholas Van Hear, Oliver Bakewell, and Katy Long, *Drivers of Migration* (2012): 1–43. Presented at the Migrating Out of Poverty Research Programme Consortium, Falmer, Brighton BN1 9QN, United Kingdom: Arts B, University of Sussex. Retrieved from http://migratingoutofpoverty.dfid.gov.uk/files/file.php?name =wp1-drivers-of-migration.pdf&site=354.

9. M. King Hubbert, "Nuclear Energy and the Fossil Fuels," *Resilience*, March 8, 2006, https://www.resilience.org/stories/2006-03-08/nuclear-energy-and-fossil-fuels/.

10. Kenneth S. Deffeyes, *Hubbert's Peak: The Impending World Oil Shortage*, new edition (Princeton: Princeton University Press, 2009), ix.

11. U.S. Energy Information Administration, December 5, 2019, https://www.eia .gov/todayinenergy/detail.php?id=42176.

12. Michael T. Klare, *Blood and Oil: The Dangers and Consequences of America's Growing Petroleum Dependency* (New York: Penguin Books, 2005), 185.

13. Michael Schwartz, "Military Neoliberalism: Endless War and Humanitarian Crisis in the Twenty-First Century," *Sociologists Without Borders / Sociologos Sans Fronteras* 6, no. 3 (2011): 190–303, 197.

14. Patrick Cockburn and Tom Dispatch, "We Have Reached an Age of Disintegration: How Greedy Neoliberalism and Deadly Wars Are Destroying Modern Life," June 28, 2016, https://www.alternet.org/2016/06/too-many-wars-middle-east-and-north-africa/?akid=14393.81723.V19cY5&rd=1&src=newsletter1059189&t=8.

15. UNHCR, Global Trends, *Forced Displacement in 2018*, https://www.unhcr.org/5d08d7ee7.pdf.

16. Leila Ahmed, *Women and Gender in Islam: Historical Roots of a Modern Debate* (New Haven: Yale University Press), 153.

17. Wajahat Ali, Eli Clifton, Matthew Duss, Lee Fang, Scott Keyes, and Faiz Shakir, *Fear, Inc. The Roots of the Islamophobia Network in America* (Center for American Progress, 2011), 15, 129, https://cdn.americanprogress.org/wp-content/uploads/issues/2011/08/pdf/islamophobia.pdf.

18. Halima Kazem, "Funding Islamophobia: $206m went to promoting 'hatred' of American Muslims," June 20, 2016, https://www.theguardian.com/us-news/2016/jun/20/islamophobia-funding-cair-berkeley-report.

19. Ali et al., *Fear, Inc.*, 3.

20. Ibid.

21. Rabbi Bruce Warshal, "A Jewish problem: Anti-Muslim hatemongers," *Sun Sentinel*, January 23, 2013, http://articles.sun-sentinel.com/2013-01-23/opinion/fl-jjps-warshal-0123-20130123_1_anti-muslim-muslim-presence-muslim-man/2.

22. Swathi Shanmugasundaram, "Anti-Sharia law bills in the United States," February 5, 2018, https://www.splcenter.org/hatewatch/2018/02/05/anti-sharia-law-bills-united-states.

23. For Christian Zionism and premillennial dispensationalism, see Samuel Goldman, Introduction to *God's Country: Christian Zionism in America* (Philadelphia: University of Pennsylvania Press, 2018).

24. Louise Cainkar, "Fluid Terror Threat: A Genealogy of the Racialization of Arab, Muslim, and South Asian Americans," *Amerasia Journal* (2018): 27–59, 27.

25. Ibid., 35–36.

26. Ibid., 43.

27. Cedric J. Robinson, *Black Marxism: The Making of the Black Radical Tradition* (Chapel Hill: University of North Carolina Press, 2000).

28. Michel Foucault, *Society Must Be Defended: Lectures at the Collège de France, 1975–1976* (New York: Palgrave, 2003), 255.

29. Vikash Singh, "Race, the Condition of Neo-Liberalism," *Social Sciences* 6: 84 (2017): 1–16, 9, https://www.mdpi.com/2076-0760/6/3/84.

30. Ibid., 50–51.

31. Dave Clark, "How the US plans to welcome 10,000 Syrian Refugees,"

September 11, 2015, https://www.yahoo.com/news/us-plans-welcome-10-000-syrian
-refugees-053252486.html?ref=gs.

32. Ibid.

33. Homeland Security. Retrieved from https://www.dhs.gov/immigration
-statistics/yearbook/2019.

34. Brittany Blizzard and Jeanne Batalova, "Refugees and Asylees in the United
States," June 13, 2019, https://www.migrationpolicy.org/article/refugees-and-asylees
-united-states.

35. Presidential Documents, Executive Order 13780 of March 6, 2017, "Protecting
the Nation From Foreign Terrorist Entry into the United States," *Federal Register*
82:45 (2017), https://upload.wikimedia.org/wikipedia/commons/7/7b/Executive
_Order_13780.pdf.

36. Shoba Sivaprasad Wadhia, "Trump's Travel Ban Two Years Later," January 30,
2019, https://www.acslaw.org/expertforum/trumps-travel-ban-two-years-later/.

37. Jens Manuel Krogstad, "Key facts about refugees to the U.S.," October 7, 2019,
https://www.pewresearch.org/fact-tank/2019/10/07/key-facts-about-refugees-to-the-u-s/.

38. https://www.miryslist.org/events/.

39. Deborah Vankin, "Why Ai Weiwei was compelled to take on the global
refugee crisis in his new documentary," October 6, 2017, http://www.latimes.com
/entertainment/arts/la-ca-mn-ai-weiwei-human-flow-20171006-htmlstory.html.

40. National Immigrant Justice Center, "A Timeline of the Trump
Administration's Efforts to End Asylum," https://www.immigrantjustice.org/issues
/asylum-seekers-refugees. See also Anne Flaherty and Quinn Owen, "Leaked memo
shows Trump administration weighed separating families at border, Sen. Merkley
wants Nielsen investigated for perjury," January 18, 2019, https://abcnews.go.com
/Politics/leaked-memo-shows-trump-administration-weighed-separating-families
/story?id=60459972.

41. Talk by Jed Leano, "Southern Border Crisis: US Policy and the UN
Convention on Refugees," November 19, 2109, Claremont, Calif.

42. Associated Press, "More than 5,400 children split at border, according to new
count," October 25, 2019, https://www.nbcnews.com/news/us-news/more-5-400
-children-split-border-according-new-count-n1071791.

43. Homeland Security, "Migrant Protection Protocols," January 24, 2019, https://
www.dhs.gov/news/2019/01/24/migrant-protection-protocols.

44. RAICES: The Refugee and Immigration Center, Action: "You Can Help Stop
MPP," November 20, 2019, https://www.raicestexas.org/2019/11/20/you-can-help-stop
-mpp/?ms=20191223_newsletter.

45. Catherine E. Shoichet, "Inspectors found nooses hanging in cells at an
ICE detention facility," October 3, 2018, https://www.cnn.com/2018/10/03/politics
/immigrant-detention-adelanto-oig-report/index.html.

46. Tom Dreisbach, "Despite Findings of 'Negligent' Care, ICE to expand
Troubled Calif. Detention Center," January 15, 2020, https://www.npr.org/2020/01/15

/794660949/despite-findings-of-negligent-care-ice-to-expand-troubled-calif-detention
-center.

47. Businesswire Press Release, "The GEO Group Signs Contracts with U.S.
Immigration and Customs Enforcement for Five Facilities in California Totaling
4,490 Beds," December 23, 2019, https://www.businesswire.com/news/home
/20191223005099/en/.

48. Email communication from NK, January 20, 2020. Authors have been
assigned initials for reasons of privacy.

49. Ibid.

50. Communication from JH, January 12, 2020.

51. Communication from BH, January 9, 2020.

8

Iftars, Prayer Rooms, and #DeleteUber

Postsecularity and the Promise/Perils of Muslim Labor Organizing

C. Melissa Snarr

On January 28, 2017, the newly inaugurated United States president issued one of his first executive orders: a temporary freeze on all refugee resettlement for one hundred and twenty days, an indefinite freeze on Syrian refugees, and a ninety-day travel ban on persons from seven majority-Muslim countries. Across the nation, protesters mounted rallies and lawyers rushed to airports to volunteer support to affected travelers. In New York City, the primarily Muslim and Sikh immigrant New York Taxi Workers Alliance (NYTWA) took their own symbolic action. Within hours, these low-wage workers coordinated a work stoppage by yellow cab, green cab, and black car drivers and refused to pick up fares from the John F. Kennedy International Airport from 6 to 7 P.M. that Saturday evening.[1] The action was press-worthy in and of itself, but when Uber, the ride-hailing company, announced on Twitter that it was dropping its surge pricing at that time, supporters of the taxi drivers interpreted the action as "scabbing," or directly undercutting/crossing a picket line. They launched a social media campaign #DeleteUber, and within a week over two hundred thousand users did just that. Uber eventually apologized for their actions and promised a three-million-dollar legal defense fund to support drivers affected by the executive order.[2] In the face of daunting federal power, the NYTWA and its allies literally stopped traffic at one of the busiest airports in the world and interrupted business as usual in the boardroom of one of the fastest growing companies in the nation.

The actions of both the new president and of the NYTWA demonstrate the postsecularity of current U.S. politics and some labor organizing. The increased presence and persecution of Muslim low-wage workers in the United States invites us to consider not only the ways in which secularization in the

United States is empirically complex, but also how—what I term—"selective secularism" discourses have supported the merging of certain Christian and free market ideologies over time, much to the detriment of minority religious communities. Understanding how these dynamics ostracize Muslim low-wage workers better positions activists and allies to advocate for new forms of worker justice organizing. In the end, only by disrupting these secularist discourses and emphasizing intersectional organizing that includes religious identity will unions and related forms of organized labor be able to meet the needs of non-Christian immigrants and refugees.

The Presence and Persecution of Muslim Low-Wage Workers

Currently, Muslims make up only one percent of the U.S. population; however, they are the fastest growing religious community in the United States, and the Pew Research Center predicts Muslims will represent two percent of the population by 2050, surpassing Jews as the second largest religious constituency in the United States.[3] Approximately fifty-eight percent of U.S. Muslims are immigrants and roughly fifty-six percent of those Muslims have arrived since 2000.[4] These immigrants (many of whom are refugees) enter a political economy that favors the wealthy elite, hollows out the middle class, increases the number of working poor, and is structured by systemic race- and ethno-centrism.

We see this interstructuring of race/ethnicity, religion, and class in at least two areas: the divided economic distribution of U.S. Muslims and the disproportionate number of federal Equal Employment Opportunity Commission (EEOC) cases they endure. Economically, Muslim Americans are a decidedly bifurcated community. Although U.S. Muslims are, on average, more highly educated than the general public, their educational attainment does not mirror a similar economic attainment. U.S. Muslims are as likely as the general population to report a household income in excess of $100,000, but they are 10 percent less likely to report incomes in the "middle class"—or between $30,000 and $99,000 (35 versus 45 percent)—and are more likely to report a household income below $30,000 than the general population (40 versus 32 percent).[5] A greater percentage of Muslims also consider themselves underemployed (29 to 12 percent) than the general U.S. population as they struggle in part-time, low-wage jobs.[6] Although a wealthy Muslim elite certainly exists in the United States, the majority of Muslim Americans could be considered working poor, and these economic struggles cut across demographics in terms of national origin, age, and ethnicity.[7]

Even before they can secure a job, many Muslim candidates often expe-

rience discrimination. As information management scholars Alessandro Acquisti and Christina Fong's research shows, when the social media profiles of
job applicants include religiously identifiable information, Muslim job applicants in Republican-dominated counties had a 13 percent lower callback rate
than Christian candidates.[8] The scholars submitted job applications to 4,000
employers while simultaneously creating related social media identities with
varied personal information (for example, pictures in a hijab or posting about
a religious holiday). While there was no notable difference in invitations for
interviews based on persons who identified as gay or straight in their social
media profiles, they found a significant difference based on religious identity
in Republican-dominated counties (the same was not true in Democratic-
majority counties).

Once employed, Muslims face a disproportionate amount of discrimination
in the workplace. While only 0.8 percent of the adult U.S. population identifies as Muslim, in 2017 around 23 percent of all religious-based discrimination
charges were related to Muslim identity during this time.[9] In the ten years
after September 11, 2001, the EEOC saw a 250 percent increase in cases related
to employment discrimination against Muslims.[10] In that decade, the EEOC
pursued 90 related lawsuits against companies and increased their efforts on
educating employers and employees about the workplace rights of Muslims.[11]
Under the Obama administration, the EEOC also added a new priority area
in its *Strategic Enforcement Plan* that "focused on backlash discrimination
against those who are Muslim or Sikh, or persons of Arab, Middle Eastern
or South Asian descent, as well as persons perceived to be members of these
groups, as tragic events in the United States and abroad have increased the
likelihood of discrimination against these communities."[12] While the EEOC is
still pursuing Muslim-related cases, Trump's EEOC chair appointee removed
any special emphasis language related to Muslim, Sikh, Arab, Middle Eastern, or South Asian identity in the agency's 2018–2022 plan, and the EEOC
has stopped publicly releasing statistics related to Muslim religious workplace
discrimination.[13] Yet even as we discuss the EEOC, we should remember that
Title VII federal laws do not extend the same workplace protections to many
lower-skill workers (for example, home health-care and domestic workers and
independent contractors such as taxi drivers). These laws also do not extend
to those in private businesses with fewer than fifteen employees, and certainly
not to those paid under the table.[14]

While we have little data related to unprotected workers, we do know
that Muslim workers covered by federal law are regularly denied requests for
religious accommodations. In 2017, New York City charged Pax Assist, the
company that coordinates wheelchair services at John F. Kennedy Interna-

tional Airport, with discrimination for denying Muslim workers' request to move their break times in order to pray and to shift their meal times during Ramadan so they could break their fast after sunset (i.e., Iftar). According to the complaint, a supervisor informed the employees, "We don't care about Ramadan. We'll give you a break on our time, not your time."[15] Similarly, a Wisconsin manufacturer reversed its policy of allowing two additional five-minute breaks for prayer by sending out a notification that the company "does not allow for unscheduled breaks in production."[16]

"Secularism" and Muslim Workers

The grounds for these refusals reside in the contestation of what reasonable accommodations for religion entail in the workplace. Title VII of the Civil Rights Act of 1964 requires that an "employee's sincerely held religious beliefs or practices" must be accommodated "unless the accommodation would impose an undue hardship (more than a minimal burden on operation of the business)."[17] The EEOC goes on to specify that "an accommodation may cause undue hardship if it is costly, compromises workplace safety, decreases workplace efficiency, infringes on the rights of other employees, or requires other employees to do more than their share of potentially hazardous or burdensome work."[18] As many recent cases have shown, however, the definition of undue hardship is built on a primarily Christian (Protestant) definition of religious belief and practice, which assumes religious faith can be maintained primarily by privatized belief. In this construction of reality, two additional five-minute breaks for prayer or moving an employee meal break until after sunset constitutes a significant disruption of economic practices and a religion that is out of its proper (private) bounds. Here we see an economic system whose secularity actually erases the public presence of *Muslim* workers whose bodily practice of faith contests the supposed secularism of the workplace. The public presence of Muslim workers' religiosity both holds a revealing mirror to the alleged "neutrality" of the economic sphere and constitutes Muslims' claim to their rightful place in the postsecular political and economic life of the United States.

By invoking the phrase "postsecular" political and economic life, I do not intend herein to debate empirically whether and how secularization happened in the United States, let alone other parts of the world.[19] As sociologist José Casanova and many others argue, classic secularization theory, with its roots in a certain understanding of modern European history, assumed that with the differentiation of the "religious (ecclesiastical institutions and churches)" from the "secular institutional spheres (state, economy, science, art, entertainment, health and wealth, etc.)" religion would be largely privatized and slowly decline.[20] Or as religion scholars Janet Jakobsen and Ann Pellegrini explain, the "secularization narrative" assumed that rationalization, enlightenment, social-structural differentiation, freedom, privatization (of religion), universalism, and modernization/progress all hung together.[21] Yet the varied empirical trajectories of secularization have not held together neatly and many parts of the world have seen the continued public vibrancy and growth of religion, including the United States.[22] The sustained influence of white evangelicals in the 2016 and 2020 U.S. presidential elections and the rebirth of Religious Freedom Restoration Acts (RFRAs) in states across the nation evidence just some of this empirical complexity. Religion has not just faded from the public and political sphere even as its contours are shifting.

I am most interested, however, in how the supposed *empirical* secularization of the economic sphere in the United States actually upholds a certain *ideology* of selective secularism that imports a Protestant vision of belief and work that marginalizes other religious communities. Whereas secularization theory was meant to be an empirical-historical analysis, secularism, Casanova explains, "elaborated . . . into philosophies of history and normative-ideological state projects, into projects of modernity and cultural programs, or . . . an epistemic knowledge regime."[23] Secularism became a goal and disciplinary system of political and social actors. This disciplinary regime has also been in service of a particular vision of the political economy as "secularism's freedom from religion [is] also freedom for the market."[24] We hear echoes here of Max Weber's argument that Protestantism, particularly Calvinism, provided the "spirit" of capitalism when it sacralized everyday jobs, encouraged a zeal to work (as devotion to God), and animated a worldly asceticism that renders accumulation of wealth a moral ideal.[25] While Weber argued that *overt* religious dimensions largely faded from capitalism, these Protestant origins helped elevate the rational pursuit of economic gain to a primary moral end for individuals and communities. With this history in mind, Jakobsen and Pellegrini argue that "recognizing the co-origination of secularism and market-reformed Protestantism unmasks the national and religious particularities that have come to pass as a universal secular . . . [secularism] in its dominant, market-based incarnation constitutes a specifically Protestant form of secularism."[26] The economic sphere is not merely empty of moral and even religious assumptions; rather, certain forms of belief and practice are policed and expunged when they do not align with its forms of differentiation that sacralize efficiency and capital accumulation.[27]

The organizing by Muslim immigrant workers highlights how the current economic configurations demand the privatization of certain forms of religious practice while lionizing the freedom of the market and the Christian traditions that support rather than disrupt the free market's rationalized, uninterrupted production of owner wealth. The secularism of the economic realm is contested precisely when primarily black/brown Muslim bodies require current production or service practices to pause, realign, and respect the physical, public practices of a faith other than Christianity. Companies in numerous industries (for example, meatpacking, rental car, wheelchair assistance) have made claims that adding break times for prayer or shifting mealtimes for iftars constitutes an undue burden on their business. Their seeming secular reasoning is most often exposed through the offhand insults of "We don't care about Ramadan. We'll give you a break on *our* time, not *your* time."[28] The "our time" here is not just the time of a neutral economic sphere (as if it is empty of religion) but rather one imbued with a supposed secularism that prioritizes certain forms of religious belief and practice. We can almost hear them saying: You can certainly believe what you want (religion as interiority focused belief) and practice your faith on the weekends (themselves defined by Christian Sabbath practices), but efficient, productive "secular" work is your call here in this company and economy.

For my purposes, to name postsecularity as relevant to current labor organizing is not to enter into historical debates about whether religion disappeared and now is back in political and economic life.[29] Moreover, while I find Jürgen Habermas's argument for the "post-secular" as "regulative ideal" appealing when it encourages secularists to engage respectfully with religious persons, this is also not my primary focus.[30] Rather, what is more illuminating of the intersection of labor dynamics and growing religious pluralism in the United States is how postsecularity invites us to examine the ideology of selective secularism and its attendant oppressions. A postsecular awareness can help us see how the construction of the supposedly neutral, that is, secular, economic sphere is a site where secularism often covers over the religious assumptions of businesses and how they undergird discrimination against minoritized religious persons. Postsecularism does not imply secularization has disappeared or is irrelevant as an analytical category, but rather that the ideology of the secularization narrative is contested. Or as religious theorist Donovan Schaefer explains, "It may be best to think of the *post* in *postsecularism* as indicating that the secularization narrative has been placed under erasure, in Derrida's sense: it has been theoretically disrupted—deconstructed, situated in a genealogy that locates it in a particular European imperial-intellectual context—but it continues to shape systems of power-knowledge-affect."[31] Understanding how the secularization narrative has shaped our economic life becomes particularly important for noticing what kinds of discourses, bodies, and protests are allowed in the economic sphere and what kinds of resistance may be required.

Postsecular Intersectional Labor Organizing

We see some of this postsecular resistance in the collaborations of Muslim immigrants with union and labor organizers who are beginning to take their concerns more seriously. In 2016, the Services Employers International Union (SEIU) partnered with employees from the subcontracted security firm, Security Industry Specialists, that patrols Amazon's headquarters in Seattle.[32] The employees, led by two young Somali Muslims, complained that the security firm's low-wage employees were not allowed to use the prayer rooms reserved for directly employed Amazon workers; about 500 of the security firm's 800 employees are Muslim. SEIU helped coordinate a "pray-in" outside Amazon's headquarters that drew attention to the issue and assisted three security firm employees in filing complaints about retaliation for voicing their concerns and working with the union. The pray-in, led by a local imam, included clergy and employees from multiple faith traditions on colorful prayer rugs in front of the headquarters. Muslim security guards spoke of having hours reduced when they asked for access to the prayer rooms utilized by Amazon's high-tech employees and they complained about supervisors who told non-Muslim employees to blame their Muslim fellow employees for having to take on more shifts during Ramadan. Amazon eventually granted the security guards' request to share its company prayer rooms, and the main leaders of the protest have begun to focus their efforts on unionizing the security firm.

New worker solidarity organizations such as the NYTWA, which was instrumental in the taxi boycott mentioned at the beginning of this chapter, are also important players in this postsecular political economic climate. Started in 1996, the NYTWA now has over 19,000 members in New York City and six affiliates in other cities. Because taxi drivers are considered independent contractors and not employees, they cannot form a formal union and are forced to build power largely outside the National Labor Relations Act. That status means that any collective they form lacks automatic dues contributions, that no one is required to recognize them at the negotiating table, and that workers do not have minimum wage or overtime protections, or receive social security contributions. As the Executive Director of NYTWA, Bhairavi Desai, explains, "Everything we have done, all of the progress we have made, it comes from our workers, our members, going out onto the streets and building a militant activist-oriented movement."[33] NYTWA clearly knows how hard the struggle is for recognition and progress, and recognizes how intersectional its members' identities are as a 90 percent immigrant, overwhelmingly Muslim and Sikh low-wage workforce. Desai narrates the shifting nature of worker justice and its religious associations over the past several decades:

> The Yellow Cab went from being kind of a cultural icon, a symbol of New York City to a symbol of Muslim workers. We would see profanities carved into the taxi with a knife. Already, drivers are twenty times more likely to be killed on the job than other workers. We are one of the most visible immigrant and Muslim workforces. Our members tend to be on the frontlines of that hate and violence.[34]

Desai and the members of the NYTWA know that increased political activism entails significant risks. Any action by the mostly Muslim immigrant drivers can lead not only to lost wages but also to increased surveillance, policing, and deportations. This risk is part of the reason that she thinks the #DeleteUber campaign resonated:

> People out there know that taxi drivers are really hard working and that people really struggle day to day to make ends meet. The idea that they would put their incomes on the line and it would be a workforce that is so vulnerable, particularly in these times, to surveillance and deportations and further policing, that they would be the ones to stand up. It seemed to really touch people and we were so moved by their reaction. I think it was a beautiful start to solidarity with our movement.[35]

Her insights point to the disproportionate risks that Muslims, particularly those in working poverty, endure in their everyday lives, as well as how that threat often dampens the possibilities of organizing and protest. That dilemma only increased under the extreme stain of COVID shutdowns, as unemployment and deaths increased, and the 2020 Presidential election campaign, which ratcheted up incendiary rhetoric. The economic precarity of indigent, immigrant Muslim communities is amplified by the fact that Muslim immigrants are far more likely than U.S.-born Christians to be the focus of homeland security and anti-terrorism surveillance and policing and thus discouraged from activism.

Empowering Surveilled People

Because Islamophobia views Muslim identity itself as a "presumptive threat," the current model of Countering Violent Extremism (CVE) focuses its antiterrorism and national security policing primarily in Muslim American communities.[36] As legal scholar Khaleed Beydoun traces, CVE "links radicalization—

or propensity for radicalization—with Islamic piety" and therefore targets outwardly observant Muslims, particularly those who are moving from being secular to more devout in their ritual practice and physical appearance.[37] Those persons who "express their faith conspicuously" (praying in public, wearing a beard or hijab, and so on) are the most likely to be surveilled, and urban-dwelling, recently immigrated, indigent Muslim Americans are more likely to display a visibly nonsecular presence.[38] This disproportionate surveillance and community policing, combined with lack of access to skilled criminal and national security legal counsel, leads to more arrests and harsher sentencing for indigent Muslims.[39]

Despite this reality, discussions of Muslim Americans and their experiences of poverty are rare in academic literature and even interfaith forums dominated by religious economic elites.[40] As Beydoun contends,

> [The] incompatible caricaturing of indigent Americans and Muslim Americans facilitates the erasure of indigent Muslim Americans from both scholarly and advocacy interventions and consequently leaves their distinct struggle ignored and unmitigated. This erasure has never been more dangerous than it is today—the vulnerability of indigent Muslim Americans to "racialized poverty," "Islamophobia," and "countering violent extremism" (CVE) policing is at an all-time high (and on the uptick).[41]

The religious, racial, class, and legal precarity of Muslim low-wage workers in the United States thus requires organizing models that do not perpetuate the selective secularism narratives that uphold the current political economy.

Resisting Secularity's Fragmentation of Identity

The NYTWA offers one form of resistance to the fragmentation of identity that certain forms of secularity require of Muslims workers. As Desai articulates,

> You can't compartmentalize peoples' reality and their humanity. I remember, after 9/11, . . . our members being subject to a lot of verbal abuse and physical assaults, and at the same time they lost so much work, because all of these streets were closed down and they still had to pay for their lease out of pocket. We did a survey and we found that one out of four drivers had received an eviction notice from their home . . . At the same time, they were contending with the fact that this country was beginning to discuss military action within the Middle East in the same countries where many of the members were from.

> You can't keep somebody whole and ignore a large part of their life
> and particularly one when it comes to something as deeply rooted as
> racism and workplace violence, which given that we represent a work-
> force that's in the public, the two often intersect in drivers' daily lives.[42]

Her attention to the wholeness of workers' lives should be the marker of post-secular labor organizing. Muslim low-wage workers in the United States cannot extricate themselves from the web of religious, racial, and class dynamics that enwrap them in our political economy. They exist in a postsecular realm that is not concomitantly post-racial or post-class.

Accounting for wholeness in organizing is important, then, for at least three reasons. First, the demographic intersections of these workers mean that these workers are vulnerable both in terms of their complex needs and their surveillance by authorities. Activism entails risks of cultural violence, anti-terrorism scrutiny, and immigration status jeopardy. Second, resisting the fragmentation of these workers' identities is also vital because many of these low-wage immigrant and refugee workers are literally rebuilding their lives after being persecuted abroad for a dimension of their identity. Bringing their whole lives into organizing is a crucial form of support and respect for persons who have survived significant trauma. Finally, social movement theory also teaches us that persons are more likely to join and sustain activism if they have significant value salience with a movement.[43] Narrow self-interest rarely sustains leadership development and endurance; we build and sustain power better from the fullness of who we are.

Fortunately, more labor unions and worker justice organizations are beginning to take this kind of postsecular intersectional organizing seriously. Yet there are also disturbing examples of not just ignorance but intentional dismissal of this approach to worker justice. In 2017, the EEOC ruled against both Cargill Meatpacking Solutions and the Teamsters Local No. 455 for their treatment of Muslim workers.[44] Cargill had fired more than 150 Muslim workers when they walked off the job during tense negotiations about whether employees should be allowed to take prayer breaks during their shifts. The EEOC found that the workers had been discriminated against because they were Black, immigrants from Somalia, and Muslim. They found Cargill responsible for creating "a hostile work environment" for Muslim employees "based on their religion, race and national original, including making disparaging racial, ethnic and religious comments and by requiring them to choose between their religion and work."[45] But the EEOC also found the Teamsters did not properly represent their union members "by historically failing to pursue grievances on their behalf relating to religious accommodation and by failing to intercede, advocate for or represent" the Black, Somali Muslim workers.[46] This finding followed a previous ruling against the Teamsters local when they were found to have retaliated against Muslim union members (threatening to prevent promotions, and so on) who refused to pay dues when the Teamsters would not address the prayer break requests.

By saying all that matters for workers are increases in wages and benefits, this Teamster local embraced a secularism that, by disguising its preference for a particular ethno-religiosity, not only discriminates against minority religious traditions but ultimately undermines the long-term building of worker power. Instead, worker dignity must include honoring the fullness and integrity of persons: a view of this world that does not reduce people to *homo economicus* (or economic humans). In many ways, the presence and activism of low-wage Muslim workers invites us all to consider more deeply the ways that *homo religiosus* (our religious nature) might disrupt and contest how dominant selective secularism upholds inequity and inequality in the political economy.

The realities of U.S. Muslim low-wage workers and their courageous risks challenge those who value equity and justice to take up the task of postsecular intersectional worker organizing. Muslim organizing shows us how particular strands of Christian free market ideology have constructed our political economy and encourages us to imagine what full-body faithful resistance to the grind of production might look like. For those of us who are in the Christian majority, we may even hear a summons to our own salvation (or being made whole) and an invitation to remember and/or think anew about how a more fulsome Christian faith might restructure capitalisms.

Notes

1. Sarah Jaffe, "Beating the Muslim Ban: An Interview with Bhairavi Desai," Progressive.org, February 16, 2017, http://progressive.org/api/content/c648fbe4-f45b-11e6-86b6-0aea2a882f79/.

2. Mike Isaac, "What You Need to Know About #DeleteUber," *New York Times*, January 31, 2017, https://www.nytimes.com/2017/01/31/business/delete-uber.html.

3. Pew Research Center, "U.S. Muslims Concerned About Their Place in Society, but Continue to Believe in the American Dream: Findings from Pew Research Center's 2017 Survey of U.S Muslims, section 1: Demographic Portrait of Muslim Americans," *Pew Research Center's Religion & Public Life Project* (blog), July 26, 2017, http://www.pewforum.org/2017/07/26/demographic-portrait-of-muslim-americans/. This is the most recent comprehensive survey completed of U.S. Muslims.

4. Ibid.

5. Ibid.

6. Ibid.

7. Ibid. As this report notes, the current Census categories (white, Black, Asian, Hispanic, multiracial, and other) make it very difficult for persons from the Middle East and North Africa to answer. Persons from this region are by default categorized as "white," yet they are rarely considered "white" in dominant U.S. culture and experience many attendant discriminations of those persons more traditionally identified as brown/black in the U.S. cultural and political imaginary.

8. Alessandro Acquisti and Christina M. Fong, "An Experiment in Hiring Discrimination Via Online Social Networks," *Management Science* 66, no. 3 (March 2020): 1005–24.

9. U.S. Equal Employment Opportunity Commission, "Religion-Based Charges Filed from 10/01/2000 through 9/30/2011 Showing Percentage Filed on the Basis of Religion-Muslim," accessed October 17, 2017, https://www.eeoc.gov/eeoc/events /9-11-11_religion_charges.cfm.

10. U.S. Equal Employment Opportunity Commission, "What You Should Know about the EEOC and Religious and National Origin Discrimination Involving the Muslim, Sikh, Arab, Middle Eastern and South Asian Communities," accessed October 17, 2017, https://www.eeoc.gov/eeoc/newsroom/wysk/religion_national _origin_9-11.cfm.

11. Acquisti and Fong, "An Experiment in Hiring Discrimination Via Online Social Networks."

12. U.S. Equal Employment Opportunity Commission, "Strategic Enforcement Plan FY 2017–2021," accessed October 17, 2017, https://www.eeoc.gov/eeoc/plan /sep-2017.cfm. Karim Lakhani, "Workplace Discrimination Against Muslims," *On Labor* (blog), February 15, 2017, https://onlabor.org/workplace-discrimination-against -muslims/.

13. U.S. Equal Employment Opportunity Commission, "Strategic Enforcement Plan FY 2018–2022," accessed November 22, 2019, https://www.eeoc.gov/eeoc/plan /strategic_plan_18-22.cfm. On the cessation of public statistics: see U.S. Equal Employment Opportunity Commission, "Religion-Based Charges Filed from 10/01/ 2000 through 9/30/2011 Showing Percentage Filed on the Basis of Religion-Muslim," https://www.eeoc.gov/eeoc/events/9-11-11_natl_origin_charges.cfm, accessed November 22, 2019. In 2018, the EEOC won a $4.9 million judgment against the United Parcel Service for relegating workers who wore beards for religious purposes to backroom or non-supervisory roles. In 2019, a judgment was also made against Greyhound for not allowing a new female driver to wear an abaya (full religious covering) even though she had passed all Maryland commercial driving requirements.

14. Khaled Beydoun, "Between Indigence, Islamophobia, and Erasure: Poor and Muslim in 'War on Terror' in America," *California Law Review* 104, no. 6 (2016): 1493.

15. Ben Kochman, "City charges Queens wheelchair service company discriminated against Muslim employees during Ramadan," *New York Daily News*,

January 26, 2017, http://www.nydailynews.com/new-york/queens/pax-assist
-discriminated-muslim-workers-city-charges-article-1.2955662.

16. Jason Silverstein, "Wisconsin Manufacturer Takes Away Muslim Prayer," *New York Daily News*, January 17, 2016, http://www.nydailynews.com/news/national
/wisconsin-manufacturer-takes-muslim-prayer-breaks-article-1.2499671.

17. U.S. Equal Employment Opportunity Commission, "What You Should Know: Workplace Religious Accommodation," accessed October 24, 2017, https://www.eeoc
.gov/eeoc/newsroom/wysk/workplace_religious_accommodation.cfm.

18. Ibid.

19. Jürgen Habermas, "Notes on a Post-Secular Society," *Signandsight* (blog), June 18, 2008, http://www.signandsight.com/features/1714.html.

20. José Casanova, "The Secular, Secularizations, Secularisms," in *Rethinking Secularism*, ed. Craig Calhoun, Mark Juergensmeyer, and Jonathan VanAntwerpen (New York: Oxford University Press, 2011), 54.

21. Janet R. Jakobsen, *Secularisms* (Durham, N.C.: Duke University Press, 2008), 5.

22. José Casanova, *Public Religions in the Modern World* (Chicago: University of Chicago Press, 1994).

23. Casanova, "The Secular, Secularizations, Secularisms," 55.

24. Jakobsen, *Secularisms*, 2.

25. Max Weber, *Protestant Ethic and the "Spirit" of Capitalism and Other Writings*, translated and with an introduction and notes by Peter Baehr and Gordon C. Wells (London: Penguin, 2005).

26. Jakobsen, *Secularisms*, 3.

27. Interestingly, the highest number of successful religious accommodation cases in the United States is on behalf of Seventh Day Adventists who will not work on Sunday. Thus, while this "sectarian" Christian practice is now expunged from the dominant selective secularism of the U.S. political economy, simultaneously it is the most successfully defended by the government. Maryam Jameel, Leslie Shapiro, and Joe Yerardi, "More Than 1 Million Employment Discrimination Complaints Have Been Filed with the Government Since 2010. Here's What Happened to Them," *Washington Post*, February 28, 2019, https://www.washingtonpost.com/graphics/2019
/business/discrimination-complaint-outcomes/.

28. Kochman, "City charges Queens wheelchair service company discriminated against Muslim employees during Ramadan."

29. I am appreciative of Kristin Stoeckl's insight that it matters whether one places a hyphen when discussing post-secularity/postsecularity. The former implies a "timely succession"; a society that was once secular no longer is so (a form of "regime change"). But without the hyphen, we begin to discuss the "coexistence of religious and secular worldviews" and the tensions that creates. Kristina Stoeckl, "Defining the Postsecular" (unpublished paper presentation), February 2011, http://
synergia-isa.ru/wp-content/uploads/2012/02/stoeckl_en.pdf.

30. Habermas, "Notes on a Post-Secular Society." I am also not engaging, in this chapter, the phenomenological and normative work of Charles Taylor on

the epistemological option of belief and the immanent frame that structures our process of finding meaning in this world. Charles Taylor, *A Secular Age* (Cambridge: Belknap Press of Harvard University Press, 2007).

31. Donovan Schaefer, "Defining Postsecularism: A Response," *Bulletin for the Study of Religion* (blog), April 16, 2014, https://bulletin.equinoxpub.com/2014/04 /defining-postsecularism-a-response/.

32. Josh Kelety, "Amazon Prayer Rooms Now Available to Muslim Security Contract Employees," *The Seattle Globalist* (blog), May 17, 2017, http://www .seattleglobalist.com/2017/05/17/amazon-prayer-rooms-available-muslim-security -contractors-protests/65470.

33. Jaffe, "Beating the Muslim Ban."

34. Ibid.

35. Ibid.

36. Beydoun, "Between Indigence, Islamophobia, and Erasure: Poor and Muslim in 'War on Terror' in America," 1487.

37. Ibid.

38. Ibid., 1463.

39. Ibid., 1499.

40. Ibid., 1492.

41. Ibid., 1465.

42. Jaffe, "Beating the Muslim Ban."

43. David Snow and Robert Benford, "Master Frames and Cycles of Protest," in *Frontiers in Social Movement Theory*, ed. Aldon D. Morris and Carol McClurg Mueller (New Haven: Yale University Press, 1992), 133–55.

44. Noelle Phillips, "Cargill, Teamsters Union Violated Muslim Workers' Civil Rights in Dispute over Workplace Prayer, Federal Agency Rules," *Denver Post*, August 10, 2017, http://www.denverpost.com/2017/08/10/cargill-meatpacking -teamsters-local-union-455-muslim-workers-civil-rights-prayer/.

45. Ibid.

46. Ibid.

PART IV

Thresholds in Gender, Sexuality, and Christianity

9

Slogan, Women's Protest, and Religion

Kwok Pui-lan

On January 21, 2017, I participated in the Women's March in Boston amid a huge crowd of about 175,000 people. Some of the female marchers wore pink hats and waved homemade signs while chanting "Women! United! Can never be defeated!" as they hit the streets of Boston to protest the election of Donald Trump and to express solidarity with our society's vulnerable people.[1] Across the United States, women and men, both young and old, took part in similar marches—with crowds estimated to be as massive as 500,000 in Washington, D.C., 400,000 in New York, and 250,000 in Chicago.[2] What began as a Facebook post by a Hawaiian grandmother named Teresa Shook the day after Hillary Clinton lost the presidential election blossomed into a worldwide protest that drew a total of about 2.6 million people. They marched on the first day of President Trump's tenure to protest his new administration and to fight for reproductive rights, gender and racial equities, queer people's rights, immigration reform, health-care protection, workers' rights, and other issues.[3]

The Women's March follows a long line of women's protests and reform movements in the United States, spanning from the abolitionist movement, the temperance crusade, and the suffrage movement in the nineteenth century all the way to the second-wave feminist movement, which began in the 1960s. In this chapter, I explore three major slogans that emerged from American women's protests—slogans that had global impacts and ramifications. My interest in slogans in political speech and rhetoric is inspired by the work of cognitive linguist George Lakoff. He has studied how the framing of political discourse influences the ways people think, respond to, and elicit certain social and political behaviors. He writes, "Frames are mental structures that shape the way we see the world. As a result, they shape the goals we seek, the plans we make, the way we act, and what counts as good and bad outcomes of our actions. . . . Reframing is social change."[4] Lakoff applies his research to study how conservatives and liberals formulate their worldviews and their moral reasoning.[5] He notes that conservatives and liberals have different moral systems that shape their political discourses. He points out that both conservatives and liberals use the metaphor of "family" when talking about morality and politics, though they have different priorities and emphases. The conservatives use a "Strict Father" model, which emphasizes that life is difficult and the world is a dangerous place.[6] By contrast, liberals use a "Nurturant Parent" model, emphasizing instead relationships, mutual interaction, care, and protection.[7] When these two family-based models are applied to politics, they give rise to divergent modes of moral reasoning about what is good for society, as well as different opinions about the role of government, social welfare, crime, gun control, abortion, and other social issues.

Prompted by Lakoff's study, I investigate the moral reasoning behind women's protests in different historical periods by looking at some of their important slogans. These slogans allowed women to break from traditional barriers and construct new understandings of female identity so that they could enter the public realm to effect social change. In the nineteenth century, an important slogan or guiding principle was "For God and Home and Native Land." During the 1970s, it was "Our Bodies, Ourselves." These slogans not only shaped the moral worldviews of reformers and protesters, but also elicited strong feelings and emotions both from those who said them and those who heard them. I have selected the hashtag #MeToo as a contemporary example of these powerful slogans, particularly because it underscores how social media and the Internet have fundamentally changed our political communication and grassroots organizing.

For God and Home and Native Land

In the nineteenth century, American women who participated in social reforms and protests had to justify their right as women to work for reform in the public realm. Traditional understandings of women's primary roles at the time cast them, almost exclusively, as wives and mothers, which relegated their activity to the domestic sphere. To mobilize women to step outside of the home and participate in reform movements, specifically to demand women's rights and suffrage, female reform leaders had to challenge traditional notions of "true womanhood," which was characterized by piety, purity, submission, and domesticity.[8] Thus, the slogan "For God and Home and Native Land" allowed women to both affirm their domestic roles while also expanding their influence into the public sphere.

This slogan connected religion, family, and nation to rally women for social change. In the 1870s, thousands of American women participated in the temperance movement by holding prayer meetings in saloons and in the streets by confronting liquor dealers face-to-face, picketing drinking establishments, and applying social pressure to recalcitrant community members at mass temperance meetings.[9] They argued that alcoholism destroyed the sanctity, purity, and harmony of the family because men drank while women and children suffered. The reformers sought to expand women's spaces by bringing "the womanly role of housekeeping and children to bear on all institutions."[10] One of the mottos of the Women's Christian Temperance Union (W.C.T.U.) was "the W.C.T.U. is organized mother-love." When the W.C.T.U. elected Frances E. Willard as president, she referred to "the ballot for home protection" when she argued for women's right to vote.[11]

Willard and other reformers believed women were angels of the home and that they were, by nature, more pious, faithful, and pure. Moreover, these reformers truly believed God had ordained these women to elevate society according to domestic virtues. Wearing white ribbons, these crusaders—who were mostly middle-class, married women—went into their communities as guardians of public morality to save husbands and sons from the curse of drink and moral depravity. Influenced by evangelical Christianity, these women performed their work of soul saving and conversion with religious zeal. This evangelizing temperance movement was strongest in the cities of the Mid-Atlantic and Midwestern states, regions in which Charles Finney and the Revival Movement had been most influential.[12] Women proclaimed they were "taking up their cross for Christ" by organizing prayer meetings in the streets and confronting tavern owners in their watering holes. Indeed, in her *Woman and Temperance*, Willard writes, "to help forward the coming of Christ into all departments of life, is, in its last analysis, the purpose and aim of the W.C.T.U."[13]

For women to extend their domestic, angelic roles beyond the home into the public arena, protesters and social reformers had to reinterpret biblical teachings that previously barred them from doing so. Some of these firebrands and even a few male supporters began questioning passages (i.e., 1 Cor 14 and 1 Tim 2) that relegate females to second-class status. These progressives emphasized instead texts that speak to how God created men *and* women (Gen 1:27); how both sons *and* daughters will prophesy because God pours out the Spirit on both men *and* women (Acts 2:17–18); and how, in the body of Christ, there is neither male nor female *for all are one* (Gal 3:28). Willard cited the Galatians passage as support for her argument that at least in a Christian home, husband and wife should be equal "peers in dignity and power."[14] While subsequent, more radical women's rights activists, such as Elizabeth Cady Stanton and Matilda Joslyn Cage, would later ground their arguments for gender equality in natural rights philosophy, Willard and the temperance leaders based their protests on evangelical Christian beliefs.[15]

Prompted by their evangelical zeal, these American, Christian women saw their housekeeping roles not as limited in scope to this nation alone, but, rather, as extending to the whole world. They donated funds, organized women's missionary societies, and by the late nineteenth century, saw an increased number of female missionaries sent to foreign lands. Conversion of "heathen" mothers was commonly held as a key to Christianizing the "heathen" nation.[16] Missionaries introduced Western ideas about marriage, family, parenting, and hygiene to "heathen" mothers and initiated social reforms against practices such as polygamy and foot binding. They instead promoted social values such as female literacy and health care. The W.C.T.U. became an international organization with branches in different parts of the world. While some of these reforms contributed to the emancipation of indigenous women, the superimposition of Western values on non-Western families and women, in many cases, also reinforced cultural superiority and imperialism.

The motto "For God and Home and Native Land" succeeded in rallying several hundred thousand American women behind a movement of reform and protest based on notions of evangelical domesticity. By the late 1880s, the W.C.T.U. had grown to be the largest women's organization in the United States. It went beyond its original focus on temperance to include causes such as women's suffrage, prison reform, conditions of working women, peace and arbitration, and health reform. The reform movement had a strong patriotic favor, as displayed by its motto "For God and Home and Native Land." Many American Christian women, including Willard, believed that the United States represented the best hope for a truly democratic society based on Christian values and that the country was to be a shining example for all other nations.[17] They firmly believed in both the sanctity of marriage and an educated and enlightened motherhood, which they thought would uplift the nation. They based their understanding of the family and motherhood on heterosexist assumptions. Andrea Smith argued that the building blocks of the nation-state have been the heteropatriarchal family and genocide of Native people. As a result, Native women must continually contest heteropatriarchy as they challenge male-dominated sovereignty while simultaneously struggling for racial justice.[18]

The motto "For God and Home and Native Land" was also premised on

white, middle-class racial and class biases. Many white women failed to acknowledge that their "native land" originally belonged to Native Americans
and that they participated in settler colonialism. In addition, the construction
of the public and private spheres, coupled with the belief that women were
domestic angels, only worked for women who had the means to stay at home
because they could depend on their husbands financially. Many Black women
during the time worked in white homes as "domestics," thus the "private"
realm of white women was these Black women's "public" workplace. Poor
women simply could not afford to stay at home: They had to join the increasingly industrial labor force in late–nineteenth-century America. Women born
into poverty often had to work long hours in factories, in abysmal working
conditions, and could not afford time off to participate in any of their rich
counterparts' protests.

   During the Jim Crow era, many white women, especially in the American
South and Midwest, supported racial segregation policies under the guise of
protecting their children and their households. To protect racial purity, many
states enacted anti-miscegenation laws to forbid the marriage of white women
to non-white men. Supporters of these laws argued that if white women were
protected from interracial liaison, they would purify and invigorate the nation.
The argument goes on: White women's reproductive capacity could either
strengthen or weaken the nation because they carried in their genetic makeup
the power to enforce racial purity. In the 1950s, during the massive effort to
desegregate public schools, white women organized rallies and protests in support of segregation laws and the "separate but equal" policies. They organized
campaigns, wrote letters to newspapers, lobbied local and state officials, and
distributed pamphlets and surveys to fight against school desegregation to protect their children from mixing with Black children. They argued that desegregation of schools would lead to the decline of family, schools, the state, and
the nation. The rhetoric of protecting the home and the anti-integration arguments employed by white women had deep roots in the South and across the
nation. As Elizabeth Gillespie McRae observes, "White women took central
roles in disciplining their communities according to Jim Crow's rules and were
central to massive resistance to racial equality. White, segregationist women
capitalized on their roles in social welfare institutions, public education, partisan politics, and popular culture, to shape the Jim Crow order."[19] They also
provided a political education that mobilized generations and trained activists
to fight for white "family values" and supremacist politics.

   The moral reasoning behind "For God and Home and Native Land" influences American politics to our present day. In the 1970s, conservative icon
Phyllis Schlafly used the rhetoric of protecting traditional gender roles and

saving the endangered family to unite and mobilize women to join pro-life and pro-family rallies against the Equal Rights Amendment and abortion. Although she was a lawyer, author, and activist, Schlafly basked in the image of herself as the perfect wife and mother.[20] The Christian right, especially James Dobson's "Focus on the Family," has championed "family values" to shore up moral authority and uphold conservative standards of behavior. They have fought against liberalism and pushed back against the feminist movement. After the defeat of Hillary Clinton in the 2016 election, some commentators pointed to the strength of this antifeminist movement. About 53 percent of white women voted for Donald Trump, which substantially helped to elect him. Kim Phillips-Fein argues that the supporters of Schlafly and other conservative leaders in the 1970s were foremothers of the women who voted for Trump in 2016. She notes that there were, in fact, two women's movements, "two equal mobilizations, struggling over the role of women in America, each with its own well-intentioned supporters, divided in their vision of the nation and their sense of the place of families and women within it."[21] One of these women's movements did not challenge male authority in the family and home, but focused on gaining greater economic and political power for women, while the other represented a more radical edge by focusing on women's consciousness-raising, gender equality, reproduction freedom, and queer issues. I now turn to the latter women's movement, often called the second-wave feminist movement, which affected women not only in America, but worldwide.

Our Bodies, Ourselves

In the 1960s, as women marched in the streets to support the civil rights movement and protested the Vietnam War, they became even more critically aware of gender discrimination in the church and in society. In her landmark book *The Feminine Mystique*, Betty Friedan shed light on the plight and general dissatisfaction of American women in the 1950s and 1960s.[22] She dubbed this feeling "the problem that has no name." She said that women were pressured to stay at home and take care of children because of the "feminine mystique": an idealized image of feminine domesticity that arose in the 1950s. As women resisted traditional gender roles, a new slogan, "Our Bodies, Ourselves," emerged that shaped women's perception of themselves, their sexuality, and their struggle for freedom. This slogan derived from the book *Our Bodies, Ourselves*, first published in 1971. Since its initial publication, the book has become a feminist classic and has been translated into thirty different languages, reaching millions of women worldwide.[23] The ability of women to make choices and decisions about their bodies became a defining issue for the second-wave feminist movement.

The second-wave women's movement did not place women's responsibility in the familial context. It rejected marriage and procreation as women's destiny and aimed to empower women to take control of their bodies, sexuality, and reproduction to fight societal pressure that limits women's freedom. The authors of the book noted that "until very recently pregnancies were all but inevitable, and biology was our destiny: because our bodies are designed to get pregnant and give birth and lactate, that is what all or most of us did."[24] With the introduction of the contraceptive pill, women were rid of the fear of pregnancy and could delay motherhood while they established careers. The Supreme Court's landmark decision in *Roe v. Wade* (1973) gave women the right to make decisions about abortion. Abortion offers women choices about whether to have children and when to have them.

Proponents of the slogan "Our Bodies, Ourselves" argued that women can take charge of their bodies because they are moral agents who can make responsible decisions about the most important matters affecting their lives. They asserted that women are grown-ups and not inherently dependents. They are subjects of their own destiny, and are not dependent on the family, church, or state to make decisions for them. For too long, these institutions have treated women as children or as morally weak, not to be trusted with moral decisions. Second-wave feminism asserted women's right to protect their bodily integrity and boundaries. Thus, this feminist movement fought against rape, domestic violence, and sexual harassment by organizing campaigns such as "Take Back the Night." Advocates argued that for women's bodies to flourish, women also need to have access to education, employment, health care, political power, and so forth.

Against the backdrop of the second-wave feminist movement, feminist theology has contributed to the recovering of women's bodies as something positive — as blessing instead of curse. Rosemary Radford Ruether described how Christian theology, influenced by Greek philosophy, had valorized the mind over the body. Thus, because women were associated with nature and physicality, much of Christian tradition denigrated them. According to her, even though women, like men, are created in the image of God, they symbolized to many in that tradition the lower self. This prejudice was underscored by women's physical and sexual nature. Instead of a patriarchal anthropology, Ruether proposed a positive view of women's bodies and an egalitarian relationship between the sexes. She argued, "There has been, throughout the entire history of Christianity, theologies of woman's original equality with man, restored in Christ."[25] Other radical feminist scholars, such as Mary Daly, argued that Christianity is irredeemably sexist and cannot be reformed or rehabilitated.[26] Feminist scholar Carol P. Christ looked beyond Christianity to rediscover the ancient Goddess traditions of Old Europe. Feminist rituals in the Goddess movement emphasize the natural cycles of women's bodies and their alignment with cycles of nature.[27] In debates surrounding abortion, Christian feminist ethicists, such as Beverly Wildung Harrison, marshaled resources from both the Bible and the Christian tradition to support women's right to choose how their anatomy would or would not be an incubator for human life. Harrison places moral debates on abortion within the larger context of the historical struggle of women to become subjects in their own lives.[28]

The motto, "Our Bodies, Ourselves," aimed to establish a moral worldview that unites women based on their shared experience of having female bodies. But gender is only one of the characteristics that mark the body. Cherríe Moraga and Gloria Anzaldúa intervened in the white women's movement by coediting the foundational text of radical women of color, *This Bridge Called My Back* (1981).[29] Using poetry, interviews, personal essays, and testimonials, the anthology explores, in Moraga's words, "the complex confluence of identities—race, class, gender, and sexuality—systemic to women of color oppression and liberation."[30] In Christian theology, Womanist, *Mujerista* and Latina, Asian American, and Native American scholars also began to articulate theology based on the intersections of multiple identities and oppression. In her article "The Color of Feminism," Womanist theologian Delores S. Williams challenges racism in both the women's suffrage movement and the second-wave feminist movement. She points out that the understanding of patriarchy in white feminist theology is insufficient and biased: While white feminists criticize patriarchy, they also benefit from white-controlled American institutions. These white institutions provide resources for white women's development and afford them protection, while Black women may not enjoy these benefits. By pointing their fingers at men, white feminists do not account for the horizontal violence of white women against other women.[31]

As the body became a site of contestation in cultural criticism, poststructuralist theory, and queer theory, the slogan "Our Bodies, Ourselves" has been subjected to further scrutiny. Queer theorist Judith Butler contests the binary construction of gender and, in her *Bodies That Matter*, she further interrogates how heterosexual hegemony and regulatory norms of "sex" constitute the materiality of bodies, gender, and sexual difference. She points out that the exclusionary practices of heterosexism allow the formation of certain subjects, while simultaneously producing other abject beings who are relegated to the "unlived" or "uninhabitable" zones of public life.[32] In other words, Butler asks us to rethink how the boundaries between *"our* bodies" and *"their* bodies" have been constituted, demarcated, and maintained. Butler's challenge was taken up by queer theologians, such as Marcella Althaus-Reid, whose *Indecent Theology* questions deep-seated heterosexist ideologies in Christian theology. Introducing and using the concept of "unveiling," Althaus-Reid undresses our assumptions of both the masculine body of Christ and the feminine ideals embodied by Mary the Virgin. She argues that all theologies are sexual, and either conform to decent, heterosexual norms or opt for indecent and queer perversions of heteropatriarchy.[33]

After Hillary Clinton lost the election, many asked what it would mean for feminism and its future that the first female candidate of a major political party lost, while a billionaire with a record of both admitted and alleged harassment, misogyny, and insults toward women won. Columbia University's Mark Lilla published a widely read essay, "The End of Identity Liberalism," in which he questions whether American liberalism has focused too much on identity politics and diversity issues, such as race, gender, and sexuality.[34] For him, such a focus can be divisive, rather than unifying, and further, the democratic process needs principles to unify people. He argues that we must engage more in conversations about class, war, political economy, and the common good. Lilla's essay has elicited much debate, with some racial minorities arguing that what Lilla dismisses as just "identity politics" actually address real problems of discrimination. But I think Lilla has a point in that the feminist movement has focused overwhelmingly on gender, race, and sexuality, while ignoring issues of class, poverty, and working people's plight, in a society divided by a widening gap between the rich and the poor. Some women in the Global South do not want to be associated with the term "feminism" because it is often taken to mean Western women's fight for sexual freedom. For feminism to have a future, the bodies that matter must include the bodies of gendered subalterns—those who are relegated to the margins of society, who are forced to migrate and inhabit borderlands, and who do not benefit from the neoliberal economy. The American feminist movement must broaden its concerns and work in solidarity with women in other parts of the world, who toil under military conflicts, war, migration, and gender-based violence of all kinds.

#MeToo

In early 2017, following widespread allegations of sexual abuse by film producer Harvey Weinstein, the "#MeToo" movement spread, virally, as a hashtag on social media. On October 15, 2017, at the suggestion of a friend, American actress Alyssa Milano posted on Twitter: "If all the women who have been sexually harassed or assaulted wrote 'Me too' as a status, we might give people a sense of the magnitude of the problem."[35] Responses of high-profile actresses and celebrities led to widespread coverage and discussion of sexual harassment in Hollywood and in wider society. Sexual harassment survivor and activist Tarana Burke coined the phrase "Me Too" on Myspace in 2006. Today, the #MeToo hashtag has been translated into dozens of languages, and the #MeToo movement has become a catalyst for millions of women to share their stories and experiences about sexual harassment and abuse, thereby showing the pervasive nature of misogynistic behavior. The willingness of so many women to come forward and share their experiences created an atmosphere that makes more women feel comfortable to admit that they, too, have been victims of sexual abuse. Since then, we have seen many powerful men in media, entertainment, politics, education, business, and medicine accused of sexual misconduct rebuked, censored, or even fired.

In many parts of the world, sexual harassment and assault have been associated with shame and many women have not had the courage to speak out. The #MeToo movement became a rallying cry and shone a spotlight on how sexual abuse and harassment inflict suffering and pain in women's bodies, psyches, and spirits. Indian women who work as domestic workers claimed their place in the global #MeToo movement when they fought for a safe workplace because Indian sexual harassment laws to protect women in the informal sector are poorly implemented.[36] In Greece, after Olympic sailing champion Sofia Bekatorou revealed in 2020 that she had been the victim of sexual assault, the #MeToo movement took off as more and more Greek women broke the wall of silence, accusing university professors, journalists, state officials, and politicians of sexual abuse.[37] The #MeToo movement has also inspired and spawned new movements. For example, during the mass demonstrations against an extradition bill in Hong Kong in 2019, some female protesters complained that the police had sexually assaulted and harassed them. Protesters launched the "#ProtestToo" movement to bring awareness to the public of sexual misconduct by law enforcement.[38]

Social media and information technology have transformed contemporary social protests and movements. Social media is more than just the networking websites Facebook or Twitter: It includes a broad and growing portion of the Internet designed as platforms to allow users, or groups of users, to create and exchange content in an interactive and collaborative fashion. In *Tweeting to Power: The Social Media Revolution in American Politics*, Jason Gainous and Keven M. Wagner describe how the nature of the political world and of people's political participation has changed because "social media presents an entirely new paradigm on how people engage with each other. Instead of waiting for traditional media to explain limited elements of the news, the networker is interacting with not just the news itself but with entire networks of acquaintances without limits from borders or geography."[39]

Using social networks, women initiate social protests and movements, finding like-minded people to join their cause while bypassing traditional political parties or organizations along the way. Social media enables women to connect with people in other parts of the world instantaneously while simultaneously creating virtual communities. By 2010, 22 percent of American Internet users used social media websites for political activities. This percentage is likely to increase as more and more people access social media through mobile devices.[40] Additionally, people are increasingly consuming news through social media. They are more likely to pay attention to news or events their friends post or tweet, and they may be more motivated to join an event after seeing that their friends are going. Furthermore, organizers and participants of political protests no longer need to depend on traditional news outlets because they can broadcast the event, post pictures, and share experiences and comments, all on social media platforms.

The Internet has drawn more women into the political process through their social networking, tweeting, blogging, posting on websites, responding to posts, and creating news content. Women are dominating the blogs, and they make up a majority of people who use social media. Nisha Chittal writes:

> Social media democratized feminist activism, opening up participation to anyone with a Twitter account and a desire to fight the patriarchy. By removing the barriers of distance and geography, sites like Facebook, Twitter, Tumblr, and Instagram have made activism easier than ever, facilitating public dialogues and creating a platform for awareness and change.[41]

The use of social media as a tool for organizing enables women to form a broad-based resistance movement by amplifying new voices while also mobilizing these new voices across multiple fronts.

There are many other examples of how women have used social media for protests and activism in recent years. For example, women in Texas protested an abortion bill in 2013 by posting online with the hashtag #StandwithWendy, in support of State Representative Wendy Davis through her thirteen-hour filibuster. In 2015, women called out sexism in Super Bowl advertisements in real time using the hashtag #NotBuyingIt. The top trending, feminist hashtag on Twitter in 2015 was #BringBackOurGirls, which protested the kidnapping of two hundred schoolgirls by Nigeria's Boko Haram. Twitter reported that some 5.5 million users have used the hashtag.[42]

More recently, in the summer of 2020, after the killing of George Floyd, an unarmed Black man, protests broke out across the United States and other parts of the world in solidarity with "Black Lives Matter," a movement started by three Black women—Alicia Garza, Patrisse Cullors, and Opal Tometi. The Black Lives Matter movement is a decentralized movement, which uses social media, and other means, to rally people, organize activities, and sponsor events. In September, after the school year began, Anthea Butler, a Black female scholar of religious studies and Africana Studies, sent out a tweet saying that she would strike for a few days to protest police brutality. Many professors took part in what became the "#ScholarStrike" to show their solidarity against police violence and racial injustice. They paused their classes, led teach-ins about racial violence, and protested against the over-policing of college campuses.[43]

Some may question whether "hashtag activism" and cyberfeminism can bring any real change. There are a bevy of limitations, drawbacks, and criticisms for social media organizing. For example, the prominence of the #MeToo movement in media coverage, because of its association with Hollywood, has overshadowed activism for women's rights in other parts of the world that predate the emergence of #MeToo. These other, global campaigns include #MeshBasita in Lebanon, HarassMap in Egypt, and the "Shefarers" in the Philippines.[44] Advocates of the #MeToo movement have been criticized, first, for abandoning due process in favor of virtual courtrooms populated by faceless Internet users and, second, for pursuing a form of witch hunts, reminiscent of American McCarthyism during the Red Scare immediately following World War II. Still, the #MeToo movement, in conjunction with other social network activism, has created social awareness and, in some cases, succeeded in pressuring politicians, agencies, and companies to change their behavior.

The power of the Internet and social media has attracted the attention of feminist scholars of religion. As Gina Messina-Dysert, in her TED Talk, said, "Technological spaces, they have grown and create a space for us that has not existed in the past. And social media has propelled forward the online feminist movement. . . . In fact, feminist blogs have been called the consciousness-raising group of the twenty-first century." She argues that these technological changes have enabled a "new feminist revolution in religion" because the digital world offers women a voice. A practicing Catholic, Messina-Dysert notes that men have dominated traditional leadership roles while suppressing women's participation. Now women can share religious ideas and form communities that reach across nations and geographical areas freely, thanks to the Internet. The blog "Feminism and Religion," which she cofounded in 2011, provides a platform for scholars and activists to have conversations around religious and social issues. These conversations oftentimes lead to further organizing and activism. After three years, the blog had readers from 181 countries with about half a million hits per year. Such online spaces are desperately needed for women. Messina-Dysert notes, "Online space has become sacred space."[45]

In the groundbreaking book *Feminism and Religion in the 21st Century: Technology, Dialogue, and Expanding Borders*, contributors explore many issues related to women, religion, and activism.[46] Womanist scholar Monica Coleman explains how feminist, religious activists can use blogging to reach across boundaries. Through blogging, she can discuss discriminatory practices of the church and explore issues, such as miscarriage and depression, which churches seldom discuss. For instance, Mormonism does not allow for women to be ordained or to have equal position with men in the church, and in 2013, an "ordain women" movement was organized online by members of the Mormon Church, ultimately garnering 711 signatures. Online communication enabled this activist movement. In Roman Catholicism, some activists organized virtual communities, with one author even asking to what extent we can call these communities church "congregations." Similarly, a Jewish leader explored the use of social media to expand her synagogue beyond the confines of brick-and-mortar walls. By live-streaming services of a synagogue in Los Angeles, that particular religious community has reached out to people who cannot physically attend the services. During the Covid-19 pandemic, many faith communities have likewise broadcast their religious services on social platforms. Rounding out a list of female adherents of "People of the Book," an Islamic moniker for Muslims and their fellow Jewish and Christian siblings in the Abrahamic streams of faith, Muslim women have created websites to help women study their tradition and ask pressing questions of their faith and its leaders. Muslim women who either may lack proficiency in Arabic or, alternately, who are not allowed to share academic or worshipping space with men unrelated to them, now have access to imams, articles, and resources that are of interest to them, thanks to the power of social media and various other online platforms.

Social media enables an increasing number of feminist scholars, especially women of color, to intervene and disrupt white, mainstream, and male perspectives on religion. Feminist theologian Grace Ji-Sun Kim who has maintained an active presence on the Internet through social media, podcasts, and YouTube interviews, explains her reason for doing so:

> We do not have diverse voices in the mainstream religion, politics, and society. We must have diverse voices. We need to hear voices especially

from women of color and Asian American women. Social media provides such a platform for various voices to be heard and it is good that I can share my voice through such an open platform.[47]

The Internet allows feminist scholars and religious leaders to reach beyond their classrooms and religious communities so that they may then generate interest and mobilize people to pay attention to, or to be involved in, various causes ranging from postcolonial studies to mental health issues and same-sex relationships.[48] Lea F. Schweitz, a professor in science and religion, launched a blog/website to explore her theology of urban nature. She wants to use the site and social media to bridge the divide between scholarship and activism. Through her combination of story, natural history, philosophy of nature, and beautiful photography, she hopes to bring readers to an immersive experience centering on the wonder of nature. She writes, "Part of the reason that I am so excited about social media scholarship is the ways in which it can be public, personal, and activist . . . Pursuing this scholarship through social media allows me to share a wider range of stories and voices and to bring images and aesthetic experiences to bear on the ideas."[49] Like Schweitz, I have used blogs and social media to combine intellectual work with activism. My blog has helped me reach an international audience that I could not have imagined. Blogging has also changed my writing and thinking, and it has made me more alert to what is happening around the world.[50]

Conclusion

The three slogans that emerged from the women's protest movements recounted in this chapter point to the expansion of women's roles and spheres: first, from the family, or the "domestic"; next, out into the entire American nation; and, finally, on to the whole wide world. Each slogan generated a moral worldview that enabled women to reflect on their identity and social position so that they could subsequently take action and push for social change. The motto "For God and Home and Native Land" did not refute feminine domesticity but extended motherly care and love to the public realm. In contrast, the slogan "Our Bodies, Ourselves" challenged biology as destiny while also emphasizing women's autonomy and control of their sexuality and reproduction. This slogan argued that women should demand equality with men and seek a fulfilling life, rather than being defined by traditional gender roles. Finally, the hashtag #MeToo points to a moral worldview that recognizes the bodily integrity and dignity of women while underscoring that it is not shameful for women who have been sexually harassed or abused to speak out. The use of the Internet, particularly social media, enables global and transnational connection and mobilization.

However, no slogan is perfect: each of these slogans presents valid challenges and contestation for their detractors (and honest proponents!). In the case of "For God and Home and Native Land," the "home" has been modeled mostly after the white, middle-class family. To protect the purity of the white family, white women organized grassroots movements to support racial segregation and Jim Crow laws. The slogan "Our Bodies, Ourselves" promotes the sociopolitical interest of white, heterosexual, female bodies. Women of color did not find their interests represented by the white second-wave feminist movement and, consequently, had to organize their own resistance. Lastly, the #MeToo movement obscures lesser-known women's movements in other parts of the world and may target people unfairly or, worse, for revenge.

Religion serves as a backdrop in the conceptualization and mobilization of women's protest movements. In the nineteenth century, female reformers drew from evangelical domesticity in arguing for "For God and Home and Native Land." The second-wave women's movement and liberal feminist theology reinforced each other in championing women's right to choose by mutually supporting the motto "Our Bodies, Ourselves." Today, as conservative religious voices dominate the media, the Internet becomes a critical space for progressive feminist voices. As religion continues to be an important force in social life, women's protests will not be effective without continued mobilization of religious communities.

Notes

1. "175,000 Were on Hand for Women's March for America in Boston," WCVB 5, January 21, 2017, http://www.wcvb.com/article/womens-march-for-america-will -impact-traffic-and-parking-in-boston/8614813.

2. Anemona Hartocollis and Yamiche Alcindor, "Women's March Highlights as Huge Crowds Protest Trump: 'We're Not Going Away,'" *New York Times*, January 21, 2017, https://www.nytimes.com/2017/01/21/us/womens-march.html?_r=0.

3. Heidi M. Przybyla and Fredreka Schouten, "At 2.6 Million Strong, Women's Marches Crush Expectations," *USA Today*, updated January 22, 2017, https://www .usatoday.com/story/news/politics/2017/01/21/womens-march-aims-start-movement -trump-inauguration/96864158.

4. George Lakoff, *The All New Don't Think of an Elephant! Know Your Values and Frame the Debate* (White River Junction, Vt.: Chelsea Green Publishing, 2014), xi–xii.

5. George Lakoff, *Moral Politics: How Liberals and Conservatives Think*, 2nd ed. (Chicago: University of Chicago Press, 2002).

6. Lakoff, *Moral Politics*, 65–68.

7. Lakoff, *Moral Politics*, 108–11.

8. Barbara Welter, "The Cult of True Womanhood, 1820–1860," *American Quarterly* 18 (1966): 152.

9. Susan Earls Dye Lee, "Evangelical Domesticity: The Origins of the Women's National Christian Temperance Union under Frances E. Willard" (Ph.D. diss., Northwestern University, 1980), 11–12.

10. Carolyn De Swarte Gifford, "Women in Social Reform Movements," in *Women and Religion in America*, vol. 1: *The Nineteenth Century*, ed. Rosemary Radford Ruether and Rosemary Skinner Keller (New York: Harper & Row, 1981), 301–2.

11. Gifford, "Women in Social Reform Movements," 302.

12. Lee, "Evangelical Domesticity," 126.

13. Frances E. Willard, excerpt from *Woman and Temperance* in Ruether and Keller, *Women and Religion*, 326.

14. Willard, *Woman and Temperance*, 327.

15. Carolyn De Swarte Gifford, "'The Woman's Cause Is Man's'? Frances Willard and the Social Gospel," in *Gender and the Social Gospel*, ed. Wendy J. Deichmann Edwards and Carolyn De Swarte Gifford (Urbana: University of Illinois Press, 2003), 23–24.

16. Patricia R. Hill, *The World Their Household: The American Woman's Foreign Mission Movement and Cultural Transformation, 1870–1920* (Ann Arbor: University of Michigan Press, 1985), 5.

17. Gifford, "'The Woman's Cause Is Man's'?" 24.

18. Andrea Smith, "Dismantling the Master's House with the Master's Tools: Native Feminist Liberation Theologies," in *Hope Abundant: Third World and Indigenous Women's Theology*, ed. Kwok Pui-lan (Maryknoll, N.Y.: Orbis Books, 2010), 72–85.

19. Elizabeth Gillespie McRae, "How the 'Grassroots Resistance' of White Women Shaped White Supremacy," *Jezebel*, January 31, 2018, https://pictorial.jezebel .com/how-the-grassroots-resistance-of-white-women-shaped-whi-1822340338.

20. Douglas Martin, "Phyllis Schlafly, 'First Lady' of the Political March to the Right, Dies at 92," *New York Times*, September 5, 2016, https://www.nytimes.com /2016/09/06/obituaries/phyllis-schlafly-conservative-leader-and-foe-of-era-dies-at-92 .html?_r=0.

21. Kim Phillips-Fein, "The Two Women's Movement," *The Nation*, June 19–26, 2017, https://www.thenation.com/article/two-womens-movements. She cites the work of Marjorie J. Spruill in her observation.

22. Betty Friedan, *The Feminine Mystique* (New York: Norton, 1963).

23. "History," in Our Bodies Ourselves: Information Inspires Action (website), accessed October 27, 2017, http://www.ourbodiesourselves.org/history. The original title of the book was *Women and Their Bodies* and was changed to *Our Bodies, Ourselves* in 1971.

24. "Preface to the 1973 Edition of *Our Bodies, Ourselves*," in Our Bodies Ourselves: Information Inspires Action (website), http://www.ourbodiesourselves.org /history/preface-to-the-1973-edition-of-our-bodies-ourselves.

25. Rosemary Radford Ruether, *Sexism and God-Talk: Toward a Feminist Theology* (Boston: Beacon, 1983), 99.

26. Mary Daly, *Beyond God the Father: Toward a Philosophy of Women's Liberation* (Boston: Beacon, 1973).

27. Carol P. Christ, *Laughter of Aphrodite: Reflection of a Journey into the Goddess* (San Francisco: Harper and Row, 1987).

28. Beverly Wildung Harrison, *Our Right to Choose: Toward a New Ethic of Abortion* (Boston: Beacon, 1983).

29. Cherríe Moraga and Gloria Anzaldúa, eds., *This Bridge Called My Back: Writings by Radical Women of Color* (Watertown, Mass.: Persephone Press, 1981).

30. Back cover of Cherríe Moraga and Gloria Anzaldúa, eds., *This Bridge Called My Back: Writings by Radical Women of Color*, 4th ed. (Albany: State University of New York Press, 2015).

31. Delores S. Williams, "The Color of Feminism, Or Speaking the Black Women's Tongue," *Journal of Religious Thought* 43, no. 1 (1986): 42–58.

32. Judith Butler, *Bodies That Matter: On the Discursive Limits of Sex* (New York: Routledge, 2011), vi–viii.

33. Marcella Althaus-Reid, *Indecent Theology: Theological Perversions of Sex, Gender and Politics* (London: Routledge, 2001).

34. Mark Lilla, "The End of Identity Liberalism," *New York Times*, November 18, 2016, https://www.nytimes.com/2016/11/20/opinion/sunday/the-end-of-identity -liberalism.html. He has extended his arguments in his book *The Once and Future Liberal: After Identity Politics* (New York: Harper, 2017).

35. Alyssa Milano (@Alyssa_Milano), "If all the women who have been sexually harassed or assaulted Wrote 'MeToo,'" Twitter, October 15, 2017, https://twitter.com /Alyssa_Milano/status/919659438700670976.

36. Jayshree Bajoria, "#MeToo: India's Domestic Workers Are Sending Smriti Irani Postcards Demanding Safe Workplaces," Scroll.In, January 31, 2021, https:// scroll.in/article/984874/metoo-indias-domestic-workers-are-sending-smriti-irani -postcards-demanding-safe-workplaces.

37. "#MeToo Movement Takes Off in Greece," Deutsche Welle, accessed January 30, 2021, https://www.dw.com/en/metoo-movement-takes-off-in-greece /a-56304797.

38. Jessica Hiu-tung Tso, "Hong Kong 'Freedom Cunt': Sexual Violence and Crucifixion," in *Hong Kong Protests and Political Theology*, ed. Kwok Pui-lan and Francis Ching-wah Yip (Lanham, Md.: Rowman and Littlefield, 2021), 117–32.

39. Jason Gainous and Kevin M. Wagner, *Tweeting to Power: The Social Media Revolution in American Politics* (New York: Oxford University Press, 2013), 3.

40. Aaron Smith, "22% of Online Americans Used Social Networking or Twitter for Politics in 2010 Campaign," Pew Research Center, January 27, 2011, http://www

.pewinternet.org/files/old-media/Files/Reports/2011/PIP-Social-Media-and-2010 -Election.pdf.

41. Nisha Chittal, "How Social Media Is Changing the Feminist Movement," MSNBC, updated April 6, 2015, http://www.msnbc.com/msnbc/how-social-media -changing-the-feminist-movement.

42. Chittal, "How Social Media Is Changing the Feminist Movement."

43. Skylar Mitchell, "What You Need to Know about the #ScholarStrike and What It Means to Protest during a Pandemic," CNN, September 1, 2020, https://www .cnn.com/2020/09/01/us/professors-plan-protest-scholar-strike-trnd/index.html.

44. Mariz Tadros, "The Fight for Women's Rights Beyond #MeToo," *ASEAN Post*, January 18, 2021, https://theaseanpost.com/article/fight-womens-rights-beyond -metoo.

45. Quotes are from Gina Messina-Dysert's TEDx Talk, "The New Feminist Revolution in Religion," YouTube, November 18, 2014, https://www.youtube.com /watch?v=VMb1UkkZsR8.

46. Gina Messina-Dysert and Rosemary Radford Ruether, eds., *Feminism and Religion in the 21st Century: Technology, Dialogue, and Expanding Borders* (New York: Routledge, 2016).

47. Grace Ji-Sun Kim, "Constructive Theology," in *Theologians and Philosophers Using Social Media: Advice, Tips, and Testimonials*, ed. Thomas Jay Oord (San Diego: SacraSage Press, 2017), 251.

48. See Kwok Pui-lan's blog, http://kwokpuilan.blogspot.com; Monica Coleman's blog, http://monicaacoleman.com; and Elizabeth Kaeton's blog, http://telling-secrets .blogspot.com.

49. Lea F. Schweitz, "Science and Religion," in *Theologians and Philosophers Using Social Media*, 378. See her blog/website, Wild Sparrows, at https://wild sparrows.com.

50. Kwok Pui-lan, "How Blogging Has Changed My Thinking and Writing," *Kwok Pui-lan* (blog), January 19, 2012, http://kwokpuilan.blogspot.com/2012/01/how -blogging-has-changed-my-thinking.html.

10
LGBTQ+ Politics and the Queer Thresholds of Heresy

Ju Hui Judy Han

Disputes over heresy are not new or uncommon. Mainline Protestant denominations have historically declared minor sects and radical theologies to be heretical to the Christian faith, especially when they challenge prevailing norms in doctrine or ideology. However, when the largest evangelical denomination in South Korea, the Presbyterian Church in Korea (Hapdong), began investigating Reverend Lim Borah (Im Pora) of the Sumdol Hyanglin Church in 2017 and subsequently declared her ministry heretical, they charted new ground: theologies and ministries that accept and affirm the inclusion of lesbian, gay, bisexual, transgender, and otherwise queer (LGBTQ+) individuals were now officially considered heretical, at least in this corner of the Presbyterian church. This set an example—a warning—for those within the South Korean church who were becoming interested in queer theology and LGBTQ-accepting ministry. It also signaled to the minority faction against same-sex marriage within the Presbyterian Church (USA) that the Korean Presbyterian Church would join them in opposing the tide of change.

Two years later, the Korean Methodist Church followed the lead of the Presbyterians and put on trial Reverend Yi Dong-hwan, a Methodist minister who gave a blessing at the 2019 Incheon Queer Culture Festival. Yi shared the stage with Lim Borah, leading a ceremony to welcome and celebrate LGBTQ+ Christians, wearing a rainbow stole, and tossing handfuls of colorful flower petals from a small basket. For this, the church suspended Yi for two years for violating the Korean Methodist Church's doctrine against homosexuality. Both cases against Lim and Yi involved straight-identified cisgender clergy who advocated for LGBTQ+ equality and tolerance, and both cases demonstrated the capacity of Protestant denominations to use heresy charges to delegitimize dissenting minorities.

Other heresies and cults have also been in Korean headline news in recent years. Sewol ferry, which capsized and killed 304 passengers in 2014, was quickly linked to a little-known religious sect and its leaders who owned the ship, shrouding the ferry disaster with rumors of cult conspiracy. Heresy rumors and conspiracy theories subsequently obfuscated the criminal investigation, confusing public discourse and confounding survivors' and victims' families who sought answers and accountability. In another example, the downfall of President Park Geun-hye—impeached in 2017 and imprisoned for nearly five years—took place amidst a massive corruption scandal and no small part of this involved rumors of her long-standing connections to a close family friend and cult leader. Allegations that Park invited shadowy cult members and summoned "shamanistic rituals" in the official presidential residence helped turn the public opinion against her, though this aspect did not end up playing a formal role in Park's impeachment proceedings.

The COVID-19 pandemic in South Korea starting in 2019 involved two religious groups familiar with heresy charges. A fringe Christian group known by the name of Sinch'ŏnji—discussed again later in this article—became demonized as the culprit for the country's earliest and largest cluster of coronavirus infections. But when the government later imposed sanctions against in-person church services to prevent the spread of COVID-19, Sinch'ŏnji was not alone in objecting to the state's regulation of religious assembly. Representing the Christian Council of Korea (CCK or Han'gich'ong), a national flagship organization for evangelical Christians, was an outspoken pastor named Ch'ŏn Kwang-hun, previously considered heretical by the very organization he now heads. He defied new rules against public assembly and incited anti-government protests, urging churchgoers to resist COVID testing and defy mask wearing protocols. It should be noted that these mass protests led by Ch'ŏn were different in many ways from the protests against mask mandates and shelter-at-home policies in the United States. For example, compared to the United States where the Trump administration at the federal level stoked protesters' hostility against local public health advisories, the anti-mask protests in South Korea were primarily national evangelical organizations that stood opposed to the liberal national government in power. But similar to the United States where white evangelical Christians were often the most vocal in seeking religious exemptions from vaccine and mask mandates, Christian conservatives in South Korea likewise led the fights against COVID policies.

These examples of so-called heresies and fringe religious groups suggest a complex geography of religion in contemporary South Korea. Heresy charges or cult accusations are a contested terrain with tensions and frictions between minority and majority, heterodoxy and heresy. Adding to this complexity is the word *idan* in Korean, a remarkably ambiguous and pliable term that refers to everything from heterodoxy to heresy, fringe insiders and cultish outsiders. The threshold of *idan* is unstable, both ambiguous and intrinsically political.

It is in this context of religious politics that this article asks: How do heresy charges shape contemporary LGBTQ politics? On the one hand, I show how beleaguered Presbyterian denominations in South Korea have used heresy declarations to discredit and stigmatize advocacy for gender equality and LGBTQ+ acceptance, a familiar political maneuver with historical precedents. However, it would be a mistake to conclude that heresy declarations simply stifle dissent. Just as important are the ways in which heresy declarations spotlight the existence of dissent, providing glimpses of non-normative, non-conforming, and counterhegemonic contestations. Heresy controversies in fact expose the limits of dominant power and norm enforcement. Dissident practices in the margins provoke the orthodoxy at the center, forcing the center to define itself against the challengers; heresy declarations essentially define the very thing that they seek to reject.

LGBTQ+ Advocacy as Heresy

On June 15, 2017, Reverend Lim Borah of the Sumdol Hyanglin Church in Seoul received an unexpected registered letter from the Hapdong denomination of the Presbyterian Church in Korea (PCK).[1] Sent by a committee charged with investigating heresy allegations, the letter from Hapdong asked Lim to submit a number of evidentiary materials—books, articles, sermons, and audiovisual recordings, especially concerning her work on the Korean-language translation of an edited book titled *The Queer Bible Commentary* (2006). This letter was peculiar; not only was it asking her to submit self-incriminating evidence, but it also came from an evangelical denomination with which Lim has no formal affiliation. Reverend Lim is a pastor ordained in the more liberal and ecumenical Presbyterian Church in the Republic of Korea, commonly known as Kijang.[2] The denominational distinction is significant here. Since neither Lim nor her ministry fell under the institutional purview of the more conservative and evangelical Hapdong Presbyterian, she was under no obligation to comply with their heresy investigation. Hapdong could say whatever they wanted about Lim ministering to LGBTQ+ communities and "promoting homosexuality," but they could not demote her or suspend her since she is not a member of their denomination. At the same time, Lim would not be able to explain or defend herself since she was not part of this institutional process. Lim did not comply and they did not wait.

The letter from Hapdong soon spiraled into a multidenominational effort to condemn Lim as a heretic. To be sure, there were institutional arrangements and bureaucratic mechanisms designed to deal with these matters along the way. Even before making a public-facing heresy declaration, Protestant denominations such as Hapdong periodically hold discussions and investigations. They issue warnings, sanctions, decrees, and advisories concerning minor sects and radical theologies and update heresy watchlists on an ongoing basis. New groups, individuals, and practices are declared *idan* every year, and sometimes, a previously heretical group is redeemed after apologies or change, or both. Or simply because new authorities see the matter differently. The threshold of heresy, I argue, is intrinsically a liminal site of contradictions and transgressions, a location where numerous lines meet and part ways. Along norms and normativities, and along the porous lines of hostilities and hospitalities, the threshold of heresy adjudicates more than what constitutes an outside to the inside.

Understanding the heresy controversy over Lim in 2017 requires a closer look at the historical geography of Korean Protestantism and the institutional arrangements of religious power. Lim's case also illustrates the stakes of dissent. Lim should be understood as part of an increasing number of outspoken voices from progressive reformers and critics of conservative Christianity, LGBTQ-identified Christians and their allies both inside and beyond the church.[3] They suffer real, material consequences such as getting expelled from school and suspended from ministry. Once a denomination declares any embrace of gender and sexual nonconformity as heretical, ordained clergy and affiliated faculty can be disciplined for even suggesting that gender and sexual minorities need protection from harm and discrimination. Reform-minded seminary students in South Korea can be — and have been — blocked from advancing in their pastoral career, barred from ordination and pastoral placement in majority-conservative denominations.[4]

To characterize the case another way, Lim is a woman pastor of a small community-oriented ecumenical church singled out by the largest and most powerful evangelical denomination in the country, one that does not even ordain women as clergy. They accused her of affirming and promoting LGBTQ+ identities and practices — not of herself being an LGBTQ-identified person or engaging in subversive sexual activities but for acting as though there is nothing wrong or wicked with gender and sexual nonconformity and variance. Her alleged heresy lies not in being an LGBTQ-identified person but her allyship and advocacy that include speaking positively and affirmatively about LGBTQ+ individuals, holding events and creating spaces to support and worship with LGBTQ-identified Christians, and espousing the message of acceptance and antidiscrimination.

The question I am most interested in pursuing in this article is not whether Lim is actually *idan* and by what criteria, but rather, what political work *idan* discourse performs. On the one hand, *idan* declarations spur religious censure and social stigma in order to discredit and stifle dissent. Heresy charges mobilize a variety of institutional apparatuses to apply pressure and create public disrepute. On the other hand, the case involving Lim demonstrates also that heresy determinations are not a simple top-down institutional mechanism that enforces doctrinal borders; they in fact make legible the *struggle* between orthodoxy and heresy. Lester R. Kurtz argues that "heresy is socially constructed in the midst of social conflict" and that "the heresy hunt, in which heresy is labeled and heretics suppressed, serves as an anxiety-relieving ritual for institutional elites and facilitates their dominance within the institution."[5] Heresy declarations serve several political functions: solidify authority, define institutional boundaries, enhance group solidarity, and offer a ritual outlet for collective anxiety. To put it another way: the activity of "naming and removing heretics is a predictable aspect of rhetorical 'power-maintenance.'"[6]

This resonates with the case of South Korean queer religious politics in that the heresy controversy has made the struggle more legible. There is growing visibility of conservative Protestant-led activism against gender equality policies and human rights ordinances, against decriminalization of abortion, and against the passage of antidiscrimination measures. These efforts converge often with the political right wing that holds fast to pro-U.S. and anticommunist legacies of undemocratic presidents Syngman Rhee and Park Chung Hee, but among the various conservative camps there are intra-Protestant chasms and competition for power and influence that lead to a variety of fissures and fractures.[7] In fact, behind the public spectacles of mass rallies and political mobilization of megachurches, the Korean Protestant Church has been experiencing a crisis in leadership and declining membership, as well as a severely diminished status in public opinion.[8] Especially for these reasons—the crisis of moral illegitimacy and unfavorable reputation of Christianity—"heresy hunts" would seem politically expedient for supplying "a common enemy," focusing the energy on the heretic as a "deviant insider" who must be disciplined.[9] The idea of a heretic as a "deviant insider" alludes to Georg Simmel's discussion of strangers: those who are outsiders but inside, both near and far. Different from infidels, who are outside the faith, heretics are like strangers near the bounds of faith, "close enough to be threatening but distant enough to be considered in error."[10] To be in error means to be in need of correction. To be heretical means to be disciplined on the verge of (un)belonging.

Queer theology and LGBTQ-affirming ministry pose a threat to the conservative church status quo. The threat hails from within the Protestant Church, not outside. As such, it constitutes "the perversion within the normative," as Carolyn Dinshaw might describe it.[11] Heresy rulings attempt to push dissent to the margins and keep the critics within striking reach.[12] As Michel Foucault writes, "Where there is power, there is resistance, and yet, or rather consequently, this resistance is never in a position of exteriority in relation to power."[13] Resistance is not exterior to power. I likewise suggest that resistance in heresy is not located outside institutional power but rather adjacent to it, tethered in tension. Heresy is not exterior to the orthodoxy. In these spaces of resistance can be found the emerging "new queer vitalities."[14]

The Semantic Ambiguity of *Idan*

What becomes evident in a survey of heretical Christianity in modern Korea is that not only can the delineations of heresy be politically pliant, but also there is an enormous semantic ambiguity over the very word for heresy. *Idan* is used to denote a wide range of unorthodox positions. Heterodoxy, heresy, heretical sects, cultish movements, as well as new religions that are located quite far from mainline Protestantism are all swept under the category of *idan*.[15] For example, the 2018 heresy list released by the U.S.-based International Korean Christian Coalition Against Heresy (IKCCAH) condemns as heretical long-established minor Christian sects such as Jehovah's Witnesses and Seventh-Day Adventists, as well as fast-growing new religious movements such as Sinch'ŏnji and JMS (Jesus Morning Star) that have caused serious concern in recent years.[16] Sinch'ŏnji is considered by mainline Protestants to be an extremely aggressive and persuasive heretical Christian group and one of the most dangerous *idan*. On the doors of several Protestant megachurches in Seoul are notices that read, "Sinch'ŏnji not welcome." Given the well-known heterodoxy of the Mormon Church and the Unification Church, it is perhaps not surprising to find them on the mainline Protestants' list of *idan*. But Hapdong caused a stir—and critics' ridicule—by claiming in 2017 that not only is Roman Catholicism heretical but so were the practices of magic tricks and yoga.

Unlike the Catholic Church, Protestant churches do not have a singular centralized governing body that determines who or what constitutes *idan*. Instead, each denomination makes these decisions, sometimes conferring with one another but sometimes contradicting one another as well. Occasionally, fingers are pointed at former friends. Hapdong's heresy list in 2019 included the leader of IKCCAH for deviating from key theological doctrines. In a strongly worded report, Hapdong authorities pointed out that the IKCCAH's leader was not an ordained pastor with seminary training and stated, "This goes to show how important but dangerous it is for (untrained) lay person to conduct research on *idan*."[17] Consequently, Hapdong Presbyterian denomination now prohibits all churches, pastors, and congregation members from contributing to, subscribing to, advertising in, or supporting in any way activities associated with the IKCCAH.

The *idan* controversy over queer theology and Lim's LGBTQ-affirming ministry diverges in important ways from these heresy contentions. For one, previous heresy debates are concerned mostly with doctrinal challenges, controversial radical theologies, or doomsday groups with cultish leaders. New religious movements gaining widespread popularity under charismatic leaders have been an especially popular target for *idan* advisories and excommunication decrees.[18] According to the influential theologian and expert on *idan*, T'ak Chi'il (Tark Ji-il), there are four telltale signs of heretical Christianity: the sanctification or deification of religious leaders; religious leaders who seek to rule rather than serve their members; apocalyptic end-time prophecies; and "mind control" of behavior, information, thoughts, and emotions.[19] The online inventory published by T'ak and a monthly publication he directs, *Hyŏndae Chonggyo* (*Modern Religion Monthly*), detail many cases of heresy that meet these criteria—religious leaders who clearly contradict doctrinal orthodoxy by denying the holy trinity, for example, or claiming to be prophets, as well as figures who claim to possess supernatural or superhuman powers.

Lim does not fit this typology. She is neither a charismatic leader of a popular religious cult nor a self-proclaimed messiah. Her theological claims and activities place her squarely in left-leaning social justice activism and social gospel ministry. She is recognizable as a figure in the genealogy of Korea's liberation theology known as *minjung* theology, updated with feminist and queer intersectional inflections. It is telling that homosexuality and queer theology did not come up in any of the major *idan* scholarship until 2017, when Hapdong turned its attention to Lim. In other words, gender variance and non-normative sexualities denoted by the word "queer" were not considered heretical until then.

How Queer Became Heretical

Writing in 2016—a year before the heresy charge first surfaced—Lim describes the work of translating *The Queer Bible Commentary* as part of the emergent

Christian-centered movement seeking to counter anti-LGBTQ+ politics.[20] She presciently mentions the word "heresy" (*idan*) twice in this article—first when she points out that diverse theological frameworks that pose a challenge to the dominant authority often get denounced as "false, fraudulent, or *idan*" and a second time when she writes specifically about *The Queer Bible Commentary* and the promise of queer theology. She writes:

> [*The Queer Bible Commentary*] confirms the interconnected links be-
> tween LGBTQ+ folks and religion, Christianity, and the Bible not only
> in Korean society but even in societies where same-sex marriage has
> been legalized. The bleak reality is that in Korea, even feminist theol-
> ogy has a difficult time getting established. It is a total wasteland when
> it comes to queer theology . . . Those who are leading anti-LGBTQ+
> movements issue warnings against queer theology and try to devalue it
> as a substandard theology. Or they treat it like *idan*, not sound [Chris-
> tian] theology. But in foreign seminaries outside of Korea, queer theol-
> ogy is part of a regular and legitimate theological curriculum.[21]

In this passage, Lim rejects the normalization of anti-LGBTQ+ sentiments in South Korea and posits that another world is possible, and that indeed it already exists. She places the subordinated position of feminist theology alongside queer theology to illustrate the dominant heteropatriarchy and cis-genderism of the South Korean church.[22] This, of course, is a common rhetorical strategy—to claim that the case would unfold differently elsewhere, somewhere better—that draws legitimacy through a global comparison. By pointing to the ostensibly more LGBTQ-friendly climate outside of Korea—presumably in liberal seminaries in North America and Europe—Lim flips the minoritizing gaze and turns it around against the anti-LGBTQ+ movements. She describes the conservative leaders as myopic and unwilling to change and critiques their failure to recognize feminist and queer theology as legitimate theological fields, as they ought to be.

Nonetheless, considering its dissident and rebellious approach to interpreting the Bible, it is no surprise that the Korean translation of *The Queer Bible Commentary* (2006), published in 2021, provided a key spark for the heresy allegations against Lim. A groundbreaking publication and a collaborative undertaking that involved twenty-seven South Korean theologians, clergy, and scholars working at the intersection of religion, gender, and sexuality studies, the translation would serve the much-needed purpose of advancing queer theology and demonstrating that the Bible need not be "texts of terror."[23] By rejecting oppressive heterosexist teachings and offering interpretations that elevate the dignity of queer lives, the book seeks in part to "disarm Biblically based gay-bashing."²⁴ *The Queer Bible Commentary* suggests that, rather than a source of oppression, the Bible has "the capacity to be disruptive, unsettling and unexpectedly but delightfully queer" and deploys a range of hermeneutical approaches to highlight aspects of the scriptural text that are relevant to LGBTQ+ issues.²⁵ Given the feverish pitch of anti-LGBTQ+ rhetoric among fundamentalists in South Korea, the translators felt that this book would be an especially valuable tool to deepen the conversation.

On May 17, 2017, at a public forum celebrating the completion of the translation, the emcee described the Korean translation as part of an emergent LGBTQ-affirming movement.²⁶ Yeong Mee Lee (Yi Yŏngmi), professor of the Old Testament at the Kijang-affiliated Hanshin Graduate School of Theology and a contributing translator to the edited volume, proclaimed that queer theology in Korea must necessarily take shape as a social movement in order to foster critical public discourse. She compared this needed development to that of the original *Queer Bible Commentary*, which came about as the product of a diverse range of minoritized scholars who worked tirelessly to establish queer theology as a dynamic field of study in the United States. By saying this, Lee made it clear that *The Queer Bible Commentary* was not just a book but part of a movement. It was not just a product of activism, either; it was a provocation for a counterhegemonic praxis, a critical building block in a long-rising and ongoing movement.²⁷

Minjung Precedents and Witch Hunt

What Yeong Mee Lee points to is an important movement context for *The Queer Bible Commentary* in South Korea, one that involves the legacies of liberation theology and Korea's own minjung theology, as well as the social critique and solidarity activism that emerge from these theological traditions. Liberation theology, which originated in the Catholic Church in Latin America in the 1950s and 1960s, responded to poverty and social injustice. It was a moral and religious reaction to what it identified as immoral secular socioeconomic conditions, namely capitalism and imperialism. In South Korea, pro-democracy activists and critical scholars similarly developed minjung theology, a contextual theology of liberation, during Park Chung Hee's eighteen-year authoritarian dictatorship in the 1960s and 1970s. Inspired by Latin American and North American liberation theology, and in concert with anti-colonial independence and democratization movements throughout the Third World, minjung theology took hold as an important and critical minority voice that prioritized defiance and radical inclusion of the poor, the oppressed, and the marginalized. At the heart of minjung theology is "a concern for those who suffer exploitation, poverty, and sociopolitical and cultural repression."[28]

Lee herself is an expert on minjung theology and writes: "At its inception, minjung theology focused on the deplorable economic and cultural conditions of minjung [the masses]. As it developed, and as the context changed, later minjung theology expanded to address political and social concerns that emerged from the minjung movement for democracy in the early 1980s."[29] As the context changed, theological communities also changed. Many minjung theology–inflected networks of scholars, activists, and churches in South Korea subsequently supported human rights (*inkwŏn*) activism in which gender and sexual minority politics have emerged as a key concern.

This is not to say, of course, that one can trace queer theology in Korea entirely or solely to minjung theology or that minjung theology necessarily leads to LGBTQ-affirming ministry. Multiple queer theological traditions give context to the recent identification of queer as *idan*, just one of which is represented by the group that came together to translate *The Queer Bible Commentary*. Minjung theology is one counterhegemonic tradition; queer theory, feminist theory, and even some corners from evangelical theological traditions have developed approaches to diversify our understanding of religion, faith, and gender and sexual nonconformity.[30] It is nonetheless noteworthy to find South Korean LGBTQ+ politics and queer theology taking root at the progressive and social change–oriented intersection of minjung and minority politics, with a recognition of "the need to stand in solidarity in a shared struggle against repression and injustice," a familiar idea from minjung theology as well as a progressive minority politics.[31]

Hyanglin churches provide good examples of progressive minority politics embraced as a continuation of minjung theology. Lim's Sumdol Hyanglin was founded in 2013 as an offshoot from its famous and historic parent church, Hyanglin Church (founded in 1953), which is part of the liberal, ecumenical Kijang Presbyterian denomination. Hyanglin has an explicit anti-growth strategy proposed by the church's founder and well-known left-leaning minjung theologian, Reverend Ahn Byung Mu (An Pyŏngmu) in 1993. The policy meant the church size would remain relatively small, with the congregation capped at around 500 adult members. The church would not pursue the unfettered growth of the megachurches. Ahn's organizational model cultivates offshoot households as grown children might branch out in a family tree, such that when the need arose, self-selected congregants would break out and form another church with the blessing of the "parent" church. Still connected to each other through shared values and non-hierarchical genealogy, the Hyanglin church and its offshoots—Kangnam Hyanglin, Tŭlkkot Hyanglin, and

Sumdol Hyanglin—exemplify a model of community building that rejects the pitfalls of growth-preoccupied strategies. They share a critique of the mega-church model, avoiding the downsides of church growth such as exorbitant construction and maintenance expenses for larger buildings, a diminished sense of intimacy and fellowship, an increasing conflation of pastoral work with corporate executive management—the pastor as a CEO—and lastly, the potential for financial corruption and abuse of power.[32] The radical antigrowth approach reflects minjung theology's anti-capitalist critique of the prosperity gospel and growth-oriented development model.

The four churches that make up the Hyanglin community came together to hold a press conference on July 7, 2017, in defense of Lim. They are all part of Rainbow Jesus, a coalition of LGBTQ-affirming ministries and groups that have been building a national network. Held at the historic parent Hyanglin Church in Myŏngdong, near the frenetic city center of Seoul, the solemn press conference featured a panel of clergy and activists who defended Lim's record as a compassionate and courageous religious leader and praised her dedication to social justice activism. The panel speakers stressed that the heresy disputes were part of an ongoing historical contestation between traditions that had diverged long ago—evangelical and fundamentalist Yejang and ecumenical and liberal Kijang—and that the label of heresy has been used in political efforts to legitimate denominational dogmatism.

A representative from a queer Methodist group said at the press conference: "This is a modern-day witch hunt. This creates a scapegoat to cover up the clear and evident crisis—the crumbling church authority and declining church membership."[33] The gendered language of "witch hunt" appears repeatedly in media coverage and rebuttal documents, including the July 3 response from the Kijang Presbyterian women's group.[34] The sharply worded statement pointedly places the modern-day heresy controversy in the long historical context of women and heresy and states, "We remember in medieval history that the medieval church accused countless women of being witches and burned them at the stake as sacrificial lambs when in fact their authority was in crisis due to a famine and the plague."[35] They stressed that even with controversial positions, differences in theological interpretation should lead to open discussion and debate, not condemnation and purge.

The modern history of heresy in South Korea does feature several controversial women, though none were burned at the stake. In his 2016 book, *Han'guk Idan Kidokkyo*, theologian Heo Ho-Ik (Hŏ Hoik) traces the genealogy of modern Korean Christian heterodoxy as beginning essentially with three female heretics.[36] The first heretic he lists is Yi Sunhwa, who in 1917 founded Chŏngdogyo, and the second heretic he lists is an anonymous woman known

only as Nambang Yŏwang, or Queen of the South, who is said to have traveled widely throughout Korea in the 1920s. Heo posits that these two heretical
women were relatively inconsequential in reach and influence, but he allo-
cates an entire chapter to the third heretic, Deaconess Kim Sŏngdo (1882–
1944), who gained notoriety in the 1920s and 1930s as the founder of a new
religion called Saejugyo.

Women's religious leadership seems to elicit scorn and suspicion, especially
if they are successful. Arguing that nascent religious movements become more
established only when they successfully manage the leadership transition from
the founder's generation to the next, heresy and cult expert T'ak Chi'il implies
that women leaders are essentially a sign of failure. He suggests that in many
well-known cases of *idan*, women become de facto or temporary successors
to the founding patriarchs when there is no suitable male heir.[37] His examples include Han Hakja (1943–), widow of Reverend Moon Sun Myung and
the current head or "True Mother" of the Unification Church; Chang Kilja
(1943–), "God the Mother" of the World Mission Society Church of God;
and Chŏng Choŭn (birthdate unknown), who has emerged as the de facto
leader of the infamous Christian Gospel Mission (CGM), also known as Jesus
Morning Star (JMS), while its founder and leader Chŏng Myŏngsŏk (1945–)
serves a ten-year prison term for sexual assault. Interestingly, T'ak singles out
these women not as cases of successful leaders but as examples of a legitimacy
crisis that inevitably befalls *idan* organizations.

Not surprisingly, the statement from the Kijang Presbyterian women leaders does not try to position Lim's heresy dispute in the historical lineage of
these heretical women. As mainline Protestants, albeit marginalized by conservative evangelicals, the Kijang women would not have claimed affinity with
groups like JMS or Sinch'ŏnji, or other radical sects located far from mainline
Protestantism. In fact, the Kijang women leaders do not dispute that there are
"real" heretics out there; they just deny that Lim is one of them.

While sexism and misogyny are an important part of the "witch hunt"
discourse, gender is not the only axis of difference in heresy politics. The
Kijang Presbyterian women leaders also situate the heresy controversy over
Lim in the old feud between conservative fundamentalists and progressive
ecumenical, tracing the conflict back to the 1950s, when Korean Presbyterians
split into two camps: the ecumenical National Council of Churches in Korea
(NCC) and the World Council of Churches (WCC) on the one hand, and
on the other, the fundamentalist evangelicals and affluent megachurches who
have taken an anti-WCC position. In fact, when the WCC held its assembly
in Korea in 2013, thousands of conservative Protestants protested outside in
what was described as the most "well-organized and vehement opposition"

against the WCC since its founding in 1948.[38] The conservative formation against the WCC marked the start of escalated campaigns against LGBTQ+ rights in South Korea.

Specifically, the Kijang Presbyterian women leaders reference the historic figure of Reverend Kim Chaejun (1901–1987), a liberal theologian who was excommunicated from the Presbyterian Church in 1952 and later became the founder of the Kijang Presbyterian denomination. He had helped establish Amnesty International in South Korea and served as its first chairperson in 1972.[39] Kim's reputation as a minjung theologian and a pro-democracy activist in the 1960s and 1970s against Park Chung Hee's dictatorship has earned him a place in church history as an esteemed elder figure and a respected teacher who mentored a generation of prominent religious leaders, including Reverend Moon Ik-whan (Mun Ik-hwan) (1918–1994), a longtime leader in Protestant activism for democracy and South-North Korea reunification, and Reverend Ahn Byung Mu (1922–1996), known as a pro-democracy movement leader and a principal architect of minjung theology, as well as the founder of the Hyanglin Church, as mentioned above. But for sixty-three years, in the eyes of the conservative Yejang Presbyterians, Rev. Kim Chaejun remained officially a heretic — until 2016, when his excommunication in 1952 was finally voided.

Reminding the readers of this religio-political history, the Kijang Presbyterian women leaders' statement asks, why heresy now and why heresy again. Why now does the Yejang Hapdong Presbyterian denomination stir up another heresy dispute with Lim, a Kijang pastor? "If there is an issue with [Lim]," they retort, "we will investigate it ourselves. We must make it very clear that this is not a matter that another denomination should trouble itself with." This excerpt from their remarkable statement directs our attention again to the intersection of gender and power:

> [The Hapdong Presbyterian denomination] have willfully misinterpreted the Bible verse, "Women should remain silent in the churches," and have tolerated ludicrous statements like "Women wearing diapers should not stand at the pulpit." Their anachronistic acts include refusing to ordain women pastors and continuing to engage in gender discrimination. They should attend to addressing their own internal issues. They should stop discriminating against women and stop punishing neighbors who are in pain. We encourage them to see the plank in their own eye before looking for a speck in another's eye.

The letter suggests that the Hapdong Presbyterian denomination is conducting the heresy hunt as a diversion because it is mired in internal criticism and surrounded by voices asking for reform. It points to Hapdong's dismal record on gender equality and critiques the low status of women in the denomination's leadership as anachronistic and indefensible, and urges change. The heresy allegations have to do with much more than a theological position on homosexuality.

Conclusion

Given the fractured and decentralized landscape of Protestants—especially Presbyterians—in Korea, there appeared to be unusually swift force of support behind the heresy charges against Lim. Seven other major denominations joined Hapdong's initial standing committee on heresy, with the notable absence of Lim's own Kijang denomination, which denounced the heresy charge. On September 1, 2017, the joint heresy committee of the eight denominations—in short, the Heresy Committee—spoke in rare unison and found Lim's ministry guilty of heretical tendencies.[40] Based on this report, several Presbyterian denominations subsequently put the matter to a vote in their annual general assembly. In 2017, Hapdong became the first to officially declare Lim as *idan*. The next year, two other Presbyterian denominations would base their *idan* declarations entirely on the 2017 joint report, without taking into consideration the objections from Kijang or opening up space for further discussion.[41]

The joint report by the Heresy Committee in 2017 organized the allegations against Lim in six sections that addressed what the committee considered to be theological transgressions and political concerns. They criticized Lim's embrace of gender and sexual diversity and acceptance of non-normative family forms, and denounced her refusal to weaponize the Bible against LGBTQ-identified individuals and communities. The evidence they presented for this was Lim's visible participation in the annual Queer Korean Culture Festival in Seoul, in which she "prayed for and blessed homosexuals"; they considered this as going against the teaching of the Bible and committing apostasy. In a particularly interesting section concerning Rev. Lim's promotion of diverse family forms, the joint report cited a 2014 radio interview as an attempt to justify same-sex marriage, polygamy, and incest. The report also found fault with Lim's writing from 2012:

> People who have not had access to higher education, people who
> are not in a patriarchal heterosexual family form, people who are ill,
> migrant workers, people who for a variety of reasons came to have
> criminal records, and sexual minorities—these are the most power-
> less people among those who are powerless in this society. They are

a minority among minorities, without guaranteed basic human rights that are afforded to all people. People who were treated as minorities throughout the Bible are still, thousands of years later, excluded as minorities and yet this is still not object for our concern.[42]

The Heresy Committee expressed concern over Lim's use of the term "basic human rights" to refer to sexual minorities, stating this was tantamount to promoting the "legalization of homosexuality" and same-sex marriage. They cited the book *Hanŭnim kwa Mannan Tongsŏngae* (*Homosexuality Meets God*) (2010), in which Lim urges repentance for Christians who are "busy saying malicious things against homosexuals as if they are true and using this to conceal their own flaws."[43] In another article where she criticizes orthodox Biblical interpretation as literalism with no concern for human rights, Lim describes queer theology as "a cry against the majority of Christians who consistently respond with prejudice and ignorance."[44] The Heresy Committee states in the joint report that Lim has waged an attack against the church's orthodoxy, that she has shown defiance, and that she continues to insist that she is right and her claims are biblical. "This is no different from what other heretics always assert," the report concludes, "and such heretical claims made by Lim are rapidly spreading among homosexuals and those who support homosexuality. The Korean Church must protect the church and the faithful and let it be known that Lim Borah's ideas are heretical ideas."[45]

The heresy charges in 2017 demonstrate how queer theology and LGBTQ-affirming ministry were seen as a threat to the heteropatriarchal normativity and theological orthodoxy. But what also transpired is that the heresy controversy exposed long-standing contestations between the Left and the Right and the split between progressive and conservative currents in the Protestant church, rendering visible numerous Christians who do not agree with anti-LGBTQ+ politics or heresy charges. The heresy decision ironically made the critique of heteropatriarchy and gender and sexual normativity more legible in church history.

History suggests that the heresy controversy concerning Reverend Lim Borah and queer theology has more to do with internal crises and long-standing political struggle than consensus on gender and sexual diversity. The question of heresy reflects the shifting alignments among conservative factions in a galaxy of competing denominations and political interests.[46] As I have argued in this article, heresy declarations are an exercise of power that defines and articulates the contours of right and wrong, an effort to clarify the border between inside and outside. Heresy designations work by hardening the edges of orthodoxy, locking heresy and orthodoxy into a symbiotic relationship, "two sides of a social process through which a belief system is . . . formed *via negativa*."[47] In fact, the heresy controversy surrounding Lim spurred an occasion for anti-LGBTQ+ Protestant groups to articulate their views and flex their institutional muscles. Ironically, however, in declaring Lim and LGBTQ-affirming ministry to be *idan*, the process also revealed the defiant contours of new queer vitalities, minority solidarities that extend beyond exclusive religious or sexual identity boundaries. The threshold of heresy ends up creating visibility for non-normative ideas and contradictions rather than entirely silencing discussions or stifling dissent. Strewn over the threshold of heresy, then, are not only transgressions of gender and sexuality (*iban*) but also ideological differences and historical fissures, religious and secular minority politics.

Heresy decisions delineate a threshold between permissible dissent and dangerous deviance. In order to establish the threshold for heresy, authorities must first acknowledge the presence of the dissent, recognize its shape and iterate the nature of its threat, and determine how much dissent to permit and how much to reject. As such, heresy decisions fundamentally shape both heresy and orthodoxy, two sides of an interactive process by which institutional identities are forged and sharpened.[48] Put differently, the definition of heresy is also an attempt at defining orthodoxy. While the effort to root out heresy is tied to an effort to bolster internal coherence and strengthen hegemony, heresy declarations do not merely delegitimize a minority. They also acknowledge the contours of new vitalities and spotlight the existence of dissent.

The heresy declarations in South Korea certainly have consequences for Korean American congregations that may be located in the United States but institutionally belong to South Korean denominations. On one hand, the conservatives in the Korean diaspora would be reassured that their South Korean counterparts are fighting against LGBTQ+ acceptance. On the other hand, the heresy declarations serve as a reminder that there is dissent within and among various denominations and institutional spaces. The dissenting movements demanding LGBTQ+ equality are anchored in long transnational histories of resistance, histories that concern not only gender and sexual nonconformity but also democracy, geopolitics, and more.

Notes

1. I use the McCune-Reischauer Romanization System except in cases of personal and place names that are already known in English, for example, Lim Borah (Im Pora), Sumdol (Sŏmdol), and Seoul (Sŏul).

2. Hapdong is short for Taehan Yesukyo Changnohoe (Presbyterian Church in Korea), or Yejang Hapdong, which is more conservative and evangelical in

comparison to the smaller and ecumenical Kijang (PROK) denomination. The
Presbyterians have shown remarkable disunity: Out of 374 Protestant denominations
in South Korea in 2018, over two-thirds—286 individual Protestant denominations—
had the phrase "Presbyterian church" in their title. Presbyterians collectively
make up the majority of Protestants in Korea, and Hapdong is considered the
largest among them. It is also notorious for refusing to ordain women and mired in
controversy for standing by male pastors accused of sexual misconduct. See "2018
nyŏn Han'guk ŭi chongkyo hyŏnhwang" (Status of religion in South Korea in
2018), Ministry of Culture, Spots, and Tourism (Seoul: Ministry of Culture, Sports,
and Tourism, 2018); Kang, "Yejang Hapdong, yŏsŏng moksa ansu hŏhara" (Yejang
Hapdong, allow the ordination of women), *News N Joy*, September 17, 2019, http://
www.newsnjoy.or.kr/news/articleView.html?idxno=225138.

3. I translate *pandongsŏngae* in this article not narrowly and literally as "anti-
homosexuaity" but as "anti-LGBTQ." Though the *pandongsŏngae* Protestant
rhetoric simplifies "homosexuality" as the primary locus of sin, their discourse
usually conflates an objection to male homosexuality, repulsion to nonbinary
or variant gender bodies, and consternation over non-normative family forms.
Pandongsŏngae should therefore be understood in a capacious sense to include
objections and opposition to a variety of non-normative gender and sexual identities
and practices, including gay, lesbian, bisexual, transgender, asexual, nonbinary,
and agender. Nonetheless, that the primary target of this *pandongsŏngae*, or anti-
LGBTQ+ imagination, remains fixated on cisgender gay men and transgender
women can be seen in the prevalent use of the rhetoric that "homosexuality" will
condone anal sex and invite "men dressed as women" into the family as monstrous
daughters-in-law. I use "anti-LGBTQ" not to imply that it stands in mirror opposition
to something that might be construed as simply "pro-LGBTQ" but rather to describe
a constellation of political actors and social forces that have stressed the rhetoric
of "*opposing* homosexuality," which is the literal meaning of *pandongsŏngae*. For
a discussion of the range of homonegative views, see Dawne Moon, "Beyond the
Dichotomy: Six Religious Views of Homosexuality," *Journal of Homosexuality* 61,
no. 9 (2014): 1215–41.

4. See Pyŏngwang Yi, "'Mujigae p'ŏp'omŏnsŭ' haksaengdŭl tashi chingyehara
moksori" (Voices call to discipline again "rainbow performance" students), *News N
Net*, July 24, 2019, http://www.newsnnet.com/news/articleView.html?idxno=6677;
Yongp'il Yi, "Mujigae p'ŏp'omŏnsŭ chingyebadŭn changshindae shinhaksaeng
'chat'oisŏ' chech'ul" (PUTS student disciplined for "rainbow performance" formally
withdraws from school), *News N Joy*, August 1, 2018, http://www.newsnjoy.or.kr/news
/articleView.html?idxno=218936; Ŭnhye Yi, "Yejangt'onghap Koshiwi, mujigae
pŏp'omŏnsŭ shinhaksaengdŭl moksa koshi 'pulhapgyŏk' kyŏljŏng 'ch'onghoi
chŏngch'esŏng wihae'" (Yejangt'onghap exam committee decides to disqualify
"rainbow protest" seminary students' pastoral exam to "maintain denominational
identity"), *News N Joy*, September 6, 2019, http://www.newsnjoy.or.kr/news/article
View.html?idxno=225062.

5. Lester R. Kurtz, "The Politics of Heresy," *American Journal of Sociology* 88, no. 6 (1983): 1085.

6. Thomas M. Lessl, "Heresy, Orthodoxy, and the Politics of Science," *Quarterly Journal of Speech* 74, no. 1 (1988): 19.

7. See Ju Hui Judy Han, "The Politics of Homophobia in South Korea," *East Asia Forum* 8, no. 2 (June 2016). Some of these competitions involve questions of who has the authority to make and unmake heresy declarations. In 2012, the two largest Presbyterian denominations, Hapdong and T'onghap, led an exodus of several major denominations to leave the Christian Council of Korea (CCK or Han'gich'ong), formerly the national flagship organization for evangelical Christians. This took place in part after a rift over the new CCK leadership's reversal of heresy rulings and embrace of leaders formerly deemed heretical. The Hapdong and T'onghap denominations subsequently formed a rival national group, the Communion of Churches in Korea (CCIK or Han'gyoyŏn), which now surpasses Han'gich'ong in number of member denominations and churches as well as political power. Hapdong Presbyterian declared in 2016 that they would lead the fight against heresy. In the meantime, the beleaguered leaders of Han'gich'ong attempted to restore its legitimacy by launching its own competing committee on heresy. Kwŏnhyo Ku, "Yejang ch'onghoi, 'idan saibi kyujŏng chich'imsŏ' palkan" (Hapdong PCK general assembly publishes "heresy policy guideline"), *News N Joy*, April 19, 2012, http://m.newsnjoy.or.kr/news/articleView.html?idxno=37530; Chuyŏl Song, "8-Kae Kyodan Idandaech'aekwi, Idan Kubun Chege Tankye t'ong'il Kyŏlŭi" (Eight denominations' heresy committee resolves to unify heresy classification and sanctions), *K'ŭrisŭch'ŏn nokŏt nyusŭ*, June 5, 2018, http://cbs.kr/mFBTFM.

8. For example, in a 2017 opinion survey of individuals without religious affiliation, the majority of respondents expressed a high degree of distrust toward the Protestant church. Conducted by the reform-minded Christian Ethics Movement of Korea (CEMK), the survey found that only 20.2 percent of individuals without religious affiliation expressed that they trust the Protestant church, while 51.2 percent responded that they do not. Critics usually point to the excess of affluent megachurches and the numerous scandals of financial corruption and sexual misconduct among Protestant leaders as contributing to the negative opinion of Christianity. See Christian Ethics Movement of Korea, "2017 nyŏn Han'guk kyohoe ŭi sahoejŏk shilloedo yŏronjosa kyŏlkwa charyojip" (2017 opinion survey of levels of social trust in Korean churches), March 3, 2017, http://cemk.org/resource/2699/.

9. Kurtz, "The Politics of Heresy," 1085.

10. Kurtz, "The Politics of Heresy," 1087, 1088; Georg Simmel, "The Stranger," in *The Sociology of Georg Simmel*, translated and edited by Kurt H. Wolff (New York: Free Press, 1950), 402–8.

11. Carolyn Dinshaw, *Getting Medieval: Sexualities and Communities, Pre- and Postmodern* (Durham, N.C.: Duke University Press, 1999), 99.

12. See also Ali Qadir, "When Heterodoxy Becomes Heresy: Using Bourdieu's Concept of Doxa to Describe State-Sanctioned Exclusion in Pakistan," *Sociology*

of Religion 76, no. 2 (2015): 155–76; Qadir, "How Heresy Makes Orthodoxy: The Sedimentation of Sunnism in the Ahmadi Cases of South Africa," *Sociology of Islam* 4, no. 4 (2016): 345–67.

13. Michel Foucault, *The History of Sexuality*, vol. 1 (London: Penguin Books, 1990), 95.

14. "New queer vitalities" is a phrase used in Jin Haritaworn, Adi Kuntsman, and Silvia Posocco, eds., *Queer Necropolitics* (Abingdon: Routledge, 2014).

15. Haengŏp Chŏng, *Han'guk Kyohoesa e Nat'anan Idan Nonjaeng* (The controversy concerning heresies in the history of the Korean church) (Seoul: Han'guk Changnogyo Ch'ulp'ansa, 1999); Jeong-Min Suh, "An Understanding of Orthodoxy and Heresy in Korean Church History," *Ecumenical Review* 57, no. 4 (2005): 451–62; Han'guk Kidokkyo Ch'ongyŏnhaphoe (Christian Council of Korea), *Han'guk Kyohoe Idan Nonjaeng Kŭ Silch'e Rŭl Palk'inda* (Revealing the truth behind the heresy controversy of the Korean Church: With a focus on the objects of heresy disputes) (Seoul: Han'guk Kyohoe Idan Saibi Taech'aek Hyŏbŭihoe, 2007); Hoik Hŏ, *Han'guk Ŭi Idan Kidokkyo: Chuyo idan ŭi kyebo wa kyori pip'an* (Heresy in Korea and Christianity: Genealogy of major heresies and theological criticism) (Seoul: Tongyŏn, 2016).

16. At the International Korean Christian Coalition Against Heresy, often known by the Korean acronym Seiyŏts annual meeting in 2018, it announced that the top eight heretical groups in South Korea are Sinch'ŏnji, also known as the Church of Jesus, the Temple of the Tabernacle of the Testimony; World Mission Society Church of God; Salvation Sect; Seventh-Day Adventist Church; the Church of Jesus Christ of Latter-Day Saints (often known as the LDS or Mormon Church); Jehovah's Witnesses; Christian Gospel Mission, more commonly known as JMS (Jesus Morning Star); and Manmin Central Church. Its website (ikccah.org) also lists Catholicism, Islam, the Unification Church, and Christian Science as heretical.

17. Yi In'kyu of IKCCAH was essentially accused of making heresy determinations without formal training or license. Ch'ŏryŏng Kim, "Yejang Hapdong, Seiyŏn Yi In-Kyu Kwŏnsa Idan Kyŏlŭi" (Yejang Hapdong determines Deacon Yi In-Kyu of Seiyŏn to be heretical), *Newspower*, September 24, 2019, http://www.newspower.co.kr/sub_read.html?uid=43974.

18. See Chŏng, *Han'guk Kyohoesa e Nat'anan Idan Nonjaeng*; Suh, "An Understanding of Orthodoxy and Heresy in Korean Church History"; Han'guk Kidokkyo Ch'ongyŏnhaphoe, *Han'guk Kyohoe Idan Nonjaeng Kŭ Silch'e Rŭl Palk'inda*; Hŏ, *Han'guk Ŭi Idan Kidokkyo*.

19. The so-called BITE model draws mostly from anti-cultist activism in the United States. Chi-il T'ak, *Kyohoe wa idan: Idan taech'ŏ rŭl wihan kyohoe kaehyŏk* (The church and heresy: Reforming the church against heresies) (Seoul: Turanno, 2016); Steven Hassan, *Combatting Cult Mind Control* (Rochester, Vt.: Park Street Press, 1988).

20. This article was published on the blog of Chingusai, a long-established gay men's organization. Borah Lim (Pora Im), "Sŏng sosuja wa hamkke kŏnnŭn kil,

kŭrigo 'k'wiŏ sŏngsŏ chusŏk'-ŭi ŭimi" (Walking together with sexual minorities, and the meaning of the *Queer Bible Commentary*), *Chingusai Newsletter*, September 23, 2016, http://chingusai.net/xe/newsletter/481344?category=593886.

21. Lim, "Sŏng sosuja wa hamkke kŏnnŭn kil."

22. While "heteropatriarchy" refers to "social systems in which heterosexuality and patriarchy are perceived as normal and natural, and in which other configurations are perceived as abnormal, aberrant, and abhorrent," "cisgenderism" refers to cultural and ideological systems that deny, denigrate, or pathologize "self-identified gender identities that do not align with assigned gender at birth as well as resulting behavior, expression, and community." Maile Arvin, Eve Tuck, and Angie Morrill, "Decolonizing Feminism: Challenging Connections between Settler Colonialism and Heteropatriarchy," *Feminist Formations* 25, no. 1 (2013): 13; Erica Lennon and Brian J. Mistler, "Cisgenderism," *TSQ: Transgender Studies Quarterly* 1, no. 1–2 (2014): 63.

23. Linn Marie Tonstad, *Queer Theology: Beyond Apologetics* (Eugene, Ore.: Cascade Books, 2018), 17.

24. Deryn Guest, Robert E. Goss, Mona West, and Thomas Bohache, eds., *The Queer Bible Commentary* (London: SCM Press, 2006), 1; Tonstad, *Queer Theology*, 17.

25. Guest et al., *The Queer Bible Commentary*, xiii.

26. The forum was held at the Hyanglin Church on May 17, 2017, which was the annual International Day Against Homophobia and Transphobia.

27. The Christian-led movement to counter anti-LGBTQ+ politics within the church and beyond includes the constellation of advocacy groups and LGBTQ-affirming ministries that have gathered under the banner of Rainbow Jesus. This includes Lim's Sumdol Hyanglin Church (founded in 2013) and the other Hyanglin churches and affiliates; the Pilgrimage Church (Kilch'atnŭn Kyohoe, founded in 2013), and the Yongsan House of Sharing (Nanumŭijip, founded in 1986), with their community activism anti-poverty mission led by the young outspoken Anglican priest Min-Kim Jong Hun, a.k.a. Father Zacchaeus; the Rodem Church (founded in 1996); and the Open Doors Metropolitan Community Church (founded in 2011), a congregation of the Metropolitan Community Churches (MCC) and the Progressive Christian Alliance. The MCC is an international Protestant Christian denomination with over two hundred member congregations in thirty-seven countries that specifically reach out to LGBT families and communities. Also part of Rainbow Jesus are a queer (*iban*) women's Catholic group, a Methodist group, and feminist and other human rights advocacy groups.

28. Robert Benedetto, Darrell L. Guder, and Donald K. McKim, *Historical Dictionary of the Reformed Churches* (Lanham, Md.: Scarecrow, 1999), 199–200.

29. Yeong Mee Lee, "A Political Reception of the Bible: Korean Minjung Theological Interpretation of the Bible," *SBL Forum*, October 2005, http://sbl-site .org/Article.aspx?ArticleID=457.

30. See Siu, *K'wiŏ ap'ok'allipsŭ: Sarang kwa hyŏmo ŭi chŏngch'ihak* [Queer apocalypse: Politics of love and hate] (Seoul: Hyŏnsil Munhwa Yŏn'gu, 2018); Syum P'ŭrojekt'ŭ [Shyum Project], *Hanŭnim kwa mannan tongsŏngae* [Homosexuality meets God] (Seoul: Hanul, 2010).

31. Ju Hui Judy Han, "Becoming Visible, Becoming Political: Faith and Queer Activism in South Korea," *Scholar and Feminist* 14, no. 2 (2017), http://sfonline .barnard.edu/queer-religion/becoming-visible-becoming-political-faith-and-queer -activism-in-south-korea/.

32. Ju Hui Judy Han, "Urban Megachurches and Contentious Religious Politics in Seoul," in *Handbook of Religion and the Asian City: Aspiration and Urbanization in the Twenty-First Century*, ed. Peter Van der Veer (Berkeley: University of California Press, 2015), 133–51; Yongp'il Yi, "Hyangnin Kyohoe, tŏ k'ŭn hana wihae tchogaego tto tchogaenda" [Hyanglin Church, splits and splits again for greater unity], *News N Joy*, January 8, 2013, http://www.newsnjoy.or.kr/news/articleView .html?idxno=192978.

33. Author's field notes. Also see Ŭnhye Yi, "Im Pora idan sibi, chŏkp'ye kamch'uryŏnŭn hyŏndaep'an manyŏ sanyang" [Lim Borah heresy charges, modern-day witch hunt to hide issues], *News N Joy*, July 7, 2017, http://www.newsnjoy.or.kr /news/articleView.html?idxno=212029.

34. Chŏn'guk Yŏ Kyoyŏkchahoe [Women Ministers' Association of the Presbyterian Church in the Republic of Korea], "Im Pora Moksa e taehan idansŏng sibi rŭl chŭkkak chungdan hal kot ŭl ch'okku hamnida" [We urge an immediate stop of heresy dispute regarding Reverend Lim Borah], July 3, 2017, http://www.prok.org /gnu/bbs/board.php?bo_table=bbs_board1&wr_id=6514.

35. Chŏn'guk Yŏ Kyoyŏkchahoe, "Im Pora Moksa e taehan idansŏng sibi rŭl chŭkkak chungdan hal kot ŭl ch'okku hamnida."

36. Hŏ, *Han'guk Ŭi Idan Kidokkyo*.

37. T'ak, *Kyohoe Wa Idan*, 179.

38. Han, "Becoming Visible, Becoming Political"; Ro, "WCC General Assembly Aftermath."

39. Benedetto, Guder, and McKim, *Historical Dictionary of the Reformed Churches*, 158–59.

40. Five Presbyterian denominations (Hapdong, T'onghap, Kosin, Hapsin, and Paeksŏk Taesin) were joined by three other Protestant denominations (the Korean Methodist Church, the Korea Baptist Convention, and the Baptist Korea Evangelical Holiness Church). Hyŏngnyul Kwŏn, "Kyodanbyŏl ch'onghoe rŭl tora pomyŏ" [Looking back at denominational general assemblies], *Kidokkyo sasang* [Christian thought] 707 (November 2017): 118–24; 8-kae Kyodan Idanwi [Eight Denominations' Committee on Heresy], "Im Pora Moksa ŭi idanjŏk kyŏnghyang e kwanhan pogosŏ" [Report on the heretical tendencies of Rev. Lim Borah], *Kyohoe wa sinang* [Church and faith], September 8, 2017, http://www.amennews.com/news/articleView.html ?idxno=15607.

41. Sŭnghyŏn Ch'oe, "Im Pora Moksa 'idan' mandŭn kŭn'gŏ nŭn?" [Grounds for declaring Reverend Lim Borah as a heretic?], *News N Joy*, September 21, 2018, http://www.newsnjoy.or.kr/news/articleView.html?idxno=219887.

42. Borah Lim (Pora Im), "Kŭrŏtch'i mothal ttae enŭn yŏrŏbun to challyŏ nagal kŏt imnida: Mainŏrit'I wa Han'guk kyohoe" [Otherwise, you also will be cut off: Minority and the Korean church], *Kidokkyo sasang* [Christian thought], July 2012, 48.

43. Syum P'ŭrojekt'ŭ [Shyum Project], *Hanŭnim kwa mannan tongsŏngae.*

44. 8-kae Kyodan Idanwi [Eight Denominations' Committee on Heresy], "Im Pora Moksa ŭi idanjŏk kyŏnghyang e kwanhan pogosŏ" [Report on the heretical tendencies of Rev. Lim Borah].

45. 8-kae Kyodan Idanwi [Eight Denominations' Committee on Heresy], "Im Pora Moksa ŭi idanjŏk kyŏnghyang e kwanhan pogosŏ" [Report on the heretical tendencies of Rev. Lim Borah].

46. Borah Lim and Nami Kim, "Che 204-ch'a wŏllye p'orŏm" [204th monthly forum], Forum presented at the P'orŏm che-3 Sidae Kŭrisŭdo Yŏn'guso, Seoul, Korea, July 31, 2017, http://www.youtube.com/watch?v=DM1qaAZFppo.

47. Lessl, "Heresy, Orthodoxy, and the Politics of Science," 20.

48. Qadir, "How Heresy Makes Orthodoxy."

Acknowledgments

The editors wish to acknowledge and to thank the McFarland Center for Religion, Ethics, and Culture at the College of the Holy Cross, especially the director, Thomas Landy, and staff, Danielle Kane and Patricia Hinchliffe, for their facilitation of the Religion, Protest, and Social Upheaval conference in November 2017. We would also like to thank the Department of Religious Studies, including Alan Avery-Peck, William Clark, S.J., Caner Dagli, Gary DeAngelis, John Gavin, S.J., Caroline Johnson Hodge, Mahri Leonard-Fleckman, Todd Lewis, Joanne Pierce, Virginia Ryan, and Mathew Schmalz for their collaboration in the development of the conference and for their participation as interlocutors, session presiders, and respondents. Thanks also to our faculty colleagues across the college who also served in such roles at the conference: Kendy Hess, Nadine Knight, and Justin Poché. Special thanks to the current Religious Studies department chairperson, Mary Doyle Roche, and the former chairperson, William Reiser, S.J., for their leadership. Most importantly, a huge thank you to our colleague Benny Liew, who spearheaded the department's role in developing, organizing, and co-hosting the conference and for initiating the publication of this volume. Benny, we cannot thank you enough for your generosity, collegiality, advice, and steadfast support. Finally, thanks to the administration of the College of the Holy Cross, especially former President Philip Boroughs, S.J., and Provost Margaret Freije, for supporting collaborative research among the faculty and beyond the college. Thanks as well to everyone at Fordham University Press, above all Fredric Nachbaur for his enthusiasm for the project and his remarkable patience with us. And to our ten contributors, thank you for your chapters and for your dedication to the pursuit of justice.

Contributors

Mary Doak (Ph.D., University of Chicago) is a Professor of Theology at the University of San Diego. Her publications include *A Prophetic, Public Church: Witness to Hope Amid the Global Crises of the 21st Century* (Liturgical Press, 2020), *Divine Harmony: Seeking Community in a Broken World* (Paulist Press, 2017), and other books and articles on Christian faith, religious freedom, and public life. She is currently serving as president of the College Theology Society and is a past president of the American Theological Society (Midwest).

Nichole M. Flores is an Assistant Professor of Religious Studies at the University of Virginia. She is author of *The Aesthetics of Solidarity: Our Lady of Guadalupe and American Democracy* (Georgetown University Press, 2021). She has also published several articles and book chapters on migration, trafficking, gender, and family. She is a contributing author on the masthead at *America: The Jesuit Review of Faith and Culture*. In 2015, she was awarded the Catherine Mowry LaCugna Award from the Catholic Theological Society of America. Flores earned an A.B. from Smith College, an M.Div. from Yale University, and a Ph.D. from Boston College.

Ju Hui Judy Han is an Assistant Professor at the University of California, Los Angeles, where she teaches gender studies and Korean studies. She writes, draws comics, and gives talks about Korean/American evangelical missions and megachurches, activism and protest cultures, and queer feminist politics in Korea and the Korean diaspora. Her publications include articles in *Journal of Korean Studies, positions: asia critique, Critical Asian Studies*, and *Geoforum* as well as in edited books, including *Territories of Poverty: Rethinking North and South* (2015) and *Ethnographies of U.S. Empire* (2018). She has a Ph.D. in Geography from University of California, Berkeley.

Kwok Pui-lan is Dean's Professor of Systematic Theology at Candler School of Theology, Emory University. She is a past president of the American Academy of Religion.

An internationally known theologian, she is author and editor of many books, including *Postcolonial Imagination and Feminist Theology* and *Postcolonial Politics and Theology*. Her most recent edited volume is *The Hong Kong Protests and Political Theology*.

Zayn Kassam is the John Knox MacLean Professor of Religious Studies at Pomona College. She has authored an introductory volume on Islam and edited two volumes on gender, one titled *Women and Islam*, and the other *Women and Asian Religions*. Her current research is on Muslim migration to North America. She is also the coeditor of the *Journal of Feminist Studies in Religion*. Kassam has thrice won the Wig Award for Distinguished Teaching at Pomona College, as well as the American Academy of Religion's national award for Excellence in Teaching.

Jermaine M. McDonald (Ph.D., Emory University) is an independent scholar whose research explores intersections between race, religion, and politics in the United States.

Donovan O. Schaefer is an Assistant Professor in the Department of Religious Studies at the University of Pennsylvania. He joined the department in 2017 after spending three years teaching at the University of Oxford. His first book, *Religious Affects: Animality, Evolution and Power*, was published by Duke University Press in 2015. It explores the relationships between theories of feeling, religion, and the experience of animals. His second book, *Wild Experiment: Feeling Science and Secularism after Darwin*, considers how affect theory can be applied to science, secularism, race, and conspiracy theory.

Devin Singh is an Associate Professor of Religion at Dartmouth College, where he teaches courses on modern religious thought in the West, social ethics, and the philosophy of religion. He is also a faculty associate in Dartmouth's Consortium of Studies in Race, Migration, and Sexuality. Singh is the author of *Divine Currency: The Theological Power of Money in the West* (2018) as well as articles in journals such as *Political Theology*, *Journal of Religious Ethics*, *Telos*, and *Harvard Theological Review*.

C. Melissa Snarr is the E. Rhodes and Leona B. Carpenter Chair and Associate Professor of Ethics & Society at Vanderbilt Divinity School. Her work focuses on the intersections of religion, social change, and political ethics with particular attention to ethnographic fieldwork and sociological/political theory. She is the author of two books, *All You That Labor: Religion and Ethics in the Living Wage Movement* and *Social Selves and Political Reforms: Five Visions in Contemporary Christian Ethics*, and articles in the area of Christian feminist ethics, worker justice, and interfaith organizing.

Mark Lewis Taylor is a Professor in Religion and Society at Princeton Theological Seminary. Among his books are *Religion, Politics and the Christian Right* and *The Theological and the Political*. Taylor received the Best General Interest Book Award for his 2001 book, *The Executed God: The Way of the Cross in Lockdown America* (2nd edition, 2015). In addition to years of anti–death penalty work and prison activism, Taylor remains active in solidarity work against U.S. dominance in Central America. Further publications and resources are available at www.marklewistaylor.com.

Index